MW01281820

FRIENDS WITH WORDS

FRIENDS
WITH WORDS

Adventures in Languageland

MARTHA BARNETTE

ABRAMS PRESS, NEW YORK

Library of Congress Control Number: 2025931678

ISBN: 978-1-4197-7884-1
eISBN: 979-8-88707-522-8

Printed and bound in United States
10 9 8 7 6 5 4 3 2 1

ABRAMS The Art of Books
195 Broadway, New York, NY 10007
abramsbooks.com

"Words may be made to disgorge the past that is bottled up inside them, as coal and wine, when we kindle or drink them, yield up their bottled sunshine."

—Owen Barfield, *History in English Words*

CONTENTS

THE JOY OF LEX

YOU NEVER KNOW WHAT'S GOING to prompt someone to call a radio show to talk about language.

I'm guessing you've wondered some of those same things yourself. Why is a self-important person called a *muckety-muck*? How did *spam* ever come to mean "junk mail"? Maybe you grew up using the word *tump* to mean "knock over," then moved across the country only to find that no one knew what it meant.

Or perhaps your new coworker says things like *My car needs washed* and *The baby needs fed* and you're not sure if that's grammatically correct. (There's a long tradition of this construction in certain English dialects. See Chapter 7.) Or maybe you've always wondered if it's OK to end a sentence with a preposition. (Absolutely! If anyone objects, tell them that this so-called "rule" of grammar is nonsense up with which you will not put.) Maybe you're curious whether there's a word that means "the place on your back that you can't reach to scratch," or "the warmth of sun in winter," or "to put off until the day after tomorrow." (There's a word for each of those: *acnestis*, *apricity*, and *perendinate*. You'll meet all of them in Chapter 17.) Or maybe you wonder about that weird thing Grandma used to say. Was that just something she made up, or do other people say it, too?

I cohost the popular public radio show and podcast *A Way with Words*, and the great thing is that after two decades, we still haven't run out of things to talk about—not at all. Each week, listeners tune in to hear about word and phrase origins, slang, regional dialects, varieties of English, curious idioms, grammar, jargon, obscure terms, and words that might not exist but ought to. (I mean, shouldn't there be a word for that feeling when you hear your favorite restaurant is closing? A pun-loving caller suggested we refer to that sinking sensation as *mealancholy*, and I've continued to use that one ever since.)

Over the years, my cohost Grant Barrett and I have enjoyed thousands of conversations about topics like these with callers of all ages, from kindergartners to ninety-somethings. Our listeners reflect a wide span of nationalities, locations, ethnicities, belief traditions, and political persuasions. What connects them all is a shared fascination with language in all its forms. I like to think of our listeners as "worders." Like birders who observe those animals closely for the sheer fascination of it, without judgment, we worders love observing words and phrases in the wild, and we delight in adding those discoveries to our word-hoard.

In fact, one of the great joys of doing this show is that it's an interactive, ongoing collaboration with our listeners. If you're a fellow worder, then you're endlessly curious, and the questions you have about language are the same kind that send Grant and me down fascinating linguistic and etymological paths each week. You've introduced us to so many colorful words and phrases, brought us so many interesting debates, and shared some wonderful linguistic curiosities, from words your family held on to because a child adorably mispronounced it to your favorite tongue twisters. (Try saying *Irish wristwatch* three times fast.)

Our listeners tell us our show is a little oasis on the radio dial—a warm, welcoming, friendly place for worders of all kinds. An opportunity to tune out the worries of the world and pause to ponder the miracle of language, puzzling over questions like what that little word *it* is doing in the phrase *It's raining*—linguists call this an *expletive pronoun* or *dummy it*—and whether anyone really bothers to use the word *pneumonoultramicroscopicsilicovolcanoconiosis*. (Not unless you're just showing off, as I explain in Chapter 13.)

You can listen to hundreds of episodes where we discuss questions like these at our website, waywordradio.org, or wherever you get your podcasts. Above all, our show is about the joy of discovering the ways that words can connect us rather than divide us, about how a single word or phrase can be a window into other worlds, and how language can be a lens that reveals surprising insights about history, family, and culture.

It's astonishing, really, that humans communicate so much to each other simply with a mouthful of air or marks on a page. Right now, for example, I'm making marks on this page in the hope that they'll change the way you think about language. Cohosting the show certainly did that for me. When I joined *A Way with Words*, I was a finger-wagging stickler about grammar. But if I've learned anything hosting the program, it's this: When it comes to language, grammatical pet peeves are the least interesting thing of all. In fact, think of our show as a spay-and-neuter program for pet peeves. You'll be much happier, trust me. There's so much more to explore when it comes to language.

In this book you'll discover lots of lively stories about words and how they came to be. You'll learn about the various types of etymological sleuthing required to uncover their origins. We'll take a talking tour around the United States to celebrate the rich diversity of American English and the dialects of various regions. We'll detour a bit into my own roots and the Appalachian dialect I heard as a child, the source of my family's linguistic heirlooms that I cherish to this day. I'll also share a bit about my own nerd origins and some favorite words and phrases that you'll want to add to your own personal lexicon.

I'll also share the unlikely story of how I came to do what I do—extremely unlikely, in fact, considering that for most of my life, I was terrified of public speaking. If you'd told me I would someday cohost a public radio show and podcast reaching hundreds of thousands of listeners and speak to hundreds more at a time in shows before live audiences, I would have told you that's preposterous. (Fantastic word, *preposterous*. It's from the Latin *praeposterus*, meaning "absurd," or "in reverse order," a combination of *prae*, meaning "before," and *posterus*, meaning "coming after," or "subsequent." In its earliest sense, something preposterous was literally "out of order"—it was bass-ackwards, if you will!) In any case, to my great surprise, public speaking is now one of my favorite parts of this unlikely job, and I'll explain how that happened.

That *A Way with Words* exists at all today is equally unlikely. In 2007, the show's original producer, San Diego's public radio station KPBS, canceled the program due to a budget shortfall. That left the show's creative team—our intrepid producer Stefanie Levine, plus Grant and me—scrambling to keep producing the episodes on our own. We had no idea what we were doing; we were word nerds, not entrepreneurs. We just knew that, together with our listeners, we were building something special, and we simply had to find a way to continue. I'll tell you about our struggle to keep the show going and some of the bumps along the way. I'll also take you behind the scenes for a look at how we put the show together each week.

Finally, I'll share some of my favorite conversations with listeners. One of them, for example, called a few years ago to discuss the difference between the words *nice* and *kind*. She told us she thought of herself as "kind, but not necessarily nice." I confess that at the time I didn't find that conversation all that interesting. Years later, though, that caller and I resumed our conversation with an entirely different result. (Reader, I married her.)

But I'm getting ahead of myself. I'm sure you have your own story about how you became a worder and fell in love with language. In the next chapter, I'll share mine.

GREEK TO ME

WHEN I WAS IN COLLEGE, we English majors were encouraged to take a classical language. I had taken some Latin in high school and delighted in the process of translation, turning words over and over, looking at them this way and that, holding them up to the light, the puzzle of a sentence slowly revealing its meaning, transporting me to a distant time.

So why not ancient Greek this time? I imagined wintry evenings nestled into a comfy chair, sipping something warm as I thrilled to the epic clashes in Homer, word for Greek word. I would read the zany stories of Herodotus and the thoughtful arguments of Plato. I'd savor the poetry of Sappho, lovesick, aching, pining away—all in the original Greek. What could be better? That was the dream, anyway. It had seemed like such a swell idea.

The reality was quite different.

I soon realized that ancient Greek was harder than Latin— much harder. First, there's what linguists call the *alphabet barrier*. Some of the Greek letters looked familiar, but other squiggles were brand-new to me. Then there were all the accent marks pointing in different directions, the occasional tilde or long mark over vowels, and apostrophes above the letters at the beginning of a word to denote whether the vowel was pronounced with "rough breathing" or "smooth breathing."

Then, there was the subject matter. Ancient Greek is quite different from modern Greek, and your typical ancient Greek primer gets right down to the business of preparing you to read extremely old texts. There's no *Hello, how are you?* or *I would like some spanakopita* or *Does this train go to Athens?* No, the very first chapter of my introductory text included, I kid you not, the following sentences: *He has small armies. Have they bowstrings? The motion was slight. It was a metaphor.*

Not exactly the stuff of everyday conversation.

Not only that, the grammar itself was grueling. Greek is an inflected language—the word *inflected* coming from an old root meaning "to bend," the source also of *reflect*, literally "to bend back," and *genuflect*, "to bend the knee." Ancient Greek nouns have different endings depending on how they're used in a sentence; the nouns are "bent" at the end to indicate how they function in that particular instance. This gives these nouns a flexibility (another word from that same "bending" linguistic family) that English nouns don't have. This flexibility means that the elements of a Greek sentence can be scattered all about in what Greek scholar Andrea Marcolongo has called "an orderly anarchy" of words.

In time, I would come to relish that orderly mess. In fact, I would come to luxuriate in it. But my attempts to translate Greek in those first few days felt like running around with a bucket, trying to catch raindrops just as they were beginning to fall—one here, then one way over there, another even farther away. The old expression "It's Greek to me" took on a new and painful meaning.

A couple of weeks into the semester, it was clear that I wouldn't be able to keep up. So at the last possible second, rather than fail the class, I dropped it.

Frustrated, smarting, I made a deal with myself: I'd find someone who could tutor me over the summer in my hometown of Louisville, Kentucky, and I'd reenroll for the fall semester. Surely there was some starving graduate student I could hire to teach me the basics. I wrote to a university there to try to find one. I received a letter back, in not entirely perfect English, from an elderly retired professor of classics.

Leonard Latkovski Sr. was born in Riga, Latvia. During World War II he and his young family had fled to Germany, just hours ahead of the advancing Soviet army. Eventually, they immigrated to the United States, and he found work teaching at Louisville's Bellarmine University.

Professor Latkovski was a polyglot, completely comfortable in more than a dozen languages. A born teacher, he'd gladly tutor anyone who asked. He agreed to teach me Greek on Monday nights. I was lucky that I had Monday nights free, because it turned out that on Tuesdays, the professor taught Spanish; on Wednesdays, he taught Hebrew; on Thursdays, he taught Turkish; and on Fridays, Italian. On weekends, he noodled with Hungarian, Urdu, and a few other other languages just for fun.

That first Monday was a typical muggy summer evening in Louisville. Professor Latkovski stepped out onto his front porch to greet me in Greek.

Xaire!

A portly, gracious man, the professor took both my hands in his and kissed both my cheeks. With a grand gesture, he welcomed me into his dimly lit living room and motioned for me to be seated at one end of a worn couch. When he disappeared into the kitchen, I had a moment to look around, my eyes adjusting to the light.

There were old family photographs in wooden frames; a yellowed map of Latvia on the wall above my head; and a small table between my end of the couch and his chair with a desk lamp, a pen, a stack of books, and a pile of letter-size pages cut in half.

He returned after a moment with two cups of strong coffee, set them down, then left again. This time he returned, grinning, with a loaf of fresh homemade bread.

"Recipe from old country," he said in a heavily accented growl. "I baked just for you."

He left again, then came back a third time with a plate of butter.

"Cow cheese," he said.

When I looked puzzled, he explained that the English word *butter* comes from the ancient Greek *bous*, or "cow," and *tyros*, "cheese," making *butter* a linguistic relative of such words as *bovine*, *beef*, *bucolic*, and *bulimia*, literally, "ox-hunger."

At last, he settled into a worn, overstuffed chair. "Now we can study," he announced.

I had in hand my elementary Greek textbook, full of dreary drills, charts, vocabulary lists, and translation exercises. I had hoped the professor would look over my written work, correct my mistakes, and quiz me on those pesky noun forms. The professor tried half-heartedly to oblige. More than once, he shook his head, frowned, then muttered, "Language is not arbitrary. There is a reason for it all. Is not arbitrary!"

As the hour wore on, he looked more and more uncomfortable, shuffling his feet, and repeatedly insisted on digressing from the exercises to talk about words in other languages. After an hour or so, he declared the lesson over. He wrapped up the rest of his homemade bread for me to take home and said he'd see me in a week. I left, quite frankly, disappointed. The lesson had gone nowhere. Maybe I should just give up on Greek altogether.

Then again, the coffee was delicious, and the bread had been excellent. I decided to give it one more try.

When I knocked on the professor's door a week later, it was the same ritual all over again: the greeting in Greek, the kisses on the cheeks, the coffee, the fresh, warm bread, the "cow cheese," and the professor settling into his chair, then declaring, "Now we can study."

This time, though, something different happened. The professor snatched my textbook from my hand and tossed it on the table, with a finality that let me know it was useless to argue. We wouldn't need my book anymore, he said. Instead, he handed me a copy of the great tragedy by Sophocles *Oedipus Tyrannus*—in ancient Greek.

"We will read this," he told me.

Wait, I thought. *I've barely crossed the alphabet barrier, and we're going to read all of* Oedipus the King? *In the original Greek? This guy is nuts.*

OK, I told myself, I'll stay just long enough to be polite, then leave. Just one cup of coffee, one slice of buttered bread—OK, maybe two—then I'm out.

"We will begin with the name *Oedipus*," the professor said, then reminded me of the story of Oedipus, son of King Laius and Queen Jocasta.

An oracle had warned that any son born to Laius would grow up to kill his father and marry his mother. When Jocasta gave birth to a boy, Laius gave the baby to a shepherd with instructions to leave the boy in the wilderness to die. Laius also ensured that the infant would never be able to crawl by having his ankles pierced and tethered together. Instead, the shepherd took pity on the baby and gave him to another couple to raise. Because of the damage to his ankles, the boy always walked with a limp. As an adult, he fell into an altercation with a stranger—who happened to be his father—and fulfilled the grisly prophecy.

The professor explained that the name *Oedipus* literally means "swollen foot," a reference to his scarred and mangled feet.

"*Oedipus* comes from Greek *oidein*, which means 'to swell.' You have in English, do you not, the word *edema*, yes? Is some sort of medical term that has to do with swelling, yes?"

I nodded, unsure.

The professor continued: "*Edema* and *Oedipus* are related, you see. They come from the same linguistic root. And that's not all yet. The rest of the name *Oedipus* is from the Greek for 'foot,' which is *pous*. You see the same root in the word *octopus*, an animal with 'eight feet.' And the genitive form of Greek *pous* is *podos*, which means 'of the foot.' You see that root in the English word *podiatrist*, the 'foot doctor.'"

The word *podiatrist* reminded the professor of something else. "The Greek word for 'doctor,' you see, is *iatros*—as in the *psychiatrist* who doctors the *psyche* or 'soul.' The Greeks used the word *psyche* to mean 'soul.' And they used the same word *psyche* to mean 'butterfly!'

"And that's not all yet. From the prehistoric Indo-European root of Greek *pous* is the Latin word for 'foot,' *pes*, and its genitive form *pedis*. You see that root in the words involving feet, like *pedal*, *pedestrian*, *pedestal*, and *sesquipedalian*. Is fantastic word, *sesquipedalian*. Literally, it means 'a foot and a half long.' So, a word that is sesquipedalian is just a really big one! Is terrific word!"

By now, the professor could hardly contain his merriment. "And that's still not all yet! In Sanskrit is same thing. Sanskrit also comes from the Indo-European language. The Sanskrit word for "foot" is *padas*, like Greek *podos* and Latin *pedis*. And Sanskrit has wonderful word for 'tree,' *padapa*. You know what means *padapa*? 'The one that drinks with its foot.' Is fantastic language, Sanskrit. Very poetic! We will read Sanskrit one day," he assured.

"And that's not all yet! In Latvian and Lithuanian . . ."

It went on like that for three hours. As we made our way through the opening lines of *Oedipus*, nearly every word set the professor off on one of these etymological romps. They were dizzying excursions across the boundaries of time, culture, and language, and the hours flew by as we talked not just about language, but history, mathematics, astronomy, folklore, ancient botany and modern medicine, alchemy and the periodic table of the elements.

By the time I left that evening, with an extra loaf of warm homemade bread under my arm and a handful of notes he'd jotted to illustrate his points, I was reeling from the sheer amount and scope of information we'd covered.

At that rate, of course, it took us quite a while to work our way through *Oedipus*. In fact, it took us seven years. But I began to grasp language with an understanding that charts of noun declensions and verb forms could never offer. I came to see the common linguistic ancestors that link words in a surprising number of languages. Professor Latkovski was right: Language isn't arbitrary. Not at all. There are faintly visible etymological footprints in words we use every day—if only you know how to look for them.

When I returned to college that fall, I enrolled again in introductory Greek, and this time, I aced the class. I went on to take as many Greek courses as I could until I graduated, and I studied with Professor Latkovski during the summers and again when I moved back to Louisville.

Sometimes emergency phone calls interrupted our lessons. The professor would disappear into the kitchen, have a conversation in a language I sometimes didn't recognize, then return. "Polish woman is having baby," he told me one of those times. "I am sorry. I must go to the hospital and translate." Another time, a Peruvian heart patient was in need of help. Another time, a French speaker stranded at the airport was having trouble booking a flight home. The polyglot professor was the one to call.

I sometimes asked him how many languages he spoke. He would invariably dismiss the question with a chuckle and a shrug. Instead, he would say in all seriousness, "There are many languages I do not know." He was far more interested in how much more there was to learn, always eager for someone to show him a word or phrase he'd never seen.

In many ways, we couldn't have been more different, the professor and I. He was a staunchly conservative Roman Catholic and father of nine, known for strongly worded letters to the local newspaper about geopolitics and the decline of spiritual values in his adopted country. I was a fallen-away Southern Baptist—fallen quite far away, in fact—who rarely talked about myself or why I didn't have children, much less why there wasn't a man in my life. But the two of us shared a passion for ancient Greek, the miracle of language, those invisible connections between words, and the thrill of prying open a single word or phrase to make it give up its secrets.

We studied together like that for twelve years. Then, on another muggy Louisville afternoon, Professor Latkovski's daughter called me. She said that the professor, now eighty-five, had collapsed while out on an errand and was taken to the hospital, and they were keeping him overnight. Would I want to drop by and see him that evening?

"Of course," I said.

Even if the professor had been out of his room when I arrived, I could have guessed I'd come to the right place: Scattered around the bed and table were newspapers in three different languages.

He greeted me warmly, reaching up from the bed to take both my hands in his. *Xaire!*

He seemed in good spirits. He was eager to talk about gemstones. He'd just been reading about alexandrite, a gem known as "emerald by day, ruby by night" because of a remarkable property: If it's lit by the sun, alexandrite is blue-green. But if placed under artificial light, it changes to purplish-red. The professor was also excited to share the etymology of its name. Alexandrite is found in the Ural Mountains, and its name honors Emperor Alexander II of Russia.

"We will study gems," he said with finality, his eyes brightening as he began mapping out our course of study.

As I got ready to leave, we made plans to study again as soon as he got home.

As I turned in the doorway for a final wave, I was surprised to hear him say something to me in Spanish.

"No me olvides," he told me.

At the time, I knew only a little Spanish, and we rarely exchanged phrases in that language. Yet for some reason, instead of our usual goodbye, he'd reached for a language at one remove from us both.

No me olvides. "Don't forget me."

I thought that was a bit odd but shrugged it off.

The next morning, my alarm clock went off early. I hit the snooze button and fell right back into a vivid dream, a dream in which I had the strong sense that somewhere, a library was burning.

I was awakened again when my phone rang. It was the professor's daughter, calling to tell me that Professor Latkovski had died.

In the years since, I have been determined to carry on the professor's legacy, to pay forward the gifts he gave me, and to share the substance and the spirit of our lessons. But it would take me a long time to figure out exactly how.

CHAPTER 2

WHAT'S A NAME IN?

WE SPEND LOTS OF TIME on the show debunking etymologies that simply aren't true. No, *golf* is not an acronym for *Gentlemen Only, Ladies Forbidden*. The word *posh* wasn't inspired by tickets for the best passenger rooms on a steamship; there's no evidence such tickets were ever stamped with the acronym for *Port Out, Starboard Home*. The phrase *saved by the bell* doesn't allude to Victorian-era coffins rigged with a string and a bell so that anyone accidentally buried alive could tug on it to call for help. Nobody ever shipped crates of manure marked with the acronym for *Ship High In Transit*, and don't even get me started about the royal edict that supposedly punished people *For Unlawful Carnal Knowledge*.*

---

* It is true that the fear of being buried while breathing was indeed widespread in the nineteenth century, especially during epidemics of cholera, which can result in loss of consciousness or coma. There were even patented "safety coffins" designed to let anyone interred by mistake signal to folks above ground that they were still alive with a little jingle or by raising a wee flag. Edgar Allan Poe wrote about this fear in his short story "The Premature Burial." In any case, these worries and workarounds aren't connected to the phrase *saved by the bell*. This idiom originated in the sport of boxing, where the bell signals the end of a round. The roots of *golf* are murky, although it

Hogwash, hooey, balderdash, poppycock. None of that ever happened.

It's a shame these bogus stories get repeated, and not just because they're wrong. It's a shame because there are so many other good ones that are so much more interesting. What's more, we can prove that those other stories are true. We know about them because of the hard work of researchers who have spent years tracing them and confirming the facts through primary sources and original reporting. And so many of these word origins are so much more entertaining, so much richer and deeper, so much more instructive—and often, so much funnier.

Some of the easiest words to trace come from the names of people and places, also known as eponyms and toponyms. In this chapter, we'll explore several of them, including tales of politicians and scholars, immigrant success stories, and a scientist who named a drug for his wife.

First, let's go back to that word *debunk*. *Debunk* means "expose as nonsensical, often by ridicule." The word *debunk* usually carries a connotation of disproving an intentional deception. The etymological road to its roots is a long and twisting one. It involves a long-winded Congressman and bitter arguments over slavery, plus a bestselling novel and the author who regretted being known for it.

Not only that, the story of how *debunk* found its way into English includes a creepy party trick, which I'll tell you about only if you promise never to try it at home. Deal?

---

arrived in Middle English via Scots and may go back to an old word for "bat" or "stick." As for *posh*, it's what folks in the dictionary business call *orig. unk.*, or "origin unknown."

That's Bunk!

THE YEAR WAS 1820. THE territory of Missouri was seeking admission to the Union, sparking heated controversy over the "Missouri question": Should Missouri be admitted as a state that allowed slavery? The answer broke down largely along geographic lines. Southerners maintained that states should have the right to determine their own domestic institutions, including the right to keep people enslaved. Northerners argued that slavery was a moral outrage and shouldn't be allowed in any new states.

After long, bitter debate, a "Missouri Compromise" was proposed: Missouri could continue to allow slavery, but Maine, which had been part of Massachusetts, would also be added to the Union as a free state, and slavery would be prohibited north of a line running across the Louisiana Purchase. The passionate arguments had flown back and forth for weeks, and a vote on the compromise was imminent.

On February 25, 1820, Felix Walker, a Congressman from Buncombe County, North Carolina, who hadn't uttered a single word in the debate, rose to speak. Walker was otherwise known for his long, blustery speeches and for brushing off the concerns of his colleagues. He wasn't speaking for their benefit, he'd say. Instead, he'd tell them he was going to "talk to Buncombe" or give a speech "for Buncombe." Since he hadn't yet weighed in on the Missouri Compromise, Walker decided to get himself on the record and make a speech to please his constituents back home.

Walker launched into a windy, gratuitous speech. His colleagues were exhausted, exasperated, and ready to get on with the vote. They did their best to get him to shut up. According to a contemporary account, they kept interrupting "so clamorously and so perseveringly" that Walker delivered only a few lines before they succeeded in shouting him down.

Just how much of this speech Walker was able to give isn't recorded in the Congressional record, but we know how long it was supposed to be because Walker later published the whole thing in a local newspaper. His screed ran nearly five thousand words, and it's a doozy.

The short version went something like this: Yes, slavery is evil, but hey, it's an evil that's been around since biblical times. And you mustn't blame the poor slaveholders. After all, slavery is a condition "placed on us by our ancestors," a situation that is "now, and at this time, beyond our reach to remedy." Besides, he continued, if abolitionists really got to know enslavers, then they'd understand that "our slaves are our friends as well as our property—they were born in our houses, and raised in our families, and consequently we feel a sympathy for them and they for us." As for the enslaved people themselves, "their cares are less, and their wants are fewer than the master, in their situation they fulfill and finish the circle of life in as much satisfaction as any people, and perhaps with more contentment than if they were free." He continued digging himself even deeper: Restricting slavery infringes not just on states' rights, but the property rights of those who want to move west but would have to leave their human property behind. And that human property would be better off there anyway, since Missouri was less crowded.

Nauseating, to be sure. The speech secured Walker's reputation for blathering on to impress the folks back home—or, should I say, the limited number of folks back home who had the right to vote. Walker became so well-known for his lack of blather control that the phrases *talking for Buncombe* and *speaking to Buncombe* soon entered the lexicon as shorthand terms for such grandstanding. In some cases, the capital *B* in *Buncombe* dropped to lowercase, and the expression *to pass a measure for buncombe* came to mean "to please or mollify a constituency" and *a bid for buncombe* was "an attempt to appeal to voters."

People also began spelling *Buncombe* as *Bunkum*, using it to mean, in the words of the *Oxford English Dictionary*, "Political speaking or action not from conviction, but in order to gain the favour of electors, or make a show of patriotism, or zeal; political clap-trap."

Over time, perhaps influenced by the word *hokum*, the words *bunkum* and *bunk* came to mean "nonsense," or "insincere talk."

Now for *debunk* and that creepy party trick I mentioned, the one you promised you wouldn't try at home.

Debunking Debunk

WILLIAM E. WOODWARD WAS A newspaper reporter–turned–New York ad executive who went on to write a satire of the advertising industry featuring a so-called "professional de-bunker" who spent all his time "taking the bunk out of things." Published in 1923, the novel was a runaway success. Its title was simply *Bunk*.

A few years later, Woodward and his wife were at a small party in a Manhattan apartment, along with fellow author Upton Sinclair and his wife, Mary Craig Sinclair. Best known for *The Jungle*, his gripping exposé of the Chicago meatpacking industry, Sinclair was fascinated by the paranormal, and even wrote a book called *Mental Radio* about his wife's attempts at mental telepathy. At this gathering, the Sinclairs brought along a friend who claimed to be a psychic and who boasted he could also endure tremendous pain without flinching.

To show off his psychic abilities, Sinclair's friend invited the group to hide a pencil and left the room. When he returned, he slowly moved about, looking this way and that, and supposedly picking up the psychic vibrations from all the guests who knew where the pencil was. After ten minutes or so, the man reached into a drawer and retrieved it. Although some guests were amazed, Woodward was skeptical that this was nothing more than, well, bunk. Surely it was some kind of clever parlor trick.

Woodward grew even more skeptical as the evening wore on, tossing out increasingly snide comments, which infuriated the psychic. This was back in the days when women wore hats with long, decorative pins, and finally, in exasperation, the psychic snatched a hatpin from one of them and declared he would shove the pin through his cheek, demonstrating the superior mental powers that rendered him immune to pain.

By this time, Woodward was so annoyed that he stood up and declared that sticking a pin through one's cheek couldn't possibly hurt that much, and to prove it, he'd stick the pin through his own cheek. Another writer who was there, William Seabrook, later described Woodward's next move: "He took the hatpin, puffed his cheeks, opened his mouth like a dying fish, and began pushing the hatpin slowly into the flesh. After about five inches of it had disappeared laterally, traversing the buccal cavity, the cheek on the other side began to bulge slightly outward. The hatpin point came through. He kept pushing it until it was sticking out several inches on both sides of his head." Woodward then merrily moved to the mirror to take a gander, looking like "a portly Cupid, shot through the head with one of his own darts." Apparently the psychic's abilities hadn't predicted this turn of events. Furious, he stormed out.

Woodward later wrote: "I had never thrust a hatpin through my cheeks before, and I did it then just to see if I could. Since then I have thrust hatpins through my cheeks numbers of times. There's nothing to it; anybody can do it. Just get a clean hatpin, which must be very sharp. There's a slight pricking pain as it goes in through the skin of the right cheek, and when it comes out through the skin of the left cheek, but the slight pain stops imme-diately. While the pin is in place you can't move your tongue, or talk, and that is a nuisance."

In typical curmudgeonly fashion, Woodward later told the *New York Times* he was dismayed that his main claims to fame seemed to be sticking a needle in his cheek and coining the word *debunk*. He'd come up with the word, he said, while on a steamship returning from a European vacation. "The weather was bad, the company was worse, and the most entertaining thing I could find to read was an account of the methods used for delousing British soldiers during the last war, and I thought to myself, 'I'll do some writing. I'll write a good-natured book about these beliefs that most people have and that are not true—about *bunk*.' The word *delouse* suggested the word *debunk*—I put a *debunking* specialist into my book." Unfortunately, he added, "I became saddled with that word." In fact, Woodward later wrote, "There is only one thing in my writing life that I regret. I invented the word *debunking*, and I shall never hear the last of it. The *debunking* label is tied to me for life, and this thought makes me very sad. I cannot put a thing in print without having this ugly word thrown in my face."*

It's a shame that Woodward didn't live to see the advent of digitized newspaper databases because—wouldn't you know it?—his notoriety for inventing the word *debunk* was itself, well, bunk. It turns out Woodward didn't coin the word after all! As *Wall Street Journal* language columnist Ben Zimmer has pointed out, digging through newspaper databases reveals that the verb

---

* In short order, the word *rebunk* also joined the language. While it's not heard that often, the *Oxford English Dictionary* notes that *rebunk* has been around since the early 1930s and means to "reaffirm the truth or credence of (a statement, idea, etc., which has been debunked)." More recently, *prebunking* has come to mean the act of "pre-emptively debunking lies, tactics, or sources."

debunk was in use at least eight years before Woodward's bestselling *Bunk*. A 1915 *New York Sun* article, for example, says in reference to one of the American Legion's founders, "And yet in his quiet, emphatic way he kept boring and boring in a convincing manner, debunked and denuded of all that was not fact."

Can you imagine how much a contrarian like Woodward would have loved finding out that his own story about coining *debunk* had itself been debunked?

As for the hatpin story, though, I'm afraid he's stuck with it.

A Sound Like a Publisher

AS WE'VE SEEN, THE WORD *bunk*, is a toponym, a word that derives from the name of a place. An eponym, on the other hand, is inspired by the name of a person, whether real or fictitious. A great example of the latter is the word *blurb*, which derives from the name of a fictional person made up by a snarky poet and artist named Gelett Burgess.

First, a little background: In 1895, Burgess founded a San Francisco–based humor magazine called *The Lark*, for which he wrote and illustrated many forgettable little ditties. How forgettable? Well, try this one:

> *My Feet they haul me 'round the House;*
> *They hoist me up the Stairs;*
> *I only have to steer them and*
> *They ride me everywheres.*

Then again, this one of his probably rings a bell:

> *I never saw a purple cow*
> *I never hope to see one;*

But I can tell you, anyhow,
I'd rather see than be one!

Burgess's verse about a cow with oddly hued hide caught on and was memorized by schoolchildren across the United States. In fact, so many people happily recited it back to him that Burgess came to regret ever writing it—to the point where he expressed his irritation this way:

Ah, yes, I wrote the "Purple Cow"
I'm Sorry, now, I wrote it;
But I can tell you Anyhow
I'll Kill you if you Quote it!

Burgess wrote several more works of satire and short fiction, as well as literature for children. A few years later, he was about to publish yet another book, this one called *Are You a Bromide?* It was a mock-serious social commentary, which claimed that people belong to one of two categories: *Bromides*, who are boring and sedate, or *Sulphites*, who are peppy and energetic.

The book is etymologically significant for a couple of reasons. For one thing, it helped popularize the word *bromide*, meaning "a tiresome platitude or cliché." *Bromide* is adapted from the name *bromine*, a chemical compound then commonly used as a sedative.

The other reason this book is etymologically significant is the ingenious ad campaign to promote it. In 1907, Burgess was to be honored at the annual dinner of the American Booksellers Association. Seizing the opportunity for microtargeted publicity, Burgess printed up mock book jackets for *Are You a Bromide?* featuring shameless hyperbole, which read in part:

WE expect to sell 350 copies of this great, grand book. It has gush and go to it, it has that Certain Something which makes you want to crawl through 30 miles of dense tropical jungle and bite somebody in the neck ... when you've READ this masterpiece, you'll know what a BOOK is ... This book has 42-carat THRILLS in it. It fairly BURBLES! Ask the man at the counter what HE thinks of it!

Above all this breathless copy was a likeness of a woman with towering hair, cupping her hand to the side of her mouth as if she's shouting.

The caption reads:

MISS BELINDA BLURB IN THE ACT OF BLURBING.

And giant letters across the top of the whole thing declared:

YES, this is a "BLURB"! All the Other Publishers commit them. Why Shouldn't We?

Belinda Blurb was, of course, a figment of the author's imagination. In fact, he'd lifted the picture of her from a newspaper ad for a dentist's office. But Miss Blurb's namesake quickly caught on in the publishing world. Burgess published a fanciful dictionary of his own a few years later, defining the word *blurb* as a "flamboyant advertisement; an inspired testimonial" and "fulsome praise; a sound like a publisher."

"Severely Alone"

WILLIAM WOODWARD MAY HAVE BEEN reluctant to go down in the annals of etymological lore for *debunk*, but spare a thought for Captain Charles Cunningham Boycott. All he wanted to do was get out of the British Army, where he'd served as an officer, and settle into a second career enforcing British rule in Ireland. Unfortunately for Boycott, he got mixed up with the 3rd Earl of Erne, an unscrupulous landowner in County Mayo who charged poor tenant farmers obscenely high rent to work his fields. The wealthy elite in Ireland forced tenant farmers to pay *rack-rents*, a term inspired by the medieval torture device that ratcheted up the pain, notch by notch. In the same way, rising rack-rents stretched the farmers' meager funds until they could no longer pay. At that point, it was Captain Boycott's job to evict them.

A potato blight had returned to the country, and harsh weather plus another terrible harvest led to fears of a second potato famine, like the one that ravaged Ireland in the late 1840s and early 1850s, leading to the deaths of approximately one million people and another million to flee the country entirely. By 1879, hungry tenant farmers had had enough. They formed the Irish National Land League to fight rack-rents, withhold rent payments, hold mass rallies, and mount fierce resistance to evictions in what came to be known as the Land Wars.

In 1880, Charles Parnell, president of the Land League, gave a rousing speech to a crowd of twelve thousand, urging them to unite against the landowners. But what, he asked, should they do about any scab willing to work a farm after a fellow subsistence farmer was evicted? Rather than resort to violence, he declared, it was better simply to leave such a person "severely alone," to shun him by "isolating him from the rest of his kind as if he were a leper of old." It would be "a more Christian, a more charitable way which will give the lost sinner an opportunity of repenting."

When Captain Boycott tried to evict eleven starving tenant farmers, the locals organized to ostracize him as well. Then Boycott made the mistake of complaining to a London newspaper in a letter that's worth reading in full:

> Sir, The following detail may be interesting to your readers as exemplifying the power of the Land League. On the 22nd September, a process server, escorted by a police force of seventeen men, retreated to my house for protection, followed by a howling mob of people, who yelled and hooted at the members of my family.
>
> On the ensuing day, September 23rd, the people collected in crowds upon my farm, and some hundred or so came up to my house and ordered off, under threats of ulterior consequences, all my farm laborers, workmen, and stablemen, commanding them never to work for me again.
>
> My shepherd has been frightened by them into giving up his employment, though he has refused to give up the house he held from me as part of his emolument. Another herd on an off farm has also been compelled to resign his situation.
>
> My blacksmith has received a letter threatening him with murder if he does any more work for me, and my laundress has also been ordered to give up my washing. A little boy, twelve years

of age, who carried my post-bag to and from the neighboring town of Ballinrobe, was struck and threatened on 27th September, and ordered to desist from his work; since which time I have sent my little nephew for my letters and even he, on 2nd October, was stopped on the road and threatened if he continued to act as my messenger.

The shopkeepers have been warned to stop all supplies to my house, and I have just received a message from the postmistress to say that the telegraph messenger was stopped and threatened on the road when bringing out a message to me and that she does not think it safe to send any telegrams which may come for me in the future for fear they should be abstracted and the messenger injured. My farm is public property; the people wander over it with impunity. My crops are trampled upon, carried away in quantities, and destroyed wholesale.

The locks on my gates are smashed, the gates thrown open, the walls thrown down, and the stock driven out on the roads. I can get no workmen to do anything, and my ruin is openly avowed as the object of the Land League unless I throw up everything and leave the country. I say nothing about the danger to my own life, which is apparent to anybody who knows the country—

CHARLES C. BOYCOTT

In other words, the Parnell-style shunning was grimly effective. The captain now had no way to harvest the crops that were his responsibility. So he hired scabs to work the fields, and the outraged British government dispatched one thousand members of the Royal Irish Constabulary to protect them. The measly crops were harvested, but at a cost of some thirty times what they were worth. The agrarian resistance proved a rousing success. All of this was duly reported in the press, and as one Irish writer observed, "like a comet the verb *boycott* appeared."

Captain Boycott returned to England to live out the rest of his days, although the next year he made a trip to the United States. In April 1881, a *New York Times* headline announced "Arrival of Capt. Boycott. The Land League's Famous Victim on a Visit to This Country." The article notes that the "famous victim" chose to travel under the name "Charles Cunningham," and "only a few of the ship's officers were aware who the red-faced and rather pleasant-mannered voyager really was."

Try as he might to remain incognito, though, Boycott's name lives on—and all around the world. Today such organized ostracizing is known as a *boikotto* in Japanese, a *Boykott* in German, a *boicot* in Spanish, a *boikot* in Indonesian, and in French, a *boycottage*. In Italian, this kind of resistance now goes by the delicious moniker *boicottagio*. But there's something still more delicious about this word:

In the 1940s, Mussolini's Fascist regime tried to purge the Italian language of words adopted from other languages by forbidding their use entirely. The government decreed that Italians should replace the French borrowings *croissant*, *menu*, and *hotel* with *cornetto*, *lista*, and *albergo*. Italians weren't even supposed to say the name of Louis Armstrong; he was instead to be called *Luigi Braccioforte*. A *cocktail* was no longer a *cocktail*, but a *bevanda arlecchina*, or a "Harlequin drink"—a colorful beverage with several ingredients, named for the patchwork-wearing clown from the commedia dell'arte, Harlequin.

But the funniest thing of all was the Fascist slogan forbidding such terms that contained a foreignism right in the middle of it: *Italiani boicottate le parole straniere!* or "Italians, boycott foreign words!"

Oops.

A Shocking Discovery

SPEAKING OF ITALIANS AND EPONYMS, here's another that involves a fascinating story.

In eighteenth-century Italy, as in the rest of Europe, physicians and anatomists were trying to figure out how muscles and nerves worked together. The Greeks had long ago surmised that nerves were hollow conduits filled with mysterious, invisible spirits that caused motion and physical sensation. But by the late 1700s, a new hypothesis had begun to make the rounds. Maybe the answer involved something that had become the source of increasing fascination: electricity. (Remember Ben Franklin with the key and the kite? That was 1752.)

One of those Italian researchers, Luigi Galvani, taught at the University of Bologna and was married to his anatomy professor's daughter, Lucia Galeazzi. She became Galvani's collaborator, and together they studied the effect of electricity on nerves and muscles. During thunderstorms, they'd stick brass hooks in the spines of dead frogs and hang them on an iron rail outside their home to observe the effects of electrical charges.

They found that when a dead frog's legs touched both a metal hook and a piece of iron simultaneously, the legs twitched as if alive. In 1791, Galvani published a paper hypothesizing that

"animal electricity" was generated in the brain and then distrib-
uted to muscles via the nerves.

That idea would later prove to be wrong, but at the time, the
Galvani experiments shook up the scientific world. This idea
of *galvanism*, or "electricity generated by chemical action," was
especially intriguing to an eighteen-year-old Englishwoman
named Mary Godwin. In 1816, she and her future husband, the
poet Percy Shelley, rented a vacation home in Switzerland and
enjoyed many evenings at the nearby villa rented by their friend
Lord Byron. As Mary would later recall, "Many and long were the
conversations between Lord Byron and Shelley, to which I was a
devout but nearly silent listener."

At one point, their discussions drifted into the possibility of
reanimating a corpse. "Galvanism had given token of such things,"
she later wrote. "Perhaps the component parts of a creature
might be manufactured, brought together, and endued with vital
warmth." In 1818, writing under the name Mary Shelley, she published a novel inspired by that tantalizing possibility, *Frankenstein*.

Galvanism also intrigued an Italian scientist named Alessan-
dro Giuseppe Antonio Anastasio Volta. But Volta doubted that
animals generated their own electricity. Instead, he suspected
that the moist frog flesh had simply been the conductor for the
electricity traveling from one metal to another. Volta ran similar
experiments by stacking discs of zinc and copper or silver, and
instead of relying on animal tissue to conduct a current, he soaked
paper in brine and then stuck it between the discs. The electrify-
ing result was the first *voltaic pile*, the forerunner of the batteries
we use today. Volta's name lives on in that term, as well as in the
unit of electrical measurement called a *volt*.

Even though the Galvanis had guessed wrong about how nerves
work, they did gain a measure of linguistic immortality. When we

talk of *galvanizing* something today—public opinion, for example—we mean jolting it, as if by sending electricity along a wire.

A Father's Love

IN 1907, TWO BROTHERS, VALERIANO and Francesco, left their home in Northern Italy for the United States, and headed for California. In the Golden State, the two brothers took whatever jobs they could find—in a copper mine, in an oil refinery, in an apple orchard, and finally, in orange groves. A third brother named Giuseppe soon followed. The brothers were always inventing new ways to solve problems. When cold snaps threatened their bosses' orange crops, for example, they devised a pump system that would distribute an oily mixture across the groves more efficiently to protect the fruit and leaves.

Another brother, Rachele, who had studied engineering in Italy, soon joined them. Rachele also had training in the relatively new field of aeronautics; just a few years earlier, the Wright brothers had first lifted off the ground. Tinkering in his spare time, Rachele found a way to produce propellers made of laminated wood, making them thinner, lighter, and more efficient. In fact, his new "toothpick" propellers were such an improvement that one of them is now housed in the Smithsonian Institution.

Orders for Rachele's new product poured in from the U.S. military, and with proceeds from those sales, he and his brothers moved to Berkeley and opened a machine shop. There they built mechanical pumps of all sorts, while Rachele kept experimenting with airplane design. During the wave of immigration from Italy that followed, the brothers worked hard to bring over the rest of their siblings—Gelindo, Giocondo, Felicita, Angelina, Ancilla, Cirilla, Stella, Gilia, and Candido—and finally, their parents.

As their business continued to expand, the brothers moved into designing and building small aircraft. Then, in 1921, one of their small planes crashed, killing everyone on board, including Giocondo. Devastated, the family quit the aviation business and pivoted to manufacturing pumps for wells, swimming pools, agricultural irrigation, and filtration systems.

But the story doesn't end there.

The youngest brother, Candido, had a son named Kenny. In 1943, shortly before his second birthday, Kenny came down with strep throat, then rheumatic fever, followed by systemic juvenile rheumatoid arthritis, a debilitating condition that left his joints painfully swollen and stiff. Doctors doubted he'd live more than a few years. When Kenny was three, he was placed in a full-body cast in hopes that immobilizing his limbs would reduce joint pain and deformities. After months in the cast, his growth was stunted and his joints were still misshapen and painful, but he survived.

When Kenny was seven, his mother began taking him to a hospital for hydrotherapy, a new treatment that required sitting in a stainless-steel tub while circulating hot water provided a soothing massage. The twice-weekly treatments provided some relief, but not nearly often enough.

Candido set about designing a device Kenny could use at home every day: a pump that could be lowered into the family's own bathtub for hydrotherapy, then removed afterward. The results were so impressive that Candido and his brothers decided to refine this device enough to bring it to market. But how to get the word out?

One way was via the 1950s TV program *Queen for a Day*, a popular game show with a format that was cringeworthy, to say the least, featuring contestants who told their own hard-luck stories to a studio audience. Whichever story tugged hardest on the heartstrings was rewarded with a slew of prizes that sponsors were all too happy to supply.

In one episode, for example, a military wife wishes for a long-distance phone call and long-postponed honeymoon with her husband. Another woman wants a TV to entertain the four foster kids she looks after in addition to her own. A third wants a dehumidifier for her asthmatic husband and son. Then a mom with seven kids pleads for some domestic help during the two weeks she'll need to recover from an upcoming surgery. The primarily female audience practically breaks the Applause-O-Meter cheering for the weary mother of seven who needs someone to take over for two weeks. Go figure. As the strains of "Pomp and Circumstance" play in the background, she is crowned, draped with a robe, and seated on a throne, looking relieved to be relieved of her chores.

Then she's told that along with some other household items, she can take home a portable whirlpool bath "that gently swirls warm water" and "eases tensions in every part of your body."

As you may have guessed by now, those inventive Italian brothers were the Jacuzzis. Thanks in part to that shrewd placement on a cheesy game show, *Jacuzzi* became a household name almost overnight. Whirlpool baths were no longer just a therapeutic device but a luxurious indulgence, and as happened with other trademarked names such as *Band-Aid*, *Escalator*, and *Google*, the name *Jacuzzi* came to be broadly applied to similar products.

For his part, Kenny Jacuzzi confounded the doctors' predictions and lived to the age of seventy-five, using a wheelchair for much of his life and becoming a powerful advocate for the disabled as director of the Office of the Americans with Disabilities for the state of Arizona. He also wrote a moving autobiography called *Jacuzzi: A Father's Invention to Ease a Son's Pain.*

Ingenuity on Ice

ANOTHER EPONYMOUS TALE OF ITALIAN immigrant ingenuity begins just a few years before the Brothers Jacuzzi began making their way to America. In 1902, Francesco Giuseppe Zamboni and his wife Carmelina settled on a farm in Idaho with their one-year-old, Frank Jr. Growing up, the boy showed a knack for mechanics. The family moved to Southern California, and Frank joined two of his brothers repairing cars in a Los Angeles garage. They later opened a business helping install and maintain electrical systems in homes and businesses. In 1927, the family built an ice-making plant where they froze blocks of ice to be used in railroad cars for shipping produce. In the mid-1930s, though, the advent of air-conditioning and refrigeration suddenly made that work obsolete. The business needed to pivot, and quickly. So they kept their ice-making equipment and opened a skating rink large enough to accommodate some eight hundred skaters. They called the rink Iceland.

The idea proved to be a smashing success, but there was now another problem. The wear and tear from so many skates left the ice with divots, pockmarks, and cracks. It took three skilled workers ninety minutes to resurface the rink by hand. It was a laborious process, dragging a scraper behind a tractor, with workers following behind to scoop the shavings, spray the surface with water, pull dirty water away with a squeegee, then cover the surface with clean water and wait for it to freeze over. There had to be a better way.

Eventually, Frank came up with a motorized vehicle that could do the whole job in a mere ten minutes, and soon he was manufacturing more of them. He wanted to call this new business *The Paramount Engineering Company* after the town where their ice rink was located. But another company already owned that name, so he decided he might as well go with his own name. That's why today announcers at hockey games lead cheers not for the Paramount, but for the Zamboni as it makes its way across the ice.

Seeing that bulky machine glide by, smoothing out all those rough edges for play to begin anew, leaving that glassy mirror in its wake—it's as satisfying as oh, I don't know, seeing all those green Wordle letters finally flip over and jiggle, isn't it? And I know I'm not the only Zamboni fan. Cartoonist Charles Schulz was one as well, judging by how often his *Peanuts* characters mentioned them. Charlie Brown aptly described their allure this way: "There are three things in life that people like to stare at: a flowing stream, a crackling fire, and a Zamboni clearing the ice."

Here in California, I occasionally see tractors trundling along the beach with an attachment that scoops up litter, stray kelp, and bits of debris, then rakes the surface clean. They're variously called *sand cleaning machines*, *beach cleaning machines*, and *beach cleaners*. But in a nice example of what linguists call a *blend*, in which parts of two or more words combine to form a new word, such a machine is also called a *sandboni*.

Fennel-Scented Shoes

IT'S 490 BCE. ON A wide plain a couple of dozen miles north of Athens, Greece, a force of thirty thousand Persian soldiers is bearing down on the town. Even though the Athenian forces are heavily outnumbered, they outsmart the Persians by thinning their ranks in the middle while reinforcing their flanks, causing the invaders to panic. The Persians are routed, and an Athenian soldier named Pheidippides is dispatched to race back to the city with news of this important victory. Exhausted after the long day of fighting, Pheidippides nevertheless drops his heavy shield and runs for Athens.

When he gets there, he announces, gasping, that the Athenians have won, then keels over dead. At least that's one version of the story.

The site of the battle was just over twenty-six miles from Athens. You probably see where this is going. It was fought on the plain of Marathon, the inspiration for the name of the foot-race that now honors the Athenian victory and the heroic run of Pheidippides. I suppose we should be grateful that the word commemorating that heroism is a toponym and not an eponym. As much as I enjoy saying "Pheidippides," and as much as the word itself sounds like rubber shoe soles slapping the pavement, I'm really glad no one has to talk about training for a Pheidippides or even a Half-Pheidippides.

Incidentally, the Greek word *marathon* means "fennel." The place was so named because of the fragrant herb that grew there in abundance. And the historic battle that took place on that scented plain has indirectly inspired the formation of quite a number of other *-thons*, including *walkathon, talkathon, danceathon, bikeathon, swimathon, skateathon, sellathon, begathon, kissathon, laughathon, hackathon, codeathon, yogathon, knittathon, writeathon,* and *readathon*.

But the etymological story of the word *marathon* doesn't stop there. In one version of the legend, the valiant messenger blurts out the word *Nenikēkamen!* or "We're victorious!" just before expiring. Take a close look at that verb *Nenikēkamen*. Tucked right in the middle of this word you'll see the Greek word for "victory": *nikē*. The Ancient Greeks worshipped *Nikē* as the winged goddess of victory.

Now fast-forward more than two millennia. Employees at a Portland, Oregon, company are racing to come up with a name for a new athletic shoe that was to begin shipping the very next day. They've been batting around animal terms like *Peregrine* and *Bengal*, but those don't seem to work. They weigh names with a more scientific ring to them, like *Dimension Six*. In the end, however, the name of the swooshing goddess of victory herself outpaces all of them.

Now whenever I see marathoners running past me in their Nikes, I can't help but think I detect the faintest scent of fennel in the air.

The Cat in the Fabric

AS I WRITE THIS, I'M being stared at by our orange cat, Wolfgang. He's perched on a green chair, gazing at me with golden, chatoyant eyes. *Chatoyant*, which rhymes with *buoyant*, means "to shimmer like a cat's eyes," and is often used to describe the appearance of gemstones. Wolfgang's reminding me to mention another wonderful toponym. This one has its roots in ʿAttābīya, a district near Baghdad long known for producing a variety of textiles. The name ʿattābī came to be attached to a particular kind of cloth produced there, a watered silk with stripes. That fabric name was adopted into French as *atabis*, then shortened to *tabis*, and *tabis* found its way into English as *tabby*. From the toponymic name of the fabric, of course, it was just a short leap to the term for a cat with markings just like Wolfgang's.

The Monument in Your Mouth

WE CAN'T LEAVE BAGHDAD WITHOUT mentioning the House of Wisdom, the vibrant intellectual center that from the eighth through the thirteenth centuries drew scholars from all over the world to study mathematics, medicine, philosophy, translation, astronomy, and optics. Also known as the Great Library of Baghdad, it was for a time the greatest repository of books in the world.

One scholar there, Muhammad ibn Musa al-Khwārizmī, studied geography and cartography, wrote treatises about sundials and astrolabes, and pored over texts on mathematics and astronomy from Greece and India. Around 830 CE, while translating mathematical texts into Arabic, he became convinced that there must be simpler, more elegant ways to solve those problems. Synthesizing his own observations and elements of Babylonian mathematics, al-Khwārizmī came up with a revolutionary way of reaching mathematical solutions.

He described his method of visualizing and describing a mathematical problem and the idea of systematically "reducing" and "balancing" an equation in a book known as *al-Jabr*, the short version of a longer title in Arabic that translates as "The Compendious Book on Calculation by Completion and Balancing." The term *al-Jabr* there literally means "the reunion of broken parts" and is the source of our word *algebra*. In fact, the word *algebra* was first used in English not as a mathematical term, but as a medical one, referring to "the surgical treatment of broken or dislocated bones."

In the twelfth century, a translation of al-Khwārizmī's book into Latin revolutionized the study of mathematics in Europe and served as the principal text on the topic for the next few centuries. Another of his books introduced Hindu-Arabic numerals, astonishing Europeans with a system for calculations that was far more elegant and efficient than traditional methods involving clunky Roman numerals. This influential book's title translates into English as "Al-Khwārizmī Concerning the Hindu Art of Reckoning." Hold that thought for a moment.

The House of Wisdom and other nearby libraries were destroyed in the Mongol invasion of 1258. So many manuscripts were thrown into the Tigris that the river was said to turn black with their ink, and so many books clogged the water, they formed a bridge that could support a rider on horseback. Many of these works of scholarship live on, but countless others were lost.

Near Khiva, Uzbekistan, stands a statue honoring al-Khwārizmī, whose name suggests he may have been born there. The larger-than-life likeness depicts the great mathematician seated and turned to one side, leaning over a manuscript, his face deep in concentration. A few other monuments to his revolutionary work are scattered throughout the world.

But there's also a monument to al-Khwārizmī that stands inside the English language. It's a word that seems to be on everyone's lips these days.

Remember al-Khwārizmī's second book that introduced Hindu-Arabic numerals to the West, paving the way for major mathematical and scientific advances? The book's title was translated into Latin as *Algoritmi de numero Indorum* or "Al-Khwārizmī on the Hindu Art of Reckoning." Note the Latinization of his Arabic name: *Algoritmi*. It's the source of the word *algorithm*, or "a sequence of rules used to solve problems, perform calculations, or complete tasks." Just imagine what al-Khwārizmī would make of their use today.

MORE WORDS FROM NAMES OF PEOPLE

mesmerize

In the late 1770s, physician Franz Anton Mesmer made a name for himself as a healer with methods that were, shall we say, unconventional. He surmised that a mysterious "universal fluid" somehow connects all of us, and when the flow of magnetism within that invisible fluid is blocked, the result is illness. At first, he invited patients to drink mixtures of iron filings in water, then placed magnets at various points on their bodies to restore the proper flow. Later, he ditched the magnets and used his own body's "animal magnetism," touching patients while staring intently into their eyes as soft music played in the background. Some insisted that Mesmer had cured them, but a government investigation branded him as a charlatan. Still, the charismatic doctor's reputation lives on today in the word *mesmerize*.

silhouette

As his country's newly appointed finance minister in 1759, Étienne de Silhouette tried to shore up the French economy by slashing the national budget, raising taxes, and cutting pensions. His austere measures proved so unpopular that Silhouette's tenure lasted mere months, and the expression *à la Silhouette* came to mean something done on the cheap. His name also became associated specifically with simple portraits made with a dark figure against a light background. Speakers of English initially referred to these inexpensive portraits as *shades*, but later replaced that term with the fancier-sounding French name of an ousted government official.

tawdry

Even though seventh-century Anglian princess Etheldreda took a vow of perpetual virginity, her family married her off anyway—first to a prince who died shortly after, and later to a king of Northumbria. Ultimately, she kept her vow by fleeing to the Isle of Ely in Cambridgeshire. There she established a religious house and served as its abbess. She died in 679 after suffering from a throat tumor, which she regarded as divine punishment for vanity in her youth, when she was overly fond of ostentatious necklaces. She was canonized as St. Audrey, and in her honor, the townsfolk of Ely held an annual fair, where merchants hawked trinkets of all kinds, including frilly neckwear made of lace or ribbons called *St. Audrey's lace*. Over time, this term was shortened to *tawdry lace*, and because tacky imitations abounded, the word *tawdry* came to be associated with the idea of something cheap, gaudy, or pretentious.

Ritalin

Methylphenidate, a mild stimulant used to treat ADHD and narcolepsy, was first synthesized in 1944 by Italian chemist Leandro Panizzon. Like many researchers of that era, he first tried the drug on himself, but he felt few effects. He then offered some to his wife, Marguerite, whose nickname was Rita. She tried some before playing a game of tennis, and sure enough, Rita found herself running faster, swinging harder, and hitting the ball with better focus. Rita was so pleased with the results that Leandro named this drug for her, which is why today methylphenidate is better known as *Ritalin*.

darcin

The pheromone darcin, found in the urine of male mice, is named for one of the most recognizable characters in literature. This Minnie-magnet in mouse pee is named after Mr. Darcy in Jane Austen's *Pride and Prejudice*, the fellow Elizabeth Bennet can't resist. I always appreciate it when scientists show their love of literature this way, like Texas Tech biologist Robert Baker, who named the big-eared, leaf-nosed bat *Micronycteris giovanniae* because he's a big fan of Nikki Giovanni's poetry. For her part, the renowned poet told a reporter she was delighted that the "really cute" little bat bears her name. "Years from now, they'll say this is the Giovanni, and nobody will know why."

MORE WORDS FROM NAMES OF PLACES

jeans

The Italian port city of Genoa was once famous for producing the coarse cotton fabric known as *fustian*, which speakers of English called *Gene fustian*, from French *jean fustian*, literally "fustian from Genoa." In the nineteenth century, the name of this sturdy cloth came to be applied to trousers made either from jean or from denim. (The word *denim* itself is from French *serge de Nîmes*, serge being a type of strong, woven fabric, and Nîmes being a town in southern France where it was produced.)

dollar

To get to the roots of the word *dollar*, you have to go back to the German word *Thal*, which means "valley." It's pronounced *tall* and is cognate with the English word *dale*. Even if you don't speak German, you've already seen *Thal* tucked inside several lovely names, including *Rosenthal* ("Rose Valley"), *Blumenthal* ("Flower Valley"), and *Wiesenthal* ("Meadow Valley"). One more valley is "Neander's Valley," named for seventeenth-century pastor Joachim Neander. And yes, as you might have guessed, this valley in Western Germany is the Neanderthal, site of the famous fossil discovery that inspired the name of those early hominids, Neanderthals.

One more German *Thal* lies deep inside the word *dollar*: In the mountains of the Czech Republic is a place on the German border once called *Sankt Joachimsthal*, or "St. Joachim's valley." It was the site of a silver mine and a mint where a large silver coin called the *Joachimsthaler* was produced. Over time, this coin's name shortened to *Thaler*, then became *daler* in Low German and Dutch, and eventually found its way into English as *dollar*, first applied to certain coins from other countries, and later to the unit of American currency.

nystatin

One of the first effective antifungal medications was discovered in 1950 by two women working for the New York State Department of Health: Elizabeth Lee Hazen, a microbiologist based in New York City, and Rachel Fuller Brown, a chemist working in Albany. Collaborating long-distance, they shared test results and samples back and forth through the U.S. Mail. Upon making their groundbreaking discovery, they patented the drug, named it for their employer, and generously donated the $13 million in profits to fund further scientific research.

laconic

Sparta was the ancient capital of the Laconia district of southwestern Greece, home to a highly disciplined, militaristic society—hence our word *spartan* meaning "frugal" or "self-denying." The Spartans were also notoriously sparing with their words. According to Plutarch, King Philip II of Macedon once threatened the Spartans, declaring, "If once I enter into your territories, I will destroy ye all, never to rise again." They answered him with the single word "If." Their response became the stuff of legend, and from the Greek *Lakōnikos*, or "native of Laconia," comes our word describing anyone similarly succinct.

CHAPTER 3

MYTH INFORMATION

IT'S A FRIDAY MORNING IN June. Even before you've had coffee, you start to panic about the gigantic pile of work that awaits you at the office. You open a window and hear the sounds of the city waking up. Doors open and close as neighbors step out onto the street, and thumping music echoes from passing cars. In the distance, there's a siren's lonely wail.

You pour yourself a bowl of cereal. Still half-asleep, you pick up your phone and begin to scroll. You moved to the city in January, grateful for a job that pays more money. But you're at least as grateful to be rid of your old boss. No one should have to deal with a narcissist like that or dread running into their nemesis each day at work. Your new boss is friendly, even jovial. Best of all, she's a wonderful mentor, which is sure to open up some tantalizing new career possibilities.

The weather report says that despite a storm moving up the Atlantic coast, the mercury will rise even higher this weekend. So, between bites, you text your pal Marcus and suggest that instead of lunch in the park on Saturday, maybe the two of you should meet up at a museum where it's nice and cool. You get dressed, gather your things, head out the door, then quickly duck back in to grab a couple of nectarines for later.

Nothing special about the preceding paragraphs, right? Just a mundane description of an ordinary morning. But out of those 250 words, twenty-one have something special about them. Did you catch them? Here's the list: *Friday, June, panic, gigantic, music, echoes, siren's, cereal, January, money, narcissist, nemesis, jovial, mentor, tantalizing, Atlantic, mercury, Marcus, Saturday, museum,* and *nectarine.*

All twenty-one of these words have etymological roots in names from mythology, primarily from ancient Greece and Rome. This chapter uncovers the mythological names and notions preserved inside these and other words—an exploration that will take us down a few labyrinthine paths, along with some forays into astronomy and onomastics, the study of names, the days of the week, why a goddess stares up at you from every bowl of cereal, and a few other places in between.

Janus

LET'S START WITH THE ROMAN god Janus—a very good place to start, since Janus was the Roman god of beginnings. Janus was also the god of transitions, duality, and portals. He's usually depicted with one face on the front of his head and another one on the back, all the better to allow him to see into the past as well as the future. This two-faced deity was also the god of gates and doors. In ancient Rome, a person who guarded a door was known as a *janitor.* This Latin word was adapted into English as a similarly spelled term for a worker who looks after not just doors, but entire buildings.

As the god of beginnings, Janus also inspired the name of the first month of the Roman year, the *mensis Ianuarius,* the source of the English word *January*. His name is also faintly visible in the name of the Brazilian city of *Rio de Janeiro*. On January 1, 1502, Portuguese explorers stumbled upon a scenic bay in what is now Brazil and went on to replace the native name, *Guanabara*, with one commemorating the month of their arrival.

Janus inspired one more term that pertains specifically to linguistics. A Janus word can have two completely opposite meanings depending on context. They developed that status in several different ways.

Take, for example, the word *sanction*. *Sanction* can mean "to approve or allow," as in *The committee sanctioned the new policy*. But *sanction* can also mean "to penalize or discipline," as in *The Senate sanctioned a member of its own*. In this case, *sanction* developed multiple meanings over time. Originally, a sanction was "a formal decree," but over time, another meaning of the word *sanction* arose, specifying the penalty imposed for disobeying something that had been decreed.

Something similarly confusing happened with *peruse*. It can be used to mean "examine without paying much attention," as in *I perused some magazines while waiting for the doctor*. But *peruse* is also used to mean "examine with close attention," as in *Peruse the contract so you understand all the terms* or *Before starting to bake, he perused the recipe to make sure he had every single ingredient on hand*.

Other Janus words are homographs—that is, they look exactly alike, but arose from two different words. My favorite example is the word *cleave*, which can mean either to "adhere to," as in the Biblical injunction that *a man should cleave to his wife*, meaning that he should remain loyal and devoted to her, or *The villagers cleaved to their ancient traditions, despite encroaching modernity*.

"But," you may be thinking, "the word *cleave* can also mean 'to split,' as in what you do with a meat *cleaver*." Think about the past participles of this kind of *cleave*. There's *cloven*, as in *Unlike horses, sheep and goats have cloven hoofs*, but there's also *cleft*, as in *He has the cutest little cleft chin*, and *intergluteal cleft*, which is the anatomical term for "butt crack." This same sense of "splitting" also informs the word *cleavage*.

Here's what's happening: Even though they look alike, these two *cleaves* are entirely different words. The first *cleave*, meaning "stick to" comes from the Old English verb *clifian* meaning "to adhere." The other *cleave*, the one that involves dividing, arose from the Old English verb *clēofan*, which means "to split or divide." It just so happens that as both words developed over time, they began to be pronounced and spelled the same.

Other times, Janus words arise as the result of cultural differences. In British English, *to table something* means to "put something up for discussion" or "add it to the meeting agenda." That's because traditionally, motions in the House of Commons were literally placed on something called the Speaker's Table. In American English, however, *to table a motion* has come to mean to postpone discussion about it.

Fittingly for words named after a god with more than one face, Janus words go by several different names. Whether you call them *contronyms*, *contranyms*, *antagonyms*, and *autoantonyms*, the meaning is the same. They're words that can seem to mean the opposite of themselves. Like so much of language, it all depends on context. Here are some others:

Dust

"To remove dust," as in *He dusted the table*.

"To apply fine powder," as in *Dust the cake with powdered sugar*.

Seed

"To plant seeds," as in *We need to seed the lawn*.

"To remove seeds," as in *Don't forget to seed those jalapeños!*

Trim

"To cut or reduce," as in *We must trim our expenses*.

"To add decoration," as in *Tonight we'll trim the Christmas tree*.

Oversight

"Close control or monitoring," as in *He'll be subject to oversight*.

"An accidental omission," as in *Oops, that was just an oversight*.

Bolt

"To secure in place," as in *Bolt those two pieces together*.

"To flee," as in *I'm tempted to bolt from here*.

Clip

"To cut," as in *Fluffy got her nails clipped at the groomer's*.

"To fasten or attach," as in *The papers are clipped together*.

Buckle

"To fasten," as in *Always buckle your seatbelt*.

"To collapse under pressure" as in *A heavy snow made my roof buckle*.

Resign

"To accept reluctantly," as in *I've resigned myself to staying at my job*.

"To quit something," as in *I've resigned from my job*.

The Big Guy

THE HEAD OF THE ROMAN pantheon was, of course, the big guy himself—lustful, lascivious, lightning-hurling Jupiter. His name apparently comes from an earlier one, *Jovis pater* or "Father Jove." *Jupiter* and *Jovis pater* go back to a prehistoric root that means "daylight-sky father." That same Proto-Indo-European root branched into the Sanskrit term *Dyáuṣ Pitṛ*, which produced the name of *Dyaus*, the ancient Hindu sky god and father figure in the *Rigveda*. This same prehistoric root also produced the Greek version *Zeus pater*, or "Father Zeus," as well as the English words *deity* and *divine*.

The Romans applied the name *Jupiter* to the largest, brightest planet they could see in the sky and believed it was a good thing indeed to be born under the sign of Jupiter. Babies born under the influence of this Jovian planet were destined to be happy, cheerful, convivial, and merry. These lucky folks would be, in other words, naturally *jovialis*. In English, such sunny personalities are said to be *jovial*.

Jupiter was notorious for pursuing both goddesses and mortal women, and his marriage to the queen of the gods, Juno, was often tumultuous. As Jupiter's wife, Juno had several roles to fulfill. She was revered as the goddess of marriage and childbirth, the protector of women, and watchful advisor who monitored the finances of the Roman state. In this last role, she was known as *Juno Moneta*, and it was near her temple on the Capitoline Hill that the Romans minted their coins. Her epithet *Moneta* was adapted into the more general Latin term *moneta*, which denoted coins as well as the place where they're made. *Moneta* found its way into English both as the term *money* and the term for a place where it's made, *mint*. Juno is also honored by the name of the sixth month of the Julian calendar, *mensis Junius*, or in English, June.

The names of these ancient gods and their attributes were often slippery and shape-shifting. The gods of the Greeks and Romans, for example, didn't always correspond exactly to each other. Even within a single tradition, gods could have different names and traits. Throughout history, conquering armies often found it easier to let a version of the local gods remain, building on the religious foundation that was already there, grafting new names and characteristics onto old figures instead of imposing a whole new belief system outright.

In what is now the far western edge of the Egyptian desert, for example, the locals worshipped *Ammon*, or *Ammon-Ra*, as the sun god, and built a temple to him near the Siwa Oasis. The Greeks later incorporated that god as *Zeus Ammon*. Then the Romans came along and dubbed him *Jupiter Ammon*, a god who was depicted on coins and statues with ram's horns on the side of his head. Those horns were sometimes large, like those of a real ram, and sometimes they were small and tightly curled, like mini Princess Leia side buns. Their coiled shape inspired the Romans to call similarly spiraled fossils *Ammonis cornu*, or "horn of Ammon," the source of their modern name, *ammonite*.

One last thing before we depart from the temple of Ammon: Near this holy site lay valuable salt deposits known to the ancients as *sal ammoniac*, or literally, "salt of Ammon." *Sal ammoniac* is source of the modern English terms *ammonium chloride* and its kindred chemical substance, *ammonia*. So next time you get a bracing whiff of ammonia, remember that ram-headed Egyptian god.

A Planet-a-Day Calendar

LET'S LOOK BACK UP AT THE sky, for the planets do indeed influence earthly affairs—at least when it comes to the names of things. In antiquity, only five planets were known. Across the world, people have long noticed that these celestial bodies, along with the moon and sun, moved differently from other bright spots in the sky. Even as the stars remain in fixed constellations that move east to west across that inky expanse each night, these other astronomical objects wander right through those patterns. The Greeks referred to these errant orbs with their word for "wanderer," *planētes*, a word the Romans adopted into Latin as *planeta*. English speakers have inherited the Romans' names for those five: *Mercury*, *Venus*, *Mars*, *Jupiter*, and *Saturn*. If we point our telescope in and zoom in close, we can see the influence of each of these planets on language.

MERCURY

The fastest-moving of the planets is named for the Roman's swift-footed messenger god, Mercury, or in Latin, *Mercurius*. (The Greeks had called this wanderer *astēr tou Hermou*, or "star of Hermes," a reference to Mercury's counterpart in Greek myth.) People born under this planet's sign are said to be dexterous and eloquent, but also restless and energetic. And if they have a quick and changeable mood, they're described as *mercurial*. Similarly, the quivering metallic element *mercury* is most likely named for its mobility, which makes it useful for measuring temperature with a thermometer. Mercury is sometimes called *quicksilver*— the *quick* in this case meaning "living," and the same *quick* in the *quicksand* that swallows things "as if alive," the *quickening* inside a womb, and a phrase that combines opposites, *the quick and the dead*.

We mustn't leave Mercury without a nod to his Greek counterpart, Hermes, and his linguistic offspring. As *Hermes Trimegistus*, or "Thrice-greatest Hermes," this god was linked with the Egyptian deity Thoth, who presided over writing, occult wisdom, and the secrets of alchemy. In fact, alchemy itself is sometimes called *the Hermetic art*. In their quest to turn base metals into gold and find an elixir that confers immortality, early alchemists puzzled over how to create airtight seals for the glass containers they used in experiments. Hermes supposedly came to their aid by inventing such a seal, hence our word *hermetically*. Now, for example, a thermometer that contains mercury or some other fluid must be hermetically sealed lest it lose any of its movable metal.

One more thing about Mercury: In Germanic mythology, his counterpart was *Odin*, also known as *Woden*, the god of, among other things, wisdom, healing, travel, and communication. Hold on to that thought; we'll return to it in a moment.

VENUS

Venus was the Roman goddess of love, beauty, and fertility. Her own linguistic offspring include the word *venereal*, or "relating to sexual love." Her Greek counterpart, Aphrodite, lent her own name to the English word *aphrodisiac*, and her son Eros was the personification of *erotic* love. Because Venus lies between Earth and the sun, it goes through phases, as love is also known to do.

MARS

The Romans named the red planet for their god of war, Mars. The month of March is named in his honor. Mars also shines through such English words as *martial*, meaning "military," as in *martial law*, *martial arts*, and *court-martial*, as well as the names *Marcus*,

Mark, *Marco*, and *Martin*. The Germanic counterpart of the Roman god Mars was a one-handed god of war named *Tiw*. Hold on to that thought too, and we'll circle back to it shortly.

JUPITER

The planet named for the king of the Roman gods has a regal presence in the sky, always maintaining the same dazzling brilliance in contrast to Mars, which varies in brightness. Additionally, Jupiter moves with its own majestic grace across the heavens, not bound to the sunrise or sunset like Venus. Since we've already noted Jupiter's linguistic progeny, let's keep hurtling through outer space.

SATURN

Beyond Jupiter is Saturn, which, as it happens, is named for Jupiter's dad. Saturn was also the god of agriculture, among other things, and was honored with one of the best Roman festivals, the Saturnalia, which lasted several days around the winter solstice and featured all kinds of merrymaking, gift-giving, role reversals, and general disregard for rules and norms. During the Saturnalia, slaveowners traded places with the people they enslaved, inviting them to lavish banquets and sometimes even serving the food themselves. For these few days, the enslaved were allowed to talk back to their masters without reproach, and gag gifts were a big part of the festivities. The merrymaking hearkened back to a long-ago golden age when Saturn himself ruled the Earth. In English, a *saturnalia* is any kind of noisy, wild revelry or extravagant celebration. (A review of a 1969 John Cage recording evocatively likened the busy composition to "a twenty-two-minute block of inchoate sound that sounds like *Saturnalia* in a harpsichord factory.")

Ironically, the planet Saturn, the farthest of the known planets in those days, was considered cold and sluggish, taking its time as it moved across the sky. People born under its sign were said to be taciturn, morose, generally gloomy, and melancholic, characteristics now described as *saturnine*.

The ancients spoke of seven planets—what we call Mercury, Venus, Mars, Jupiter, and Saturn, plus the sun and the moon. They didn't consider Earth a planet because it sure felt stationary to them while everything else clearly moved.

You know what else we have seven of? That's right—days of the week. And the names of gods and planets inspired the names of those days, both in Latin as well as in several modern languages. Over the centuries, the Romans fiddled with various systems for counting the days.

Line up these Latin names alongside three Romance languages and you can easily see how the modern names of the weekdays evolved. The names for Saturday and Sunday in these languages are related to Hebrew *shabbat*, as in "Sabbath," and Latin *dominicus*, referring to the "day of the Lord," a linguistic relative of *dominion* and *dominate*.

English	Latin	French	Spanish	Italian
Monday	dies Lunae	lundi	lunes	lunedì
Tuesday	dies Martis	mardi	martes	martedì
Wednesday	dies Mercurii	mercredi	miércoles	mercoledì
Thursday	dies Jovis	jeudi	jueves	giovedì
Friday	dies Veneris	vendredi	viernes	venerdì
Saturday	dies Saturni	samedi	sábado	sabato
Sunday	dies Solis	dimanche	domingo	domenica

Something similar happens in English but with a couple of Germanic counterparts of the Romans' god. As we've noted, the ancient Romans had a habit of incorporating local deities and slapping on the name of a god they felt had comparable characteristics. For example, the Romans associated the Norse god Odin with their own Mercury, perhaps because both had many roles that included offering guidance to souls after death.

As in Latin, English speakers have the "day of the sun" or *Sunday*, and "day of the moon," or *Monday*. Tuesday honors *Tiw*, the Germanic god of war, the counterpart of the Roman war god Mars. *Wednesday* honors Odin, also known as Woden—recall that Woden is the Norse counterpart of Roman Mercury. Next comes Thursday, which honors Jove in Latin with *dies Jovis*; his Norse counterpart is the thunderous, bolt-hurling Thor, who is honored with the English day *Thursday*. The following day honors Venus in ancient Rome, and in English, the name *Friday* honors Frigg, the wife of Odin/Woden, who, like Venus, was revered as a goddess of love, whose worship sounds like a great start to any weekend.

So there you have it: Mercury, Venus, Mars, Jupiter, Saturn, plus the sun and the moon, all memorialized in names for days of the week. But before we return from outer space, it's worth looking at two more orbs out there. It would be hundreds of years after the fall of the Roman Empire before these planets were discovered. But their own mythologically inspired names—and the fights over what to call them—will take us down some fascinating etymological paths.

The Rest of the Solar System
URANUS AND NEPTUNE

The planet beyond Saturn wasn't discovered until 1781. Astronomers had long surmised that something was out there, but it took

William Herschel, a German immigrant living in England, and his powerful telescope to realize that this celestial body was not a star. He first guessed that it was a comet, but later observations by other astronomers showed that Herschel had actually pinpointed a planet.

Herschel proposed that this new planet be named *Georgium Sidus* (literally, "George's star") after his patron, King George III of England. He also called it *the Georgian planet*, or simply *the Georgian*. As you might imagine, these names honoring an earthly king of one particular nation did not go over well outside England.

French astronomers wanted to call it *Herschel*, perhaps hoping that future planetary discoveries would bear their own names. However, a German astronomer, Johann Bode, whose calculations had helped determine the planet's orbit, proposed calling this new discovery *Uranus*, a Latinized form of the Greek god of the sky, *Ouranos*, in keeping with the long tradition of naming planets for Roman gods. In ancient myth, Uranus fathered Saturn, and Saturn fathered Jupiter, and Jupiter had fathered Mars, Venus, and Mercury, so it made sense to continue the pattern of the solar system as one big, happy planet family. Arguments went back and forth.

Around the same time, German chemist Martin Heinrich Klaproth discovered a new heavy metal and lent his support to Bode's position by naming this new element *uranium*, specifically to honor the recent planetary discovery. In fact, look at the bottom row of the periodic table of elements, and you'll see these heavy metals proceeding in a similar order: the element uranium is followed by neptunium and, after that, plutonium.

The debate over what to call the planet beyond Saturn went on for more than half a century. But then the world thrilled to the discovery of another beyond that one—the eighth planet. With yet another planet identified, it made more sense to keep the mythological family intact, so astronomers agreed to call this bluish orb Neptune, after the Roman god of the sea. And as nice as it would have been for the seventh planet to have a friendly name like Herschel, or maybe even George, astronomers finally agreed to call it Uranus.

Which brings me to the pronunciation of this planet's name. You don't have to tell me that dictionaries sanction—this time in the sense of "allow"—the pronunciation *yoo-RAYN-uss*. I know they do. But seriously, why would anyone want to look up Uranus in the first place? Sit with that for a moment. Can't we all just agree to pronounce the name of this planet the way most astronomers do, which is *YOOR-uh-nuss*? Any reason we shouldn't spare parents and schoolteachers all that tittering? Besides, *YOOR-uh-nuss* is more in keeping with the word's Greek origins anyway.

Incidentally, this god's Greek name, *Ouranos*, literally means "Sky," and in Greek myth, this Sky-God got together with his sister *Gaia*, or "Earth." Ouranos and Gaia produced twelve giant, humanlike deities called *Titans*. From their name we get the English word for something enormous, *titanic*, and the use of *titan* for someone of gigantic achievement, such as a *titan of industry*. And wouldn't you know it, the word *gigantic* itself comes from another Greek myth in which the *Gigantes* were a race of savage gods with superhuman strength.

The Titans, by the way, met a bad end when a younger generation of gods known as the Olympians waged war on them, vying for dominion of the universe. The young upstarts prevailed and proceeded to divide up the spoils with the now-familiar setup: Hades as ruler of the underworld; Poseidon, whose realm was the sea; and Zeus, king of the Olympian hill.

Among those defeated gods was Cronus, a Titan whose Roman counterpart was the aforementioned Saturn. In some versions of the myth, another Titan named Atlas was a key player in the long conflict between the Titans and the Olympians. After the Titans' defeat, Zeus singled out Atlas for especially heavy punishment: He'd have to hold up the sky for eternity. The poor guy was made to stand with his heavy load at the far western edge of the world in Northwest Africa, where earth and sky were said to meet, near what are now called—not surprisingly—the *Atlas Mountains*. The Greeks described the waters beyond that shore as being "of Atlas," or *Atlantikos*, hence the name of the ocean we call the *Atlantic*.

By the Middle Ages, bound collections of maps included a frontispiece featuring an image of Atlas holding up the world, and thus the word *atlas* came to denote such reference works. And among medical professionals, the word *atlas* refers to the topmost bone in your spine—the one holding that world inside your skull.

PLUTO

The story of how Pluto got its name involves a most unlikely pair: a wealthy American businessman (and brother of poet Amy Lowell) who was also an accomplished mathematician and astronomer—and one Venetia Burney, an eleven-year-old girl in England, who thought up the name while eating breakfast.

The astronomer was named Percival Lowell, and he hailed from a wealthy Boston family. He was also a Harvard-trained mathematician and author, and in 1894, in hopes of finding intelligent life on Mars, he founded the Lowell Observatory in Flagstaff, Arizona. By the early 1900s, he and fellow astronomers were also on the hunt for the elusive *Planet X*, which calculations had led them to suspect was out there. Sadly, Lowell died in 1916 before that discovery could be made.

In 1930, a twenty-four-year-old working at the Lowell Observatory named Clyde Tombaugh spotted what they were looking for. The sensational news sped across the globe. More than a thousand letters suggesting names for the new planet poured in. In his memoir, *Out of the Darkness*, Tombaugh recalled the prickly challenge of handling the suggestions that kept coming from the widow of Percival Lowell, the observatory's benefactor. At first, Mrs. Lowell proposed that *Zeus* should be the name of the new planet. Then she decided it should be called *Lowell*. Still later, she urged that it be named *Constance*, after herself. "No one favored that name," Tombaugh wrote. "It was a touchy situation."

Fortunately, his team didn't have to try too hard to placate their benefactor because hundreds of other proposed names were pouring in. They fell into three main categories. Some people were lobbying for *Minerva*, the Roman goddess of wisdom. Others championed *Cronus*, the Greek Titan and counterpart of Saturn. Still others advocated naming it after *Pluto*, ruler of the Greek underworld. The ancients also considered Pluto the god of wealth, in part because precious minerals were located underground—in fact, his name still glints inside the English words as *plutocracy* and *plutocrat*.

In any case, *Minerva* was out because this name had already been applied to an asteroid. Tombaugh wrote that the name *Cronus* might have been considered had it not been proposed "by a certain egocentric astronomer," an explanation that begs for a backstory, but he left it right there.

That left *Pluto*. The first suggestion for that name from outside the observatory came from young Venetia Burney, whose grandfather had been reading to her over breakfast about the new planet. She'd been learning about Greek and Roman gods in school. Between bites, she piped up, "Why not call it Pluto?" As it happened, her granddad was the top librarian at Oxford University's Bodleian Library and had lots of connections among the world's top astronomers. He fired off a cable to one of them, and the rest is galactic history.

It didn't hurt that the first two letters of that name were also the first initials of the observatory's benefactor, and in fact, for years the symbol for that planet was a combination of P and L. Mindful of all the controversy before they settled on the name Uranus, the astronomical community moved quickly to approve the name for this latest discovery. The following year, the famous Disney dog first appeared in a cartoon, solidifying the name and popularity of the solar system's most far-flung planet.

Well, at least until 2006. That's when the International Astronomical Union kicked Pluto off its planetary pedestal. The astronomers had good reasons for voting to do so, despite the outcry that ensued. (For details, check out one of my all-time favorite science books, *How I Killed Pluto and Why It Had It Coming* by Caltech astronomer Mike Brown.) Although the name of Pluto didn't change, it was demoted to the status of *dwarf planet*, a shift that had reverberations beyond the world of astronomy. Later that year, the American Dialect Society, an organization of linguists, lexicographers, etymologists, grammarians, historians, researchers, writers, authors, editors, professors, university students, and independent scholars, chose *plutoed* for its "Word of the Year," noting that the verb *to pluto* had quickly come to mean "to demote or devalue someone or something."

And for anyone complaining that "Verbing weirds language," as the *Calvin and Hobbes* cartoon put it, I would point out that verbing is a natural process of language. In fact, it's estimated that at least one-fifth of English verbs came from nouns, a process known as *denominalization*. Anyone who has a problem with turning nouns into verbs is welcome to email, phone, text, fax, or message me. Every one of those verbs started as nouns. For that matter, going from top to bottom on the human body, you can *head a committee, face a problem, mouth words to a song, shoulder responsibility, hand something over, stomach an idea, foot the bill*, and *toe the line*. Further, you can also *elbow your way* into something—an example of denominalization that goes back at least as far as Shakespeare.

One other linguistic thing to note about *plutoed*: When was the last time you heard anyone use it in casual conversation? The verb *to pluto* is a great example of how the hottest, zingiest bit of new slang may be here today and floating off into the outer edges of the universe tomorrow.

Linguistic Children of Lesser Gods

A FEW MORE MYTHICAL CHARACTERS have names that live on in the English language. There's Mnemosyne, the goddess of memory, who had a fling with Zeus. Her name is a linguistic relative of that term for "lack of memory," *amnesia*, as well as the "intentional forgetting" that is *amnesty*, and the memory-assisting *mnemonic device*, like the one I use to help me remember all the planets in their proper order: *My Very Energetic Mother Just Served Us Nachos.*

From Zeus's affair with Mnemosyne came the *Muses*, those inspirational goddesses of the arts and science. Their numbers varied over the years and locations, but in general, they inspired humans when it came to such things as literature, comedy, dance, and song. Besides the noun *muse* itself, these goddesses also inspired the English words *music* and *museum*, originally a place holy to the Muses.

In some stories, Zeus fathered the goddess of divine wrath and retribution, whose job it was to reverse excessive good fortune and dole out justice to wrongdoers. Her name: *Nemesis*, from a Greek word meaning "to distribute what is due." Nemesis provided rewards for noble deeds and vengeance for evil ones, even if that justice was delayed for generations. In American English, her name has also come to denote an archenemy or longtime rival.

Nemesis brought about justice in two stories now memorialized in our language. One involved yet another of Zeus's many offspring, the half-mortal king named Tantalus, who had a thing for testing boundaries. In one version, Zeus invited Tantalus to dine with him on Mount Olympus. During the meal Zeus, confided in Tantalus about some of his secrets, which Tantalus proceeded to blab as soon as he got home. In another, Tantalus went even further: He decided to test the gods' omniscience by inviting them to a banquet where he'd cut up his own son, then cooked him and served parts of him to see if they would notice. The gods did, and they were not amused.

For his offenses, Nemesis forced Tantalus to spend the rest of eternity standing in a pool of clear water. Every time he got thirsty and reached down to take a drink, the water receded. A bough of enticing fruit hung just above his head, but when he got hungry and reached for the fruit, it pulled away. This grim image and the name of bad King Tantalus live on in the word *tantalize*.

The goddess of vengeance also played a role in the tragic story of a young man named Ameinias who fell hard for an incredibly handsome youth named Narcissus, who repeatedly spurned his advances. At last, in a final act of rejection, Narcissus gave him a sword, which the rejected youth used to kill himself. With his dying breath, though, he begged the gods to punish Narcissus for his arrogance and cruelty. Nemesis obliged, making Narcissus fall in love with his own reflection in a pond. In some versions of the story, the handsome youth can't tear himself away from his own reflection and wastes away until nothing is left but the flower now called *narcissus* that blooms along lakes and streams. His name also lives on in the egocentric personality of a *narcissist*, characterized by grandiosity, excessive need for attention, and lack of empathy.

Narcissus spurned the advances of male and female admirers alike. In later versions of the story, he's pursued by a talkative nymph named Echo. Unfortunately for Echo, she made the mistake of distracting Hera with gossip while Zeus carried on an affair behind her back. When Hera caught on, she exacted a severe punishment: She stole Echo's ability to speak, except to repeat whatever words she'd just heard. When Narcissus was out wandering during a hunting expedition, she tried to catch up with him, but it did not go well. Every time he called out, "Who's there?" Echo could only repeat, "Who's there?" and she could only watch helplessly as Narcissus proceeded to catch sight of his own handsome face in the pond and suffer unrequited and unfulfilled love himself. Her name, however, *echoes* down through the ages.

Another goddess looks out at you from every bowl of cereal. Zeus's sister Ceres, the goddess of agriculture, introduced humans to wheat and taught them how to plow the fields. Celebrated as a symbol of maternal love, she was worshipped as a "nourishing mother," or in Latin, an *alma mater*—just as a school today nourishes its students' minds.

Speaking of nourishment, *nectar* and the sweet fruit called a *nectarine* derive from the Greek word *nektar*, thought to come from roots that mean "overcoming death," and a relative of all those *necro-* words that involve death. The gods sipped nectar and feasted on *ambrosia* (from Greek for "not mortal"), and indeed this fare was said to confer immortality. This sustenance also filled their veins not with blood but *ichor*, an equally magical fluid.

(Many word nerds treasure the term *petrichor*, which denotes "the pleasant smell of rain, especially after a long dry spell." This term was coined by a pair of Australian scientists in the 1960s who discovered that the pounding of raindrops on soil and rocks—*petra* in Greek—causes certain compounds to be released and combine in the air to produce that pleasing aroma.)

Another outdoorsy god was the goat-footed Pan, who presided over woods and fields as well as shepherds and flocks. The story goes that Pan fell hard for a nymph named Syrinx and pursued her against her wishes. She fled to the edge of a river and was transformed into a reed. Frustrated, Pan let out a deep sigh, causing the reeds below him to produce a plaintive musical sound. Unsure which reed was his beloved Syrinx, he gathered up several, bound them together, and cut them to various lengths to create the musical instrument now known as a *pan flute* or *panpipes* or, in honor of the chaste and chased nymph, a *syrinx*. As it happens, her name in Greek means "tube" and inspired the word for that tube that enables birds to sing, a *syrinx*, and that tube with a needle at the end of it, a *syringe*.

As the god of forests, fields, and other lonely spots, Pan was also notorious for striking irrational fear into the hearts of people camped in desolate places. The Greeks blamed Pan for all those scary sounds that echoed across lonely valleys at night, and *panikon deima* came to mean "fear caused by Pan," a version of which found its way into English as *panic*.

Zephyrus was a cruel, vengeful Greek god of the west wind who delighted in stirring up deadly storms at sea. Over time,

though, Zephyrus mellowed. In later Greek myth, he personi-
fied the fragrant wind wafting over the Elysian Fields, where the
blessed enjoyed the afterlife. And it's that sense that inspired
our word *zephyr*, which William Shakespeare used to conjure the
very picture of mildness when he wrote: "They are as gentle as
zephyrs blowing below the violet, not wagging his sweet head."

Any discussion of words from Greek mythology must include
some of the characters from the epic poems *The Iliad* and *The
Odyssey*. We still speak of a weak spot being one's Achilles heel,
mentioned in *The Iliad* as the one place on the Greek warrior
Achilles where he was vulnerable. Achilles' nemesis was Hector,
the Trojan prince and the greatest defender of Troy. Hector was
noble and brave, and in its earliest sense in English, *Hector* was an
approving term for someone similarly heroic. By the seventeenth
century, the noun *hector* had lost its capital *H* and expanded to
mean "a swaggering braggart," or as Samuel Johnson would put
it in his 1755 dictionary, "a bully; a blustering, turbulent, pervica-
cious, noisy fellow." This sense was influenced by the behavior of
London street gangs who called themselves *the Hectors*. Today, to
hector someone means to intimidate or harass them.

Words that had their start in *The Odyssey* include, well, *odyssey*, inspired by the long and winding route that Odysseus took
after the Trojan War. The word *mentor*, meaning "a trusted guide
or counselor," comes from Mentor, the wise old friend to whom
Odysseus entrusted the tutelage of his son before going off to
fight. Another word that branched off from that is *mentee*, a term
for "protégé" that has been around since at least the 1940s.

On his way home from the war, Odysseus let his curiosity get
the better of him when his ship came within range of the Sirens,
women with the bodies of birds, whose song was so mellifluous
that they supposedly could lure men to their death. Odysseus

had his men plug their ears with wax and lash him to the mast so that he could hear their sweet song. Centuries later, a French scientist invented a device with two disks that produced a musical tone when one of them was spinning and air was forced through them. When he found that it produced sound even when placed underwater, he called it a *sirène*. He'd originally invented it to measure musical frequencies and other sounds, but the device had practical applications as well, and soon people were using versions of it at lighthouses, on boats, and eventually, emergency vehicles.

A minor character in both *The Iliad* and Virgil's *The Aeneid* is Ucalegon, an elder of Troy. I mention this because of a conversation I once had with *New York Times* crossword puzzle editor Will Shortz, in which he told me that his favorite word was *Ucalegon* (pronounced *yew-KAL-uh-gon*). I had to go looking for that word, and it wasn't all that easy to find. But it's listed in Webster's 1934 *New International Dictionary*. A Ucalegon is a "a neighbor whose house is on fire." Turns out that in the *Aeneid*, Ucalegon's house went up in flames. If you ever do need to report something like this to your local fire department, probably best to not to bother with the word *Ucalegon* and just get straight to the point.

A couple more terms before we leave this linguistic labyrinth. The first, as it happens, is *labyrinth*, a word of obscure origin. In Greek myth, the Labyrinth was a huge maze on the island of Crete. Inside that intricate structure lived the Minotaur, a fearsome monster with the head of a bull and the body of a man. Every nine years, Athens was required to send seven young men and seven young women there to be sacrificed. They were paraded in front of King Minos and his family, then led inside the Labyrinth to be devoured by the hungry monster, its name a combination of *Minos* and *tauros*, or "bull."

One year, the hero Theseus joined the other Athenian youths who were sent as tribute and paraded in front of the royal family. When the king's daughter saw Theseus, she fell in love with him and somehow managed to get him aside from the rest. Then she secretly gave him a ball of thread and told him to tie one end of the thread at the entrance and unravel it as he ventured deeper into the maze. That way, he could kill the Minotaur, then follow the thread to find his way back out. He did just that. Which brings us to the Old English word *cliewen*. In Old English, *cliewen* could mean "a globular mass" or "a round bunch" or cluster of things. But it could also mean "a ball of yarn"—and over time, *clew* came to specify the ball of yarn used by Theseus and other mythological characters to find their way out of mazes. This word later came to indicate anything that points the way or provides guidance in solving a puzzle or mystery. And today we spell it not as *clew*, but as *clue*.

As we near the exit of this mythological maze, following the long thread out, let's pause to give a couple of nods to the two-faced fellow by the door. For it turns out that Janus, the source of *January* and *janitor* and runner-up for a planet's name, was worshipped not just as the god of beginnings, but also the god of endings.

CHAPTER 4

WORD ORIGINS

I'M OFTEN ASKED WHICH WORD is my favorite, but that's like being asked to choose a favorite star in the sky. There are way too many, whether in English or other languages. If pressed, I usually say my favorite is *mellifluous*, which describes something "sweetly pleasing"—the sound of a flute, a supple writing style, a pleasant voice. Besides having a lovely mouthfeel—the tongue touching the back of the teeth, the lips coming forward before settling back with a hiss—*mellifluous* has an etymology as sweet as it is picturesque. *Mellifluous* comes from Latin *mel*, meaning "honey," making it a linguistic relative of *molasses*, *marmalade*, and the name *Melissa*. The ancient Greek word *melissa* means "bee," and may be a combination of two older words that literally mean "honey-licker." The last part of *mellifluous* derives from Latin *fluere*, meaning "to flow," from the same family of other "flowing" words, such as *fluid* and *fluent*. Something mellifluous, then, in its most literal sense, is "flowing with honey."

Mellifluous is a great example of what Ralph Waldo Emerson meant when he said, "The etymologist finds the deadest word to have been once a brilliant picture. Language is fossil poetry." Or as the nineteenth-century essayist Thomas Carlyle put it, "The coldest word was once a glowing new metaphor."

But just how do scholars dig up those linguistic fossils and discover those brilliant pictures within? One way is to compare related words in languages arising from a common ancestor, which brings us to the hypothetical mother tongue scholars call Proto-Indo-European.

The languages spoken by nearly half of the world's population—including some four hundred million native speakers of English—are thought to have descended from this prehistoric language. Scholars have managed to reconstruct its fundamental elements by using comparative linguistics to identify common features and vocabulary in its descendants. Exactly where Proto-Indo-European began is a mystery. Some believe it arose six thousand years ago on the grassy plains of Central and Eastern Europe north of the Black and Caspian Seas. Others suggest earlier origins in Anatolia, the large region of what is now Turkey, bordered by the Black Sea to the north, the Aegean to the west, and to the south, the Mediterranean. Wherever Proto-Indo-European originated, its linguistic offspring spread throughout Europe, to Iceland and Ireland in the west, and eastward to India and what is now part of Chinese Turkestan.

Like taxonomists trying to classify the biological world into increasingly specific subgroups, specialists in comparative linguistics divide descendants of this parent language into eight large families of Indo-European languages spoken today that branch out from this root like a tree: Albanian, Armenian, Balto-Slavic, Celtic, Germanic, Hellenic, Indo-Iranian, and Italic. Those linguistic branches, in turn, divide into even smaller ones. English, for example, belongs to the Germanic group, which also includes German, Dutch, Swedish, Danish, Norwegian, Afrikaans,

Icelandic, Scots, Yiddish, and a few others. In the Italic branch, only the Romance languages survive: Spanish, Portuguese, French, Italian, Romanian, and Catalan, and several others such as Sicilian, Galician, and Dalmatian.

The Indo-European language group is just one of many, however. There's the Afro-Asiatic family of languages spoken in northern Africa, the Arabian Peninsula, and parts of Western Asia, including Egyptian and Somali, plus Semitic languages such as Arabic, Hebrew, and Aramaic. Other large language families include the reconstructed mother tongue called Niger-Congo, which gave rise to some 1,500 languages spoken over most of Sub-Saharan Africa, including Igbo, Yoruba, and Zulu. There's also Austronesian, comprising languages that include Malay, Javanese, and Tagalog. The Sino-Tibetan language family comprises more than four hundred, including Mandarin, Burmese, and Tibetan languages.

Just how linguists divide all those languages into different families varies. Some of them sort the more than 7,000 living languages into 142 groups; others suspect the number of language families is closer to 400.

Not a word of Proto-Indo-European was ever written down, so how do we know that it, or something like it, existed? The answer is the strikingly consistent correspondence between various features among its descendants. These similarities are what Professor Latkovski meant when he compared the words for "foot"—Greek *pous*, Latin *pes*, Sanskrit *padas*, and their offspring. They are all cognates, or words that mean the same thing in different languages that arose from a common source.

Similarly, the Indo-European root for the number three gave rise to English *three*, Spanish *tres*, French *trois*, Swedish *tre*, Lithuanian *trys*, Albanian *tre*, Bengali *tri*, Russian *tri*, Polish *trzy*,

Greek *treis*, Irish *trí*, and Welsh *tri*. The German version evolved as *drei*, and in Dutch, *drie*, reflecting a regular correspondence between *d* and *t* sounds that often appears among certain Indo-European languages. Something similar happens with English *two* and its various cognates in other languages, such as Spanish *dos* and French *deux*, and the kindred English words *duo*, *duet*, *duel*, and the double-tongued language app, *Duolingo*. Even the word *dubious* is a cousin to all these. *Dubious* comes from the Latin *dubare*, "to hesitate to make a choice between opinions or courses of action," presumably between two of them. (Interestingly enough, the same idea of choosing between a couple of things is conveyed in the Old English word for "doubt," *tweó*, a relative of Modern English *two*.)

Correspondences such as these are addressed in more detail by what's called Grimm's law, a system of patterns named for the nineteenth-century linguist and folklorist Jacob Grimm—yep, the same Grimm who, along with the other Grimm brother, Wilhelm, published *Grimm's Fairy Tales*. Building on the work of Danish philologist Rasmus Christian Rask, Jacob Grimm formulated a pattern of consonant changes, also known as the Germanic Sound Shift, which basically went like this: Indo-European *p*, *t*, and *k* morphed into Germanic *f*, *th*, and *h*, while Indo-European *b*, *d*, and *g* became Germanic *p*, *t*, and *k*; and Indo-European *bh*, *dh*, and *gh* became Germanic *b*, *d*, and *g*.

You can see some of these changes more clearly by comparing several Latin words to their long-lost English cousins. For example, the Proto-Indo-European root that produced Latin *piscis* or "fish" (as in the astrological fish Pisces) became English *fish* and German *Fisch*. The ancient root that gave us the Latin word *pater*, or "male parent" (as in *paternity*, *patriarchal*, and *paternoster*) became English *father* and German *Vater*, with its initial *f* sound.

Like detectives reconstructing a crime scene or archaeologists inferring the entire shape of a pot from a minimal number of fragments, scholars of historical linguistics figure out the earlier forms that must have given rise to words in many different languages and connect the dots between them. By analyzing remnants of these roots in various ancient and modern tongues, they've found links between English and modern languages as diverse as Russian, Persian, Danish, Polish, Hindi, Spanish, German, French, Portuguese, and Greek, and other modern languages as diverse as Nepali and Manx, as well as with ancient ones such as Sanskrit, ancient Hittite, and Tocharian. Such correspondences offer a fascinating means of tracing human history.

Earlier, I mentioned choosing a favorite star. That's as good a place as any to begin examining some of these puzzle pieces and how they fit together.

The Proto-Indo-European root for the word "star" produced words for this celestial body in several languages. *Star* came into English through the Germanic branch of languages, making it a cognate of Swedish *stjerna* and German *Stern*, as in *Der Stern* or *The Star* magazine and the name *Morgenstern* or "morning star." All these words are also related to the Greek word for "star," *astēr*, which gives us the similar-looking English name of the starry flower, the *aster*, and *asterisk*, literally, "little star."

Greek *astēr* also shines within the word for those star-sailors better known as *astronauts*. The *-naut*, or "sailor," in *astronaut* belongs to a whole fleet of nautical words from the same root. One of them, the Latin word *navis*, means "ship" and is the forerunner of English *navy* and *navigate*. (The related Greek word for "ship," *naus*, is preserved in our word for "ship-sickness," *nausea*.)

It was once widely believed throughout Europe that stars produced an ethereal fluid that somehow influenced earthly affairs.

In the eighteenth century, for example, when an infectious fever raged throughout what is now Italy, the locals referred to it by the same name they had long used for any epidemic caused by the "evil influence" of the stars flowing in from on high. This outbreak spread far beyond Italy, and so did its name, *influenza*, or simply *flu*. The word *influenza*, or "influence," comes from Latin for "flowing in," which brings us back to all those other "flowing" words, like *mellifluous*.

Let's gaze into the night sky for just a bit longer. That luminous cloud of stars, the galaxy, takes its name from the Greek word *gala*, which means "milk." The Greeks weren't the only ones who imagined a milky splash across the sky. The ancient Romans also called it the *via lactea* or "milky way." (The related Latin word *lac*, or "milk," also appears in *lactate* as well as milky words in several other languages, such as Spanish *leche*, French *lait*, and that Italian espresso drink with steamed milk you might enjoy each morning: the *latte*.)

Now let's turn our eyes to the Big Dipper, or *Ursa Major*, literally "the Big Bear." Part of this constellation points to the North Star, found in the Little Dipper, or *Ursa Minor*, "the Little Bear." The Latin word *ursa* gave us *ursine*, or "bearlike" and the feminine name *Ursula*, plus the Spanish and French words for this animal, *oso* and *ours*.

In Greek, the same prehistoric root of these words evolved into *arktos*, or "bear," which brings us back down to earth—and specifically, to the Arctic region surrounding the North Pole. The Greek word *arktikos* literally means "of the bear" and alludes to the region "of the Bear constellation," that is, "the north." The Arctic is the home of *Ursus maritimus*, or literally the "maritime bear," more commonly known as the polar bear. Part of that region is also home to *Ursus arctos horribilis*, the grizzly whose last name isn't that hard to figure out. And of course, the related Greek word *antarktikos*, or literally, "opposite of the bear," gave us the name of the place penguins call home, the Antarctic.

All these connections, hiding right there in plain sight—if only you know where and how to look.

I find all this oddly comforting, the way these connections reveal how others before us have puzzled over their own experiences and tried their best to make sense of them, to divide the world into manageable pieces and give all of those pieces names. In other words, we're not alone. Our predecessors reached for metaphors to try to make the world legible to themselves and to each other. Over time, the words they created have tumbled and jostled against each other, evolved, grown appendages or lost pieces of themselves, developed new meanings and uses, and spun out far and wide.

For now, one more favorite word: *vestigium*. The Latin word *vestigium* means "footprint," which is useful to know, because by investigating the roots of words, we discover vestiges of the past.

Did you see what I did there? Latin *vestigium* left footprints of its own in not one, but two, English words in that sentence. Right there in plain sight. Alas, etymologies don't always reveal themselves so clearly. The origins of many words are simply lost in the mists of history, a disappointment that lexicographers record with the frustrating notation *origin unknown*, or *orig. unk*. Not very mellifluous, is it?

CHAPTER 5

NERD ORIGINS

PEOPLE OFTEN ASK HOW I ended up doing a public radio show about language. Like so many broadcasters, it's not as if I set my sights on a career in this field early and followed a straight line to get here. Professionally speaking, I've had a checkered past, and I'll probably have a checkered future as well. The common thread throughout it all, though, is that for as long as I can remember, I've been friends with words, a lover of reading and writing. Perhaps that was inevitable, since both my parents were educators.

My mother taught English for twenty-five years in the Louisville public schools. Warm, witty, and effervescent, she was beloved by her middle-school students. She knew that to compete for their attention, she'd have to make English class entertaining. She did so with a sense of humor and a flair for drama. Over the years, she built up an inventory of gimmicks to help her students learn the boring rules of grammar.

If one of them struggled with the word *cemetery*—was it *-ery* or *-ary*?—my mother would ask, "What do you do in a scary cemetery?" She'd clasp her hands to her head, her eyes wide in mock horror, then say, "You go, '*Eeeeeeeeee!*' all the way through!"

Silly, yes. But they never forgot after that.

Mom had a reputation throughout the school for her funny stories and the goofy pictures she drew on the chalkboard to illustrate her points. When a student made a grammatical error in class, my mother would stride dramatically to the chalkboard, put her hand at the top, then slowly and dramatically drag her fingernails all the way down. "That's what that sounds like to me!" she'd say as the kids covered their ears and squealed. But they learned.

The same thing happened at home. Once when I was about ten years old, I told my mother I'd been laying on the couch.

She clutched her hands to her cheek. "You were laying on the couch?" she said, feigning excitement. "Oh goody! How many eggs? Now I won't have to go to the store!"

She explained that the transitive verb *lay* means "to place" or "to set down," the thing chickens do to eggs. I should have said *I was lying on the couch all afternoon*, the word *lying* being a form of the intransitive verb *to lie*, meaning "to repose in a horizontal position."

In other words, I learned traditional rules of grammar almost by osmosis. They were part of the air I breathed. After school, Mom and I would diagram sentences together just for fun, and she let me grade her students' spelling tests, which felt like a special treat.

Raised in a tiny town in the Shenandoah Valley, my mother was steeped in the soft Virginia dialect of her father, a Baptist preacher who grew up on a peanut farm, and her mother, a church organist from East Tennessee. When my mother was surprised by something, she'd declare, "I *swan*!" or "I *swanny*!" Both expressions are thought to be a shortening of a much older dialectal phrase in Scotland and Northern England, *I shall warrant ye*, meaning "I guarantee you" or in other words, "I swear." Where she grew up, *I swan* and *I swanny* were euphemisms—a way to express surprise or indignation without resorting to swearing, which was prohibited in the Bible.

My mother also used that familiar marker of Southern speech: *fixing to*. By that she meant "getting ready to" or "intending to." I remember her often saying, "I'm fixin' to go get my hair fixed." *Fixing to* has been used this way in the American South since the 1700s. (More recently, just as *going to* was shortened to *gonna*, *fixing to* among speakers of Black English was shortened to just *finna* or *fitna*.)

My father was also an educator, a professor of Christian ethics at the Southern Baptist Theological Seminary in Louisville. Both my parents were Baptists of the Jimmy-and-Rosalynn variety.

At mealtime with Mom and my three brothers, Dad might drop in a Bible verse if it was relevant, but just as often, he'd share bits of poetry he'd committed to memory—lines from Shakespeare, Walt Whitman, Emily Dickinson, Rainer Maria Rilke, and Lewis Carroll to name just a few. My dad had a doctorate in theology, did postdoctoral work at Harvard and Columbia, and read Latin, Greek, Hebrew, and German.

In those days, the seminary itself was a great intellectual center, respectful of all faiths, and a hub of social activism. At the height of the Vietnam War, my father invited prominent antiwar protesters like Father Philip Berrigan to come speak to his classes. He also welcomed Austrian psychiatrist and Holocaust survivor Viktor Frankl, author of *Man's Search for Meaning*, to the school. Frankl was known for sketching caricatures; it would be years before I happened across friendly correspondence between the two of them among my father's papers, saw a drawing, and connected it with the friendly man with the big glasses who came to dinner one night and drew cartoons for my little brother and me.

On his nightstand, Dad kept a tattered copy of Blaise Pascal's *Pensées* on his nightstand and often quoted the French philosopher's observation: "Men never do evil so completely and so cheerfully as when they do it in the name of religion." Dad also treasured a quote from Rilke: "Be patient toward all that is unsolved in your heart and try to love the questions themselves, like locked rooms and like books that are now written in a very foreign tongue." My dad's own homespun wisdom boiled down to a line he repeated often: "Always be kind to people. You never know what burdens they're carrying." Good advice.

Years later, the Southern Baptist Convention would be taken over by fundamentalists, a tale recounted in a 1996 documentary *Battle for the Minds*, available in its entirety on YouTube. The film, which chronicles efforts by the newly conservative seminary to deny women roles as pastors, includes several conversations with my dad. Of fundamentalist Christians, he says: "They pick and choose passages to support their prejudices. These people believe in thought control. And if you don't conform with them and believe what they believe, you are out. O-U-T, out!" Dad also provides the film's one bit of comic relief when he notes that the Bible condemns adultery as a capital crime. With a twinkle in his eye, Dad says, "These people say they take the Bible seriously . . . Why don't they apply capital punishment to adultery?"

Many years later, I was complaining to him about hard-right conservatives twisting scripture for their own political purposes. He nodded. "The Bible just says love God and love your neighbor," he told me. "All the rest is window dressing." And when I was having trouble with a college assignment that involved reconciling several conflicting arguments, I called my father to vent. He listened for a long time, then said simply, "Marth, just milk all the cows you can, then churn your own butter."

All of which is to say, my father was a Baptist minister and ethics professor who read widely—so widely, in fact, that when I was in elementary school, we added a room onto the house to accommodate all his books. A few years later, his books outgrew that room, too, so we added yet another room in the basement to house his growing collection. And that didn't even include all the books on the shelves in his office at the seminary.

Thanks to my mother and father, I arrived at college already instilled with a love of language and learning—and plenty persnickety about grammar. I had some vague notion that I wanted to be a writer myself someday, so it seemed natural to major in English. Thank goodness they encouraged English majors to take a classical language, and thank goodness I nearly failed that first class, or I never would have found Professor Latkovski.

As my college years drew to a close, I faced a choice. After reenrolling in introductory Greek, I went on to take every Greek course I could. But I wouldn't be able to do graduate work in Greek without a few more classes under my belt. A program at the University of Cambridge in England would give me a chance to swot up my Greek and Latin and prepare for grad school. So I applied and got in, but didn't have the $14,000 for tuition and board. I'd have to work for a while first.

While in college, I'd had summer internships at the Louisville *Courier-Journal* and *The Louisville Times*, a pair of newspapers with a long tradition of great reporting and writing. I lined up one more internship for right after graduation, this one at *The Washington Post*, one of two interns on the national desk covering the federal bureaucracy. The other was a fellow from Yamhill,

Oregon, and one of the nicest guys I ever met, Nick Kristof. Toward the end of that summer, a top editor at the *Post*, Peter Osnos, took us aside to say that ordinarily they'd be happy to keep us on, but the town's rival newspaper, the *Washington Star*, had just folded, which meant that talented reporters with far more experience were looking for work and the *Post* was snapping them up. Osnos told us not to be discouraged, though. "Do something different," he said. "Go off and make yourselves interesting. Then come back."

Nick headed off to Oxford and made himself very interesting indeed, going on to a storied career as a foreign correspondent. As for me, I figured I'd take a newspaper job in Louisville to earn some money, then head off to Cambridge for Greek.

At *The Louisville Times*, I covered whatever they threw at me—fires, police stings, floods, a square dance convention, and much more. On Monday evenings, I continued to meet with Professor Latkovski for coffee, bread, and Greek.

Then a thrilling opportunity opened up: the medical beat. Louisville had become a major medical center, with renowned surgeons and a large hospital complex. It was a time of exciting innovations in medicine, and the challenge would be to translate that specialized information in clear, compelling ways.

Soon I was suiting up in scrubs and following doctors and nurses around with a tape recorder. And of course, because so much of the language of medicine comes directly from Greek and Latin, it often felt as if the professionals in that field were speaking poetry.

When a physical therapist referred to the tibia, that long, straight bone in the lower leg, I'd think, "Yup. *Tibia* means 'flute' in Latin. That makes sense." If she mentioned the *pelvis*, I'd say to myself, "Yup, *pelvis* is Latin for 'basin.' Picturesque!"

When a neurosurgeon pointed out the small, nut-shaped structure in the brain called the *amygdala*, I had another forehead-smacking moment. "Oh, of course! From Greek for 'almond.'"

Coronary arteries? Yup. *Coronary* from Latin *corona*, meaning "crown" or "garland." The coronary blood vessels wreathe the heart like a crown, *coronary* sharing a root with other words involving crowns, like *coronation*. (As I would later learn, Latin *corona* inspired the name of a virus with a spiky little crown, the *coronavirus*—hence *coronavirus disease*, which when shortened becomes *COVID*.)

I'd keep all those thoughts to myself, of course. But then someone would mention *anatomy*, and I'd think about how *anatomy* is from Greek *anatomia*, a "dissection," from Greek *ana*, "up," and *tome*, "cutting"—literally, "all cut up." And if you add the Greek stem *a-* meaning "not" to that cutting root, you have the term for the tiny particle once mistakenly thought to be "uncuttable," the *atom*.

Clearly, it was easy to get distracted by the etymologies that kept nudging their way into every conversation about medicine. In fact, although the medical beat was fascinating, the idea of studying Greek kept tugging at me. After three years at the *Times*, I'd just about decided to quit the newspaper when a huge story broke on my beat.

Lured by lavish funding from the Louisville-based Humana hospital chain, Dr. William DeVries announced he was moving his artificial-heart experiments to Louisville. In 1982, in a first-of-its-kind operation, the Utah surgeon removed the diseased heart of a dentist named Barney Clark and inserted a plastic-and-metal Jarvik-7 heart. Clark survived another 112 days, but remained hospitalized, dogged by complications. Two years later, backed by Humana's vast resources, DeVries was ready to try again. This second experiment would draw media coverage from around the world, and I would get to be a part of it.

Having screened numerous candidates debilitated by congestive heart failure, he settled on a fifty-two-year-old union leader from a tiny Southern Indiana town, William Schroeder. Without a new heart, Schroeder would die. The night before his surgery, his heart was so weak he could barely lift his head from the pillow. The next morning, DeVries removed the diseased portion of Schroeder's heart and replaced it with a permanent artificial heart.

The operation was a smashing success. Within days, Schroeder was wisecracking, sitting up in bed, and hoisting a can of beer. In a televised interview, the only man alive without a human heart wept with gratitude for his family and spoke of his plans for the future. Then-President Ronald Reagan called to congratulate him. Schroeder thanked him but demanded to know why his Social Security check was late. The president laughed and said he'd get right on it. The next day, a check was hand-delivered to the world's most famous heart patient.

His new heart was connected by a pair of ten-foot pneumatic tubes to a 323-pound pump that sounded like loud windshield wipers, powering the heart with puffs of compressed air. The clicking and ticking of the plastic-and-metal heart was audible over that, even several feet from the end of his bed. The artificial heart ticked loudly, constantly, almost frantic. Like a bomb.

Schroeder continued to grow stronger. But eighteen days after the device was implanted, it sent a shower of blood clots into his brain, causing a massive stroke, one that might have killed someone else. But the artificial heart kept pumping. He suffered fever, weakness, anemia, seizures, and soon after, a second stroke. Now cameras filmed a man in a wheelchair who made slow-motion gestures and could seem to stare blankly. He sometimes nodded "yes" when he meant "no." Thoughts snagged somewhere inside him.

As news about the experiment subsided and most of the media moved on, I left the newspaper and began taking graduate classes in Greek at the University of Kentucky. Maybe, I thought, I could still teach someday. For several months, I was happily reading Homer and Aristotle in Greek, *The Consolation of Philosophy* by Boethius in Latin, and freelancing on the side.

Still, I couldn't shake the epic Greek tragedy unfolding right across town. As the experiment wore on, Schroeder survived long enough to meet a new grandson, and the family held a wedding for another son in the hospital lobby so he could attend. Given the strokes, however, it was doubtful whether he'd even remember those things he'd wanted so desperately to live for. A third stroke followed, leaving him weak and only dimly aware of his surroundings. He lived like that for another 602 days.

Amid all the reporting on the medical developments, no one was telling the family's story. Not really. They agreed to let me write an as-told-to book. Finding a publisher was easy; the family had been all over the news. But it became clear as I continued reporting that I was going to have to put classics on hold again. This modern story was more urgent, after all. The ancients would still be there when I finished.

CHAPTER 6

THERE OUGHTA
BE A WORD FOR IT

SOME OF OUR MOST ENTERTAINING calls on *A Way with Words* come from listeners who think they've spotted a hole in English vocabulary and are doing their best to fill it. Sure, you can always put several words together to try to contain an idea and communicate to others. But there's something immensely satisfying when you see that concept packaged inside a single word. It's kind of like when comedians say, "Did you ever notice how . . . ?" and then go on to riff about some common experience in a way you've never thought about. Once they call your attention to it, you can't help but see it, too. Now you have a new way to think about it, plus a handy new word or phrase for describing it.

This "Aha!" experience extends beyond English as well. Have you ever encountered a word in another language that was so delicious and so apt that you adopted it into your own vocabulary? That happened to me when I come across the marvelous mouthful *Verschlimmbesserung.* Break this German word down into its component parts, and it makes perfect sense: The verb *verschlimmern* means "to aggravate" or "to make worse." The verb *verbessern* means "to make better." Together they form *Verschlimmbesserung*, which means "an attempt to make something better that actually makes things much worse." Take Brexit, for example, or New Coke, or a software update that creates many more problems than it solves.

Verschlimmbesserung has been around in German since the early nineteenth century. I'll admit that pronouncing it is a something of a workout, but it does articulate the idea so perfectly that I don't know why English speakers wouldn't want to pilfer it. Yes, if you really want to, you can always rely on the little-used English word *disimprovement*. But why bother with something so euphemistic and bland when you can have the satisfaction of spitting out those expressively exasperated German syllables?

Now that I think about it, there is another English term that conveys a similar idea. It's *the cobra effect*, and the story behind this expression is instructive. During British colonial rule in India, the city of Delhi had an overpopulation problem with venomous cobras. The sight of poisonous snakes slithering through the streets must have been unnerving. Then someone in government got the bright idea to offer a bounty for dead cobras. This snake-snuffing program enjoyed brief success—but only until shrewd entrepreneurs realized that they could make more money by breeding lots of cobras specifically to be killed. When officials caught on, they discontinued the program. The problem was that now that breeding and killing snakes was no longer profitable, the breeders simply let them go. The snakes went back to reproducing on their own and made the situation even worse. Now that's what you call a slithery *Verschlimmbesserung*.

Sometimes individual speakers coin words that never travel much farther than their own idiolect—the vocabulary and usage particular to an individual—or beyond their familect, the linguists' term for the unique combination of words and phrases used within a family.

Many of those linguistic innovators, of course, are quite young. A Florida listener told us her four-year-old son mystified everyone for a while when he kept referring to the *have-in-it*. It took a while before the family realized he meant the cabinet. The family got such a kick out of this word—it makes perfect sense, after all—that they still tell each other that this or that item is *in the have-in-it*. A Wyoming woman told us how she carefully prepared her three-year-old to meet his great-grandparents for the first time, explaining that the people he was going to meet weren't his grandparents, but his great-grandparents. The little boy puzzled over that, then went around happily announcing that he was going to meet his *grape grandparents*. Today, of course, the whole family fondly calls them *Grandma and Grandpa Grape*. And a listener named Erica in Hong Kong told us her niece was convinced that Abraham Lincoln's name was actually *Abraham LinkedIn*, and she would never hear it any other way again.

Significant others also develop a shared vocabulary, whether by combining each family's linguistic heirlooms, imbuing old words with new meaning, or coming up with entirely new words and phrases known only to each other.

A San Diego woman called us looking for a word that denotes the period of sleeplessness that may follow if you wake up in the middle of the night. She found it odd that English does have a word for a period of sleep in the middle of the day—the word *nap*—but "when you're awake in the middle of the night, you're just awake." Shouldn't there be a word for that, too? She'd been wondering about that very question during one of her sleepless nights, so she decided to call us.

We said we weren't aware of such a word in English, but suggested she might borrow the lovely French word *dorveille*, a combination of *dormir*, "sleep," and *veiller*, "wake." *Dorveille* specifies just that sort of period of being awake before going back to sleep.

I mention her story because after we aired this call, other listeners shared their own terms. A Sacramento woman said that the term she and her husband used was *squeegee*. When they got together in the early 1990s, nighttime TV often featured half-hour infomercials for cleaning products. If one of the two of them couldn't sleep, they'd turn on the tube with the volume on low. "We were fascinated that they could spend a half hour on the wonders of a squeegee. Hence our catchphrase '*Did you squeegee last night?*'" (If you don't go to sleep at all, whether due to insomnia, writing a paper, or simply having too good a time, the French have a picturesque term for that, too. Where we would say you *pulled an all-nighter*, the French will say you had a *nuit blanche*, or "white night.")

Speaking of new words, here's a question I hear all the time from people who've coined a new word: "How do I get it into the dictionary?"

Here's the thing: You can't just announce to dictionary editors that you've come up with a new word, however evocative or efficient it might be. First, when you talk about getting a word into "the dictionary," which dictionary do you mean exactly? *Merriam-Webster*? The *Oxford English Dictionary*? The *Collins English Dictionary*? The *New Oxford American Dictionary*? The *Cambridge Dictionary*? The *Macquarie Dictionary* of Australian English? The collaboratively sourced dictionary *Wiktionary*, run by the Wikimedia Foundation and edited by volunteers online? There are several major English dictionaries, not to mention many more dictionaries that specialize in topics such as chemistry, real estate, law, and astronomy.

Second, you may have invented the world's most brilliant neologism, but a word can't break through that paper ceiling until the editors see evidence—and lots of it—that many people already use your word, and that they do so in lots of different contexts. Dictionaries are a record of what's already out there, not what ought to be, and lexicographers need solid proof that a word is established in the language, or at least well on its way. They spend countless hours scouring newspapers, magazines, chat groups, social media, historical archives, newspaper databases, and other sources to see whether a term is widely used, how it's used, and if possible, when people started using it. They gather citations documenting those instances, then monitor current language use to see when the collective weight of them is compelling enough to earn a place in their pages or in the ever-expanding collections of digital dictionaries.

In other words, your chances of getting your invented word into dictionaries aren't much better than your chances of winning the lottery—or maybe winning the lottery while being struck by lightning. It does happen on occasion, but it's rare.

One way to predict whether a new word is likely to stick around is to evaluate it with a formula created by linguist Allan Metcalf, abbreviated with the sticky acronym *FUDGE*. If you're wondering whether a word has staying power, these criteria will help:

F is for *Frequency*. If a word is used frequently, then it's clear the word is filling some lexical need and has a good shot at finding its way into reference works. When the word *selfie* appeared a couple of dozen years ago, it may have sounded cutesy or even jarring, but as more and more people from all walks of life started snapping self-portraits, the word became firmly entrenched in the language. By 2013, it was Oxford Dictionaries' "Word of the Year," and was added to the *OED* shortly afterward.

U is for *Unobtrusiveness*. Metcalf put it this way in his book *Predicting New Words*: "A successful new word flies under the radar. It camouflages itself to give the appearance of something we've known all along." Take for example *doomscrolling*, or "spending excessive time poring over grim news on social media." This term took hold during the COVID-19 pandemic as people were glued to their phones. It was so apt and so evocative and useful that it stealthily slid into the English language and stayed. Ditto for *sexting*, which explains itself pretty readily, as does, for that matter, *staycation*.

In contrast, words that seem to exist less for their usefulness and more to show off a moment of cleverness—a stunt word, like *textpectation*, which denotes "a state of anxiously awaiting a text"—are likely just a flash in the linguistic pan.*

D is for *Diversity of users and meanings*. If a word is used exclusively among scientists specializing in the reproductive habits of a particular South African beetle, it's not likely to join the general vocabulary of everyone else. (I, however, would be super interested in it, so please do send any entomological esoterica my way.) On the other hand, plenty of people from all walks of life now enjoy *binge-watching* things on television, indulging in marathon sessions of successive episodes. (The word *binge* itself has been around since the 1840s, when it was an English dialectal term that meant "to soak a leaky wooden vessel in water

---

* The phrase *flash in the pan* has been around since the early 1700s, long after the flintlock muskets that inspired it. These muskets had a small pan that held gunpowder. Pull the trigger and a piece of flint struck steel, making sparks that ignited the gunpowder in the pan. If the gun misfired, there was merely a flash in the you-know-what.

in order to make the wood swell." A few short years later, *binge* came to mean "engage in a bout of heavy drinking." Today *bingeing* refers to indulging excessively in any number of activities, and *binge-watching* and *binge-watch* are natural, seamless extensions of the word.)

G is for *Generating forms and meanings*. The word *podcast* is a combination of the portable media player called an *iPod* and the *-cast* from *broadcast*. It was quickly adapted into other forms, such as *podcasting, podcaster*, and *pod*, even as iPods have become collectors' items. (Oooo, *broadcasting*! Originally this was an agricultural term that referred to planting seeds by scattering them rather than placing them in the ground in holes dug individually. In the early twentieth century, this idea of scattering was adopted for the new technology of spreading words far and wide.)*

E stands for *Endurance of the concept*. Take *mansplain*. The *OED* defines it this way: "Of a man: to explain (something) needlessly, overbearingly, or condescendingly, esp. (typically when addressing a woman) in a manner thought to reveal a patronizing or chauvinistic attitude."

When *mansplain* first cropped up in 2008, this combination of *man* and *explain* was clever, yes, but it was also memorable—a powerful, succinct way to express something so many of us have experienced, and within a decade, *mansplain* was comfortably ensconced in major dictionaries. This word also ranks high on Metcalf's *G* scale and continues to generate its own linguistic

---

*   Another term with a surprising agricultural origin: *aftermath*. The *math* in *aftermath* is an old word for "mowing." It's unrelated to the kind of *math* that involves calculations. In the fifteenth century, the aftermath was the subsequent crop of grass or hay that follows the mowing down of the first. That second crop was also called a *lattermath*. Over time, *aftermath* developed its figurative sense of "the consequences or effects of a previous significant event."

offspring. The -*splain* element is now combined with, as Wiktionary puts it, "someone who fits that description condescendingly explaining something to someone who does not fit that description (especially, something the listener has more experience of)." These variations on *mansplain* include *ablesplain*, *cissplain*, *straightsplain*, *whitesplain*, and *youthsplain*, among others.

One word that's surely racked up several points on the FUDGE scale in recent years is *fluffle*. You may have seen the photo making its way around the internet showing nine fuzzy bunnies and the caption: "A group of wild rabbits is called a *fluffle* and I've never loved the English language more."

Fluffle even sounds like what it suggests, a fluffy bundle of nose-wiggling cuteness. You almost have to smile when you say it. But you won't find this word in most dictionaries—at least not yet, although it's off to a pretty good start. *Fluffle* has been around for a couple of decades now. You'll often see it in lists of "fun facts," feel-good Instagram posts, and websites about rabbits and pet care.

What makes *fluffle* even more interesting is the story of its origin, which involves a medieval nunnery, a college prank—and as it happens, a phone call to *A Way with Words*.

First, we need to look at the history of collective nouns in English. Some of the most famous of these involve animals. *A pride of lions*, *a gaggle of geese*, and *a murmuration of starlings* are among the scores of collective nouns in *The Book of St. Albans*, published in 1486. Its author is said to be Juliana Berners, variously known as Juliana Barnes or Juliana Bernes. Supposedly Juliana was a nun who presided over a Benedictine abbey in Hertfordshire, England. I say "supposedly" because little is known about her except that she's often credited with writing all or most of this book, which happens to be one of the first ever printed in English, and among the first thought to be written by a woman.

The Book of St. Albans contains essays on falconry, hunting, fishing, and heraldry. One section, titled "The Compaynys of Beestys and Fowlys," lists 164 collective names for groups of beasts and fowls. Among them: *a charm of goldfinches, a skulk of foxes, a shrewdness of apes, an unkindness of ravens, a business of ferrets,* and *a flock of sheep.* The author of *The Book of St. Albans* didn't make up all these terms. *Flock,* for example, had already been around in this sense for hundreds of years. But Juliana, or whoever the author was, clearly had fun with some of these. In fact, the section on collective nouns for animals also includes some playfully picturesque terms for groups of humans as well, including *a rascal of boys, a pity of prisoners, a promise of bartenders, a hastiness of cooks, a discretion of priests,* and, for some reason, *a superfluity of nuns.* (I don't know. Can you ever have too many nuns?)

In the centuries that followed, other clever folks got in on the collective-noun-coining fun, coming up with such specimens as *a parliament of owls, a clowder of cats, a knot of toads,* and *a smack of jellyfish.* Still others added fanciful groups of people and professions, such as *a wince of dentists* and *a rash of dermatologists.* (Once you start these, it's hard to stop. Try it! Grant and I even invited listeners to come up with collective nouns for plants and were pleased to receive lots of brilliant suggestions, such as *a pursing of tulips* and *a greasing of palms.*)

Anyway, fast-forward to the twenty-first century. In 2023, a woman named Van Credle of Washington, D.C., was talking with her friend Danielle. Van mentioned that her mother was fond of rabbit figurines and had a huge collection of them.

Danielle says, "Oh, you mean your mother had a *fluffle of bunnies!*"

Van had never heard that word and was surprised and delighted to learn it existed.

But then Danielle told her something even more surprising. The really funny thing about it is that Danielle and her friends were the ones who made up the word *fluffle*, and one of them had added it to Wikipedia as a joke. Now, she said, you can find the word *fluffle* defined as "a group of rabbits" all over the internet.

Van was understandably skeptical, in part because she happened to be a regular *A Way with Words* listener. She'd heard enough episodes to know that it's extremely rare for a word to be coined and popularized by a single person or small group. So in 2023, Van reached out to the show to see if there was any possibility that Danielle and her friends could have been responsible for coining the word *fluffle*.

Grant told her that the linguist and *Wall Street Journal* columnist Ben Zimmer had researched this word and indeed turned up evidence that in 2007 someone had changed the "Rabbits" entry on Wikipedia to include the line "A group of rabbits or hares are often called a 'fluffle' in parts of Northern Canada."

A few years later, a Wikipedia editor deleted that line, citing lack of evidence. In the intervening years, however, the noun *fluffle* meaning "a group of rabbits" had already begun multiplying like, well, you know.

Grant told Van that there didn't seem to be evidence that the word *fluffle* existed any earlier than 2007, so it just might be that her friends did coin the word. Afterward, he put Ben and Van in touch with each other, and Van proceeded to connect Ben with two of her physics-major classmates who'd been in on the prank, Danielle Pahud and Kevin Olsen. They told Ben that over lunch one day at the University of Alberta in Edmonton in 2007, they and some friends were talking about the snowshoe hares on campus and how they compared to the wild rabbits at another university where they'd attended a conference. They wondered what the collective noun for them would be, when someone piped up that a group of rabbits should be called a *fluffle*. The group was so delighted with the term that Kevin added the word *fluffle* and its definition to Wikipedia, where it stayed for years before being taken down.

Fluffle is currently found in Wiktionary online. Time will tell whether *fluffle* makes it into other dictionaries. For that to happen, it will have to be used more widely and in different contexts. It's certainly more fun than the collective term in the St. Albans book. I mean, why settle for *a nest of bunnies* when you can have a whole *fluffle*?

I mentioned earlier that some of my favorite calls involve lexical lacunae* that listeners have pointed out and hope to fill in. Sometimes they bring us words they believe they've coined. Or they wonder if someone else has come up with a word for a particular phenomenon. Or they contact us hoping to crowdsource a new term for something they've noticed.

Here are a few examples, including invented words that denote a particular type of meal and an epithet for a particularly irritating type of motorist. At the end of this chapter, I'll also share the "What's the word for . . . ?" question that, to my astonishment, prompted more responses than any other call in the twenty years I've been talking with listeners. I'm still puzzled as to why.

---

* *Lacunae*? Great word! In Latin, *lacuna* means a "ditch" or "pit," especially one that fills up with water, and not surprisingly, *lacuna* and its plural *lacunae* (luh-KYOON-ee or luh-KOON-eye) share a common linguistic root with the English word *lake*. Today in English, a lacuna is a gap or missing part, such as a lacuna in a manuscript or a suspicious lacuna in someone's résumé.

So, herewith, what do you call . . .

That frantic cleaning you do just before company arrives

Your guests are coming in half an hour, but you've been so busy cooking dinner that you haven't left yourself any time to tidy up the place. Now what? A Montreal listener named Vivian told us she and her friends have several terms for that mad dash before guests arrive. One of them calls that frantic filling of the junk drawer or closet *making a lasagna* because "you end up with a bunch of unrelated things in layers." Another refers to it as *mummification*, both because it forms layers but also because the mum in her household is the only one allowed to do it lest things end up too disorganized. Still another friend—Vivian's friend group must do a lot of entertaining—refers to that last-minute cleanup as *stuffing the comedy closet*, an expression perhaps related to putting things in the *Fibber McGee drawer*. On the old-time radio comedy *Fibber McGee and Molly*, McGee had a closet so crammed with junk that whenever he opened the door, it all spilled out with an impossibly long cacophony of clatters and clunks.

Still other listeners call this speedy cleanup as a *scoop 'n' shove*, *swooping*, *sweeping through the middle*, *shame cleaning*, or *guilt cleaning*.

But my favorite term for this mad scramble is one we learned from an Iowa woman who called to say that when unexpected guests were on their way, her mother always yelled to the kids, "Quick! The whited sepulchre!" It's a reference to Matthew 23:27, where Jesus draws a clever analogy between hypocrites and the ancient practice of whitewashing tombs with lime: "Woe unto you, scribes and Pharisees, hypocrites! for ye are like unto whited sepulchres, which indeed appear beautiful outward, but are within full of dead men's bones, and of all uncleanness." I've adopted this one myself, considering that *the whited sepulchre* is a pretty apt metaphor for that frantic effort to make your home look presentable—when only you know all the uncleanness really lies behind those closet doors.

Those dinners at home when everyone must fend for themselves

You know those evening meals when everyone just throws together whatever random items they can find in the fridge or pantry? Our listeners have lots of unofficial names for it.

A Dallas listener told us his family calls it *having CORN*, as in *Clean Out the Refrigerator Night*, while others call it *YOYO Night*, as in *You're On Your Own*. Others call those meals of miscellaneous items *mustgoes*, as in *Everything must go*. In still other families, the weary cook simply announces that tonight's menu features *getcheroni* and *make-your-oni*.

Other names for those informal meals include *Scrounge Night*, *Snacky Dinner*, *Anarchy Dinner*, *Anything Night*, *Graze Night*, *Girl Dinner*, and *Bachelor Dinner*, as well as *self-service*, *scratch your own back*, *fridge diving*, *leftover surprise*, *skip*, *supper jump-up*, *grab and growl*, and *root hog or die*.

You can just picture these scenes: A Maryland listener told us her family calls it *crab feast* because "we scuttle around like the crabs do, eating a little of everything." A Florida woman told us the French exchange student staying with her family called those times *IKEA Nights* because it required removing all the parts out of the refrigerator and trying to assemble them.

Grant and I are not the only ones who've delighted in all these terms. When cartoonist Roz Chast asked her Instagram followers what they called this kind of free-for-all, they responded with a whole fridgeful of terms, including *having weirds*, *eek*, *mustard with crackers*, *goblin meal*, *California plate*, *spa plate*, *gishing*, *phumphering*, *peewadiddly*, *picky-poke*, *screamers, trash panda, rags and bottles, blackout bingo, miff muffer moof, going feral, going Darwin, oogle moogle, dirt night, ifits,* and *mousy-mousy.*

I think my favorite of all, though, is the one emailed to us by a listener in Bluffton, South Carolina. When her mother wanted to make those assorted leftovers sound more appealing, she'd announce to the family that the menu that night featured *Cream of Frigidaire.*

Those chunks of dirty ice in a car's wheel well

A deckhand on the Lake Champlain ferry in Burlington, Vermont, called us to ask if there's an official word for those dirty chunks of ice and salt that accumulate in the wheel wells of your car in wintry weather. He and his coworkers spend lots of time clearing them off the deck—so much that they developed several indelicate names for these chunks. Then he heard someone refer to them as *crusticles.* Is that a regional term?

Well, yes and no. *Crusticle* was the winning entry in a contest run by *The Burlington Free Press* to name what a columnist called "the repulsive wad of frozen pastry that accumulates in the wheel well of a car or truck driven on snow." Runners-up included *clunkerhofers, carmudgeons, fendercakes,* and *grism,* as well as *skurff, klinger,* and *slushapelago,* among many others.

Crusticle was chosen not only because it neatly combines *crust* and *icicle,* but also because it contains the word *rust,* a potential byproduct of said *crusticles.* Then again, our own audience has shared many other terms for this icy nuisance, including *carsicle, carnacle, carbunkle, snowlactites, snard, slud,* and *snirt.* Particularly in northern climes, where these things are common annoyance, *fenderberg* was a popular choice, along with *snowcrete,* an apt allusion to how hard these things can feel against your boot when you kick them.

Because I live in California, where such things are more novelty than nuisance, I'm partial to cutesy names like *snow goblins* and *chunkers*. But my favorite one came from the listener who was able to articulate the sense that knocking them off a car is as satisfying as popping bubble wrap—the smaller ones, anyway. He refers to those frozen chunks as *kickies*, and now so do I.

I suspect *crusticles* will hang on, so to speak, at least in some places, but the winning entries in two other oughta-be-a-word-for-it competitions are now lodged firmly in the language. One of them is *skycap*, the term applied to those airport workers who perform curbside check-in and help you with your luggage. In 1940, with the new Airlines Terminal building in New York set to open, a contest was held to invent a term for the porters who would work there. A Louisiana man, Willie Wainwright, won for suggesting *skycap*. He patterned the word after *redcap*, the term for railway porters who wore red caps to make them stand out in a crowd.

The other contest happened at the turn of the twentieth century, when a journal in London held a competition asking readers to send in their own made-up words, noting, "Most families have a few pet words of homemade manufacture, which often are *far* more expressive and picturesque than anything in Webster's Unabridged."

Entries included *whifflement*, an "object of no importance"; *conflumption*, a "muddle or catastrophe"; and *incompoop*, an "Income Tax Assessor." But another reader made a lasting contribution to the English language: the word *smarmy*, defining it as saying "treacly things that do not sound genuine." The verb *smarm*, meaning "to smear," was already in use to refer to styling one's hair by smearing oil on it. But the first instance of the adjective *smarmy*—at least the first use of it that anyone can find in print—is the one sent in for that contest.

The act of giving someone something to drink

If someone is hungry and you give them food, you're said to feed them. But what about if you give a beverage to someone? Let's say you invite someone to dinner, which means that you promise to feed and do what to them (most likely after a speedy shame-clean)? In other words, the word *eat* is to *feed* as *drink* is to . . . what?

This question came to us from a listener in the Great Smoky Mountains of Tennessee. Try as we might, Grant and I couldn't come up with a single commonly used English word that sums up "the act of slaking someone else's thirst." Many audience members wrote and called afterward with suggestions, but no clear winner emerged.

There's *quench* and *slake*, which both mean "to relieve one's thirst," but neither word is analogous to *feed*. There's the little-used word *refect* means "to refresh"—as in *refectory*, the dining hall of a convent or monastery. But *refect* doesn't specify giving liquid; it can also specify giving food.

Maybe, we thought, the answer is *drench*. Nowadays, this word usually refers to giving liquid to livestock, but that's usually forcibly administered, as when a veterinarian puts a medication down an animal's throat. In the early eighteenth century, the expression *to feed and drench* could refer to giving a person a beverage as well as food. So maybe *drench* is the best word after all. If you invite someone over with an offer to feed and drench them, do let me know how it goes.

Left-lane slowpokes who make you miss your turn

A man named Bill called us to discuss what he called a growing problem in his Southern California hometown. "Have you ever been waiting to turn left at a long traffic light, and it finally turns green, but the driver of the car ahead of you doesn't notice it right away? They've been looking at their phone for the last two minutes. Then somebody politely honks, the offending driver looks up, sees the cars ahead of him have already turned left, and takes off. But the trouble is that the gap in cars has triggered the traffic light to turn yellow, and that leaves the rest of us fuming at the red light."

Bill said that creating a new term would be the first step toward eradicating this behavior, just as the term *distracted driving* helped raise awareness of the dangers of not paying attention to the road. "If we can form a new phrase that works as a lightning rod that collects all the frustrations in society," Bill said, "maybe we can have words lead to change instead of vice versa." Could we help?

I asked if he had any candidates already.

"I was trying to think of some that started with *phone*," he said, "and then maybe the next word would also start with an *F* sound." But that didn't seem right to him. The driver might not be looking at a phone, but applying makeup, disciplining a child in the back seat, or just daydreaming. The best the three of us could come up with during that brief conversation was *lanesquatter*.

But Bill's question apparently struck a nerve with listeners, who inundated us with more terms: *lane loafer, lane lingerer, lazy lefty, lane loiterer, phonestaller, light lagger, light lingerer, light malingerer, laneygagger,* and *lane drain* (the last, of course, has the added advantage of rhyming with *lamebrain*).

I'm not sure we ever established a clear winner, although I'm leaning toward *lanesquatter*, and now that I have a word for it, I am indeed trying hard never to be one.

Grandparents who move to be near their grandkids

A Minnesota couple wrote us to say that they'd moved across the state to be closer to their grandkids, and other friends of theirs had done the same, or even moved all the way across the country. Shouldn't there be a word that means "to pull up stakes and relocate specifically to be near your offspring and offspring's offspring"? they asked. The couple was hoping other listeners would chime in with ideas. And chime in they did, with *grandsferring*, *grandfaring*, *grandnearing*, and plain old *granding*. Some suggested that such grandparents could be called *grandabonds*, or that like *snowbirds* who move to spend part of the year in warmer climes, grandparents who move to enjoy those littles and provide free babysitting might be called *growbirds*. Still another listener offered *boomergrands* and *boomergranding*, suggesting the idea of "going out and returning."

Of all their suggestions, two others stood out for me. There was *grooving*, a combination of *grandparent* and *moving*, which would probably evoke fond memories for Boomers who are now grandparents themselves. Presumably the word for those kidwardly mobile grandparents would be *groovers*. Then there was *grandsplant*, a play on *transplant*, which could also easily work as a noun, as in "Herb and I are grandsplants from Minnesota." Who knows? It might work. For now, let's all keep an eye out for "Proud Grandsplant" bumper stickers.

Here's one last example of our listeners' efforts at crowdsourcing: We had a call from a military veteran who was having a hard time finding exactly the right word to convey a particular idea. Of all the calls we've had over the last twenty years, I would have never imagined that this would be the one that prompted so many listeners to reach out. Nor would I have guessed that finding just the right answer would be so hard. In fact, I'm still mystified as to why. What's the word for . . .

The emotion exactly between depression and euphoria

In the spring of 2021, a listener name John from Bismarck, North Dakota, called us in search of a word. He was enrolled in an online program for military veterans that helps those who've returned from an overseas deployment process their emotions. John said that part of the program involved trying to identify the emotions they were feeling at any one time. "And," he continued, "the emotion I can't seem to identify is what I'm calling 'middle emotion.'"

Imagine putting all of your emotions on a horizontal line that goes from one to ten. The emotion on the far left in the number-one position is *clinical depression*. The emotion at the opposite end, in the number-ten position, is *euphoria*.

Easy enough. But, he asked, "If you are dead center in the middle, what would be the word for that?"

John said that one of his peer mentors in the class had suggested *insouciant*. John had to look up that word, which was defined as "free from worry or anxiety." That didn't seem quite right. He considered *apathy*, but that wasn't really right either. He thought briefly about the calm attentiveness suggested by *Zen*. But that didn't work for him either. "As soon as you identify the emotion or that you're feeling it, you're feeling, you're not feeling anymore."

Grant and I offered some possibilities, such as *neutral* and *carefree*. But none of those seemed to click either. At last, we tossed the question out to our audience.

The response was overwhelming.

Psychologists and psychiatrists wrote to suggest the term they used professionally was *euthymia*, meaning "a state of tranquility and well-being," from Greek *thymos*, meaning "soul" or "spirit" and *eu*, "well." Philosophers made a case for *apatheia*, from Greek for "freedom or release from emotion or excitement." Others suggested *equanimity*, from Latin *aequs* "even" and *animus*, "mind."

Scientists reached for terms from their own fields, such as *equipoise*, *homeostasis*, and *static*. One argued for *base*, as in "the middle point between alkaline and acid." Another proposed *ambivalence*, noting that *valence* is a term used in chemistry suggesting "availability for interaction."

Other listeners offered a range of terms, including *complacent*, *content*, *adequate*, *indifferent*, *beige*, *blasé*, *nonchalant*, *sanguine*, *middling*, *unemotional*, *comfortable*, *copacetic*, *tranquil*, *numb*, and plain old *ordinary*. Still others suggested *so-so*, *meh*, *OK*, *all right*, and *mellow*. Some sounded downright Zen, opting for *calm*, *centered*, *balanced*, and *serene*.

In the weeks that followed, the thoughtful responses kept coming. One listener suggested visualizing the range of emotions as a seesaw; the word for exact middle point, then, would be *level*. Or maybe, another listener suggested, we should just split the difference and simply refer to that emotional state at the halfway as *five*. Still another suggested the Greek word *ataraxia*, meaning "undisturbed," or literally, "not stirred up. "It's less a momentary emotion than the ideal state of being, whereby you're in a state of calm equanimity without fear or trouble, but also without excessive excitement," she wrote.

Finally, I was quite taken with the response from Aimee, who emailed from the West African nation of Gabon: "My first thought was *placid*, like a smooth lake without ripples. If you look at the ebb and flow of emotions, you see waves: riding the high waves of elation and crouching under the crushing waves of depression." The more she thought about it, though, the more she felt that *placid* connoted something more along the lines of contentment.

"I think John was looking for a more neutral word so if you look at a lake with no ripples, it is still. If you are without emotional ripple, you are still."

Still. I really liked that one.

Why the overwhelming response to such a seemingly simple question? Perhaps it's just that our community of listeners wanted to help someone who was doing some tough emotional work. Maybe they just appreciated the challenge he was grappling with, struggling to identify what they themselves had once felt or hoped to feel again. It's not always easy to push a feeling into a word-shaped box and have it fit perfectly.

And maybe that's part of why this question resonated so deeply with our audience. When we're trying to divide the world up into manageable, describable pieces, it's hard to find words to describe all of the range of our emotions and where one ends and another begins. It's part of the enormous appeal of John Koenig's bestselling book *The Dictionary of Obscure Sorrows*. Based on his website of the same name, the book offers invented words like *sonder*, defined as "the realization that each random passerby is living a life as vivid and complex as your own—populated with their own ambitions, friends, routines, worries and inherited craziness—an epic story that continues invisibly around you like an anthill sprawling deep underground, with elaborate passageways to thousands of other lives that you'll never know existed, in which you might appear only once, as an extra sipping coffee in the background, as a blur of traffic passing on the highway, as a lighted window at dusk," and *etterath*, "the feeling of emptiness after a long and arduous process is finally complete—having finished school, recovered from surgery, or gone home at the end of your wedding—which leaves you relieved that it's over but missing the stress that organized your life into a mission." Koenig is giving a name to emotions we've all felt but never had a word for.

As for our listener's search for that "middle emotion" between despondency and euphoria, for now, at least, I'm going with *still*.

MORE THINGS THERE OUGHTA
BE A WORD FOR

When you're excited and nervous at the same time

A fifth grader once called our show in search of a single word combining the two emotions of excitement and nervous anticipation—like you might feel on the first day of school, for example. Sure, there's *aflutter*, but listeners offered their own suggestions, including *happrehensive, anticipacious, apprecited, apprehensive, nervited, nercited*, and *antrepidacious*. Still others pointed out that there may already be a winner, *nervouscited* or *nervacited*, as used by Pinkie Pie in *My Little Pony*. As the rose-colored pony explains, "It's like you want to jump up and down and yell, 'Yay me!' But you also want to curl up in a teeny-tiny ball and hide at the same time!" Yup, Pinkie Pie, been there.

When you meet or see a radio personality for the first time

You've had this person in your earbuds or listened to them on your car stereo for years. You even develop what's called a *parasocial relationship* with them, *parasocial* being coined in the 1950s by sociologists to denote this kind of intimacy at a distance. Then one day, you happen across a photo of that radio or podcast host online, or you maybe meet them in person, and they're not at all like what you'd pictured. Not at *all*. What do you call that odd, unsettling sensation and the weird disconnect if you close your eyes again as they talk? Is it what one listener calls a *see change*? Are you experiencing what another listener described as *inconsonance*? I've had lots of longtime listeners describe that experience, like the woman who told me, "I thought you'd be taller!" (I don't know—do I sound tall?)

In any case, I tell listeners they can call those jarring experiences *hostbusters*.

When you try to walk past someone, but you both take a step in the same direction, and you both side-step the same way several times until one of you stays put or you both guess correctly

In their book *The Deeper Meaning of Liff*, Douglas Adams and John Lloyd dubbed this apologetic street dance *droitwich*. But our listeners offered up lots of other delightfully terpsichorean terms, including: *avoid-dance*, doing *the sidewalk boogie* or *the sidewalk shuffle*, or simply doing the *slidewalk*. Alternatively, you could opt for *sidewalzing*, *mall dancing*, and the *Texas you step*. My own favorite term for this little do-si-do, however, is *polkadodge*.

When you try to do something offline that's possible only on-screen

You're scribbling out a grocery list, but when you write the word *broccoli*—wait, is that two *c*'s or one?—you half expect a squiggly red line to appear underneath it telling you you've misspelled it. Or maybe you're flipping through a magazine and see an interesting photo and instinctively touch your thumb and forefinger to the page to enlarge it. Or perhaps you're reading a book and reach for the "back" button to return to the previous page. Shouldn't there be a term for that bit of muscle memory that kicks in when we're using nonelectronic objects? My personal favorite is *e-flex*—that is, *reflex* without the *r*. (For that matter, can't someone invent a "search" function that works for an entire house? I could really use one.)

CHAPTER 7

LIKE I HAD TWO HEADS

I'LL NEVER FORGET WHEN KARA, a listener from North Carolina, called to tell us a story about visiting friends in New Brunswick, Canada. The weather turned colder than expected, so they stopped into a local coffee shop to warm up. Kara was relieved to see that the shop sold lots of additional merchandise from behind the counter, including some cute, knitted caps.

She ordered a coffee, then added, "And I'd also like a toboggan."

"A what?" asked the cashier.

"A toboggan," Kara repeated. "You know, the thing you put on your head."

Now the cashier looked even more perplexed. In her world, a toboggan was a type of sled.

For a moment, each stood contemplating the absurdity of what the other had said.

A sled you put on your head to stay warm?

A woolen hat you ride down a hill?

Turns out they were both right. In much of the American South, a *toboggan* is a knitted winter cap. Originally, though, the word *toboggan* referred to a long, wooden sled used by Native Americans. French traders and trappers adapted the word from similar-sounding terms in the Algonquian family of languages. By the 1800s, the English word *toboggan* had also become a verb for riding on such a sled, and the thing people wore on their heads to keep warm while *tobogganing* was called a *toboggan cap* or *toboggan hat*. In the South, both the *cap* and *hat* dropped off, as it were, leaving Kara's word for this headwear.

We hear from listeners with similar stories all the time. I call these "Two-Headed Conversations," meaning that someone has used a word or phrase their whole life, then they go somewhere else, use it again, and no one has any idea what they're talking about. If I had a dollar for every time one of these listeners said, "People looked at me like I had two heads!" I could probably fund a public radio show and podcast for a year.

I've had some of those two-headed conversations myself. Shortly after starting college in Poughkeepsie, New York, I was hanging out with some new acquaintances when I realized that one of them was about to knock over a drink.

"Ooo, watch out!" I cried, grabbing the glass. "You almost tumped that over!"

Everyone else at the table was dumbfounded.

"*Tump*? TUMP? What the hell does *tump* mean?"

"You know, *tump*," I said. "As in '*Don't tump over the canoe*.'"

I was flabbergasted that no one knew this word. I'd heard it my whole life. Only later did I learn that *tump* is a marker of Southern speech. It may derive from a dialectal term in England, where *tumpoke* means "to fall head over heels." Or it might be a blend of *tip over* and *dump*. Or *tump* might be somehow related to *thump*. Nobody knows for sure. What I can tell you is that not one of my classmates from the Northeast had ever heard *tump* before, and looking around at them after I said it, I indeed wondered if I'd sprouted an extra noggin.

Differences in dialect show the richness and range of American English, a diversity we celebrate each week on *A Way with Words*. The particular words and phrases we have at our disposal and the way we pronounce them are packed with history—not just the history of the United States but of each of us as individuals.

Remember the *New York Times* interactive dialect quiz? Created in 2013 by *New York Times* graphics editor Josh Katz, the online quiz was based on the Harvard Dialect Survey, a comprehensive study by linguists Bert Vaux and Scott Golder. Readers who answered a series of twenty-five questions about words and phrases they regularly used were surprised to find that the results pinpointed their hometowns or places they'd lived with mind-blowing, uncanny accuracy. The quiz became the newspaper's most viewed page ever. Linguists weren't at all surprised, though. How you pronounce the word *crayon* (*CRAY-on? Cran? Crown?*) or what you call that little gray bug that curls up when touched (A *roly-poly? A pill bug? A potato bug?* Something else?) says a lot about you and where you come from.

Sometimes it's not so much vocabulary as a particular grammatical construction that's a tip-off as to where a person grew up. Soon after I moved to Southern California, I cashed in a gift certificate for a massage. A young woman named Sherry met me at the front desk and led me back to one of the rooms, where a pile of used towels still lay on the floor.

"Oh, sorry," Sherry said, scooping them up. "These towels need washed!" She left me to undress and lie face down on the table. When she returned, she squeezed warm massage oil onto her hands, then rubbed them together and began working my sore shoulders.

"So," I said after a moment, "You're from western Pennsylvania?"

Her hands stopped, mid-knead.

"Or . . . Eastern Ohio, maybe?" I said, hoping to move things along.

Her hands still hadn't moved.

"Pennsylvania," she finally replied. "But we were close to the state line and went to Ohio all the time to buy beer. How did you know?"

"You said 'needs washed,'" I said. "'These towels need washed.'"

"I did?" She hadn't noticed.

"Yes," I said. "*Needs washed* is a typical dialect feature there, as well as in Northern West Virginia and Central Indiana. It's a reflection of Scots-Irish migration patterns."

She considered this for a moment, then finally went back to kneading. I resolved to refrain from interrupting my massage again with any more linguistic insights, such as the fact that this construction is known as *infinitival copula deletion*.

I'm not always that lucky at guessing—not at all. But it's fun to try. Often, someone's pronunciation of certain words is the biggest giveaway as to where they're from. Our listeners often ask, for example, why some people insert an *R* sound into the word *wash*, saying *warsh*. Linguists refer to this as the *intrusive R* or *excrescent R*. It's another vestige of the English spoken by Scots-Irish immigrants and is often heard from people who grew up in the Midlands of the United States, roughly the inland side of the Ozarks to the upper edges of Pennsylvania, Ohio, Indiana, Illinois, and parts of Nebraska, Kansas, Oklahoma, and North Texas.

In much of the American South and South Midlands, many people pronounce the word *pen* like *pin*, so that *ten pens* sounds like *tin pins*. (This pronunciation also survives in central California, where people from the Midlands settled after fleeing the Dust Bowl of the 1930s.) That *pen-pin* shift is called a *vowel merger*, in which two vowels that once were distinct begin to sound alike. Linguists also listen for differences in the way people say the words *caught* and *cot*. In much of the United States, these words are pronounced exactly the same. But in much of New York, New Jersey, Michigan, Chicago, St. Louis, and a few other places, those vowels tend to sound different. In recent years, this similarity of sound, called the *caught-cot* merger, has become more common and will likely continue to spread.

Linguists listen for other vowel mergers as well. How you pronounce the words *merry*, *marry*, and *Mary* or whether *Dawn* and *Don* sound the same in your mouth, for example, will differ according to where you're from. Then there's what's called the *fill-feel merger*, in which the words *fill* and *feel* sound the same. It's heard mostly in much of the American South, west-central Texas, and a few other places, including parts of Utah. I'm particularly fond of the *fill-feel* merger of this one because it figures in one of my all-time favorite stories about linguistics. It concerns an attempted robbery that went hilariously wrong.

In 2008, a man in a hunting cap and sunglasses marched into a Salt Lake City restaurant called Café Trio. The man approached the cashier and held out a plastic bag, then gave the employee an order: "Fill the bag. Don't make me hurt you."

The frightened cashier slowly reached out . . . and felt the bag.

"You've got to be kidding me!" cried the would-be robber, who fled empty-handed.

A spokesman for the Salt Lake City Police described the bungled robbery this way: "The employee thought the suspect said 'feel' the bag," noting that perhaps that moment of linguistic confusion gave the suspect "a chance to rethink his life of crime." (I love this merger mishap so much that years later when I was in Salt Lake to give a speech, I made a point of dropping by Café Trio for lunch. I had a nice chat with one of the servers about the incident. I highly recommend their tomato soup.)

Over the last several decades, vowels have been shifting around in a fascinating way in the Inland North of the United States, which includes the cities of Syracuse, Buffalo, Chicago, Milwaukee, and other areas along the shores of the Great Lakes. There, the word *caught* began to sound more like *cot*, and *cot* sounds more like *cat*, and *cat* now sounds like *kit* or *key-at*. This so-called Northern Cities Shift is the result of a complicated phonological process. Simply put, when people begin pronouncing one vowel differently, shifting the position of the tongue, it causes a chain reaction that's a bit like musical chairs, as vowels jostle for position in the mouth. As a result, speakers in this region tend to pronounce *tech* like *tuck*, and *kid* like *kud*, and the phrase *The bus went around the block* sounds more like *The boss around the black*. Although these changes have been quite noticeable in the late twentieth and early twenty-first centuries, new research suggests that this vowel-chain shift is now waning.

In fact, accents around the country are continually shifting and changing, however slowly. A 2023 study led by University of Georgia linguist Margaret Renwick analyzed the speech of Georgia residents born between 1887 and 2003. It found that by the late twentieth century, younger white speakers had begun drifting away from traditional-sounding Southern speech. A Southern Vowel Shift produced the stereotypical "Southern accent" in which, for example, *nice white rice* sounds like *nahs whaht rahss* and the words *beet* and *bait* sound more like *buh-eet* and *buh-eyt*. However, those features seem to have peaked with the Boomer generation. Those vowels are now flattening out and fading, to the point where younger Georgians who are white now sound more like Californians. Renwick and her team are now analyzing changes in the speech of Georgia's Black residents, and around the country, others are studying the effects of the language of immigrants and other groups on local pronunciations.

Linguists get excited about these vowel mergers and shifts—very excited. In part, that's because these changes enable us to watch language evolving in real time. Toss in additional factors such as geographic isolation, migration, and cultural mingling, then add a few thousand years, and you start to get a sense how the great diversity of Indo-European languages today might arise from a single source and spread across much of the world.

Besides listening for variations in pronunciation and grammatical constructions, linguists also take note of people's vocabulary. Sometimes a single word or phrase can be a tip-off as to where someone grew up.

I remember a listener named Ivan who called to tell us about traveling to Maryland for a stay at a friend's home. While he was there, she told him she needed to run out to the store to pick up a few things. As she was leaving, she said to him, "OK, *retten up* while I'm gone."

Ivan nodded and went on to enjoy a relaxing morning at his friend's home. When she returned, he could tell immediately by the look on her face that she was disappointed.

"You didn't *retten up*!" she said.

That's when Ivan learned that by asking him to *retten up*, she was asking him to tidy up the house. Particularly in Pennsylvania and in other nearby states, including Maryland, *retten up* is a variant of *redd up*, which means "to put in order" or "to straighten up." This expression is yet another a vestige of the language of Scots-Irish immigrants. *Redd up* and its many variants are still used in Scotland, Ireland, and parts of England today.

Dialects don't stop and start at state lines, of course. In fact, linguists don't always agree on exactly how to map out different areas of American dialect. Generally speaking, though, if you drive from north to south along the Atlantic coast, you'll hear more diversity of dialect than if you start at one point on the East Coast and drive due west—again, a reflection of the migration patterns of early immigrants from the British Isles.

In the seventeenth and eighteenth centuries, people from different parts of the British Isles established settlements at various points along the Eastern Seaboard and brought their accents, vocabulary, and quirks of grammar with them. The Puritans who arrived in Massachusetts came primarily from the southeast of England. The aristocrats who settled in Virginia tended to come from the south and west of London. Quakers who settled in Pennsylvania came mostly from the North Midlands of England. Later, immigrants from northern England, Northern Ireland, and the border regions of Scotland put down roots in western Pennsylvania and in Appalachia. Over the next three centuries, the English language traveled west across the continent like a great wave, then smashed into the Rocky Mountains, scattering this way and that.

That's vastly oversimplified, of course, but this early history of English in the United States helps explain why, for example, it's easy to distinguish the language of someone from New York and a person from North Carolina, but much harder to differentiate between the language of a person who grew up in Oregon and someone who grew up in, say, Wyoming. Dialect differences tend to be subtler in the West. Increasingly, though, the picture is complicated by factors such as greater mobility, the internet, social media, and the arrival of other immigrants whose own languages cross-pollinate the vocabulary and pronunciation in the dialects of American English. As we saw with the word *toboggan*, the languages of Indigenous peoples are also part of this rich linguistic mixture.

One of the most delightful ways to explore regional vocabulary is to thumb through the *Dictionary of American Regional English* (*DARE*), a glorious compendium of dialect. First published in 1985, with a digital version in 2013, it's based on the work of lexical fieldworkers who fanned out across the country in vans dubbed "Word Wagons." They interviewed more than 2,700 Americans in more than 1,000 communities across the country from 1965 to 1970. *DARE*'s six volumes make for serendipitous browsing among more than sixty thousand words and phrases heard around the United States. The digital version (daredictionary.com) offers more ways to search and sort these terms and some delicious digital recordings of how people in various parts of the country spoke half a century ago.

Sadly, some of these words and phrases have been dying out, and the dictionary merely serves as a historical record of their use, a snapshot in time. Others are alive and well, especially among older Americans. They include vocabulary for a wide range of topics: local food and drink, weather phenomena in certain regions, exclamations and sayings, leisure activities particular to those areas, and other vestiges of this country's history.

How about if we follow some of those footprints by taking a road trip of our own to check out words and phrases you're likely to hear in various parts of the United States? As with any long drive, this linguistic journey will be most enjoyable if we worders take breaks to get out and stretch our legs along the way. So for now, let's start with some of the verbal scenery you may well encounter while traveling around New England and down the Eastern Seaboard.

CHAPTER 8

ROAD TRIP! NORTHEAST AND MID-ATLANTIC: CULCH TO LEMON STICKS

FOR THIS LEG OF OUR journey through American dialect, let's hop in the Worder Wagon and start at the northeasternmost part of the United States, then work our way halfway down the coast. Again, remember that dialect differences don't start and stop where one state ends and another begins; sometimes bits of vocabulary will vary even from town to town. In any case, here's a small sampling of words and phrases and patterns of speech to listen for when traveling in this part of the country.

New England
MAINE
If you're a Mainer, you don't want *culch* in your *dooryard. Culch* originally meant the layer of debris, such as clamshells or gravel, to which oysters attach themselves. In Maine, *culch* can be used more generally to mean any kind of trash or rubbish, and a *dooryard* is the area right outside your front door. In Maine, you might

ask for coffee with just a *dite* of cream, the word *dite* meaning "a very small amount."

Folks in that state may respond affirmatively with a sharp intake of air, often rendered in writing as *Aup!* It's what linguists call the *pulmonic ingressive*, sometimes referred to as the *Gaelic gasp*, and it's heard not just in parts of Maine and Scotland but in many other places. If you've never heard it before, this little sound can be disconcerting. A listener named Jonathan once called our show to say that when he rented a flat in Dublin, his Irish landlord gasped that way so often that Jonathan feared the poor fellow was ill. Over time, though, he realized the man was perfectly healthy; that breathy noise was just his way of saying "Yes" or "I agree."

VERMONT

If you're frustrated or exhausted in Northern Vermont, you might heave a sigh and moan, *"I've had the radish!"* It's possible that this statement derives from a French phrase from across the border, *je n'ai plus un radis*, or "I'm depleted"—literally, "I no longer have a radish."

A Vermonter may also ask you how you think something will *sugar off*—whether, for example, an investment will produce dividends or how an election will turn out. In Vermont, *sugaring off* is literally the process of converting maple syrup into sugar, so if you wonder how something sugared off, you wonder what happened when all was said and done. If you're surprised by how something sugared off, you might exclaim *Jeezum Crow!* This euphemism for *Jesus Christ!* isn't unique to Vermont, but many Vermonters are proud to claim it as their own.

NEW HAMPSHIRE

In New Hampshire, pranksters traditionally enjoy *Beggar's Night*, which occurs either on or near Halloween. It's a night for all sorts of mischief, such as draping trees and shrubs with toilet paper, pelting windows with hard corn kernels, and the old ring-the-doorbell-and-run trick, known elsewhere in the U.S. by names like *ding dong ditch*. In Vermont, on the other hand, this yearly occurrence is called *Cabbage Night*, a vestige of the days when young vandals would gather up rotting cabbages and leave them strewn across neighbor's porches. The smelly aftermath probably left many a Vermonter grumbling that they'd had the radish.

MASSACHUSETTS

Moving on down into Massachusetts, you're sure to hear the modifier *wicked*, meaning "extremely," as in *wicked good*. The word *wicked* used this way follows the same pattern of other negative adjectives repurposed as adverbs, as in *It's awful cold out there*.

If you're wicked hungry, you can hop in the car and head to the local *spa*, or "neighborhood variety store," for a quick bite. If you want to ride in the front passenger seat, claim it quickly with *I hosey that!* The word *hosey* may derive from *holdsie*, as in *I put a hold on*.

At the spa, younger folks buying a soft drink will call it a *soda*, while older folks still call it a *tonic*. For something more substantial, try a *frappe*. A frappe is what's known elsewhere as a *milkshake*—that is, a combination of milk, ice cream, and flavoring. If you ask for a *milkshake* in Massachusetts, it won't have the ice cream. There, a milkshake is just milk that's just, well, shaken, along with some chocolate syrup or other flavoring.

If you take the ferry out to Nantucket Island, you'll learn that newcomers are known as *off-islanders*, *wash-ashores*, or *coofs*.

If there's a *slatch*, or "a short interval of good weather," take the opportunity to head off for a *rantum scoot*, that is, "a walk with no particular destination in mind."

RHODE ISLAND

In Rhode Island, you don't drink a *frappe*, you drink a *cabinet*. This name for "a milkshake with ice cream" supposedly comes from the days when old-fashioned soda jerks kept ingredients for this treat in a cabinet. Prefer a caffeinated pick-me-up? Then you want *coffee milk*, or "milk mixed with coffee syrup," which is the state's official drink. Blend in some ice cream and you'll have a *coffee cabinet*. For that matter, you could drink your coffee cabinet with a *New York System*. This Rhode Island favorite is hot dog topped with mustard, chili, onions, and celery salt. When hot dog were first sold there in the early 1900s, they were marketed as *New York Systems* to suggest that the product was just like the ones you could get at Coney Island.

CONNECTICUT

Connecticut residents are rightly proud of their thin-crust, coal-fired, Neapolitan-style pizza called *apizza* and pronounced *ah-BEETZ*. The name *apizza* is a remnant of *la'pizza* from the language of Italian immigrants who settled in and around New Haven. This two-syllable pronunciation of *apizza* is the result of what linguists call *apocope* (*ah-POCK-uh-pee*), or the loss of a final sound or sound. Apocope is also at work in some Italian Americans' pronunciation of *prosciutto* as *pro-ZHOOT* and mozzarella as *mutza-DELL*.

Shopping for bargains in the Nutmeg State? Stop by a *tag sale*. That's what most of the rest of the country calls a *garage sale* or a *yard sale*. The name *tag sale* tag probably refers to adding stickers with the asking prices for all those unwanted items, and it originally referred to fundraisers where a tag was given as proof that you donated something.

NEW YORK

In the boroughs of New York, sellers display their unwanted items on the stoop of their buildings, hence the name *stoop sale*. The word *stoop* comes from the Dutch word for "a flight of stairs," *stoep*.

A single preposition can also mark you as a New Yorker: When queuing up for something, you don't stand *in line*, you stand *on line*. Some people have speculated that this usage derives from the lines painted on the floor at Ellis Island indicating where immigrants should stand while waiting to be processed, but there's no definitive evidence to support this story.

Another prepositional giveaway that you're a New Yorker: Do you *call in* sick to work? Or do you *call out*? Most Americans *call in sick*, but New Yorkers tend to *call out sick*. What's more, firefighters, police officers, and other civil servants in New York, Boston, and other East Coast cities have their own expression for skipping work because they're not well: They *bang out sick*.

The New York specialty called an *egg cream* is usually made with milk, chocolate syrup, and seltzer—but oddly, no eggs or cream. Since this refreshing drink arose among Eastern European Jews who settled there, some speculate that the *egg* part derives from Yiddish *echt*, or "authentic." Then again, in the early 1900s, New Yorkers enjoyed all kinds of drinks that really did have eggs or frothy egg whites in them to make them richer— egg lemonade, egg coffee, egg phosphates, egg-and-celery phosphates, and eventually egg-and-chocolate beverages; it's more likely egg creams were just a less pricey version. The bottom line is no one's sure how this drink got its name.

Mid-Atlantic

NEW JERSEY AND PHILADELPHIA

In New Jersey, you'll see lots of *jug handles*. In the Garden State, a jug handle is a short stretch of road that loops around and lets you make turns at intersections without crossing in front of oncoming traffic. In Jersey, if you're heading to the coast, then you're said to go *down the shore*. That's true even if you're in South Jersey heading northeast. The *down* in *down the shore* simply indicates movement from inland to shoreline. Once you're at the shore, you can *go to the beach*, where you'll see *shoobies* and *bennies*, terms the locals use for tourists. *Bennies* come from around New York. Nobody knows why, although it's been suggested that this name derives from the *beneficial* rays they soak up on the beaches or that *BENNY* is simply an acronym for places they're from: *Bayonne, Elizabeth, Newark, and New York*. (Always be suspicious of etymologies that involve acronyms! They're almost never true.) The story behind *shoobies* is much clearer. Shoobies are tourists from the Philadelphia area who descend on beach towns in South Jersey for the day or a weekend getaway. In years past, such visitors took the train from Philly, carrying *shoebox lunches*—their midday repast packed in a sturdy cardboard shoebox.

Philadelphians, by the way, are known for their distinctive pronunciation of *water*, which sounds like *wooder*. They're also famous for their use of the word *jawn*, which substitutes for other words in lots of different instances, as in *Can you hand me that jawn over there?* or *Have you seen that new jawn on Hulu?* and *So many jawns, so little time*. Although Philly likes to claim this multipurpose term as its own, *jawn* originated in New York City during the early twentieth century from *joint*, slang for "a place where people come together," giving rise to such terms such as *gin joint* or *juke joint*. By the 1970s, this sense of "things joined together" expanded to mean "business venture" or "artistic collaboration," such as that trademark phrase movie posters for Spike Lee films, *A Spike Lee Joint*. Over time, joint morphed into *jawn*, and now this Swiss Army knife of a word marks casual users as likely from Philadelphia.

We'll visit the western part of Pennsylvania later on our way back up.

DELAWARE

Because this state is divided by the Chesapeake and Delaware Canal, you'll also hear folks in Delaware speak in terms of locations either *above the canal* or *below the canal*. If someone says they're from *Slower Lower*, it means they're from the part of the state south of the canal, where life is more rural and relaxed than bustling Wilmington, with its proximity to Philadelphia.

And don't tell someone there that you're *going to the shore*, or you might leave your listener *baggin' up*. To *bag up* means "to crack up with laughter," a term largely confined to that state. Some Delawareans may tell you they're going to the shore, but most say they're *going to the beach*. And in Delaware, a *baby coach* isn't someone hired to make your infant smarter; it's a baby carriage. Once you get to the beach, you may see many a *Mom-mom* and *Pop-pop* out with a baby coach, those two names being popular for grandparents along the Mid-Atlantic coast.

MARYLAND

Instead of saying they're going to the beach, Marylanders say they're going *down the ocean*, which can sound more like "downy ayshun." Or if they're in Baltimore, they might just cool off by sipping on a *lemon stick*. That's a stick of soft peppermint stuck into a chilled lemon; Baltimoreans swear that combining the tart juice and sweetness that way is quite refreshing. In Maryland, you don't register your car at the *DMV*. There, *DMV* is short for "District of Columbia, Southern Maryland, and Northern Virginia." Instead, head for the *MVA*, or *Motor Vehicle Administration*.

The friendly term of address *hon* isn't exclusive to Baltimore, although many locals claim it as their own. This word has had its share of controversy, though. In the early 1990s, someone with a paintbrush added a comma and the word *hon* to the *Welcome to Baltimore* sign at the city limits. After that word was removed, an editorial vandal stapled the word *hon* to the sign, only to have it repeatedly torn off. Some residents welcomed the change, but others felt that *hon* failed to represent the city's predominantly Black population and that the sign should read *Welcome to Baltimore, bro*.

Before we head farther south on our linguistic tour, let's get out and stretch our legs for a bit.

CHAPTER 9

THE ALLURE OF *ALLURE*

AFTER FINISHING THE ARTIFICIAL-HEART BOOK, I decided
that at least for a while, I'd continue studying with Professor Latkovski and try to support my etymological habit by freelancing.
Meanwhile, another book began taking shape. As the professor
and I continued our tutorials, I found myself with stacks of index
cards on which I'd scribbled bits of lexical information he'd told
me about or that I'd come across on my own. One shoebox full
of them became two, then three, then four. As I sifted through
them, organizing them into piles, one stack was getting larger
and larger. Each of those cards had something to do with flowers.

What if I took the names of flowers as a starting point for
the same sorts of etymological romps the professor and I enjoyed
each week? The long-leaved *gladiolus*, for example, takes its name
from Latin *gladium*, or "sword," a relative of the sword-wielding
gladiator. The word *pansy* comes from French *pensée*, or "thought."
(Remember *Hamlet*'s Ophelia when she says, "And there is pan-
sies, that's for thoughts"? Some pansy blossoms actually do look
like a little elfin face crinkled up in thought, although Germans
see a scowling *Stiefmütterchen*, or "little stepmother.")

Then there's the Greek word that means "flower" itself, *anthos*, the source of *chrysanthemum*, or "golden flower," and "a flower with a tail," *anthurium*. And of course, there's one of the loveliest words in all of English, *anthology*. An anthology is literally "a gathering of flowers"—a literary bouquet, if you will.

That pile of cards turned into my first book on word origins, *A Garden of Words*, published just months after Professor Latkovski's death.

AN ANTHOLOGY FOR YOU

Daisy
In Old English, this flower was called *dæges éage*, literally "day's eye," inspired by the fact that some varieties of this cheery blossom close up their petals at night, then open again in the morning.

Iris
In Greek and Roman myth, Iris was the personification of the rainbow, a goddess who "runs on the rainy wind," flying along foamy seas to deliver messages from Mount Olympus. In one story, Iris firmly resisted the advances of Juno's philandering husband Jupiter, and in gratitude, Juno created a flower in her honor, with blooms that, like her own shimmering robes, come in a whole rainbow of colors.

Geranium
The pointed seed pods of this flower inspired the geranium's name, which comes from Greek *geranos*, or "crane," a bird with a long, pointed bill. In fact, another name for *geranium* is *cranesbill*,

also a reference to this grallatorial bird. (*Grallatorial?* Great word! It applies to long-legged, wading birds such as cranes, herons, and storks, from Latin *grallator*, literally "one who walks on stilts.")

Lupine

The English adjective *lupine* means "wolflike" or "ruthlessly predatory," from Latin *lupus*, or "wolf." The flower called *lupine* is so named because it thrives in poor soil, giving the impression that it "wolfs" nutrients from the earth. Actually, the opposite is true: Lupine is a nitrogen-fixing plant, meaning that it enhances the soil by converting nitrogen into a form that other plants can use.

Tulip

The gaily colored tulip was introduced to Europe from Turkey, where it was called *lale*. However, the shape of its blossom is said to have inspired its name in English, which comes from Turkish *tülbent*, "turban," a word adapted from Persian for "turban," *dulband*.

Nasturtium

In Latin, *nasturtium* means "a kind of cress." The ancient writer Pliny contended that this name comes from *nasus*, "nose," and a form of *torquere*, meaning "to twist," a reference to the blossom's piquant, peppery taste. If that's indeed the case—and no one's entirely sure—then this flower's name is etymologically related to "nose" words such as *nasal* and *nostril* and "twisting" words, such as *torque* and *torment*.

Around this time, I met a Louisville artist named Debra Clem and fell hard. Deb specialized in oil painting, at once realistic and magical, and usually large-scale oils of human figures.

She revered the greats of the Renaissance—Michelangelo and Caravaggio—as well as Artemisia Gentileschi and Hans Holbein, and her paintings reflect their influence. Deb dreamed of being an art professor, but academic positions in her field were extremely rare, so she took adjunct teaching positions when she could. Students adored her. "Art is teachable," she'd tell them. "You weren't born knowing how to speak French, were you? Anyone can learn to draw." She got amazing work out of them, too—even the ones who'd insisted they couldn't even draw a stick figure.

I was drawn to Deb's keen mind and abundant talent. (You can see what I mean at her website, debraclem.com). Conversations with Deb were endless, interesting, and all over the map. By that point, I'd reached my early thirties and was delighted to settle down with a partner with whom I clicked with on so many levels.

I continued researching and writing on my home computer. It was a boxy, twenty-six-pound Kaypro with a nine-inch black screen where the glowing green letters appeared, and 64 KB of RAM (that's 64 kilobytes, mind you, not megabytes). At the time, in 1991, just over 1 percent of Americans had ventured online, but a former newspaper colleague, Robin Garr, began urging me to join CompuServe, the world's first major commercial online service. Get online, he said, and I could connect with people all over the world to discuss languages, travel, cooking, pets, gardening, photography, politics, and more.

That sounded nice, but then again, going online would mean buying a dial-up modem, connecting it to my phone line, getting it all to work, and learning a whole new computer program. "Eh, maybe I'll try it someday," I told him.

A few days later Robin mentioned a friend he'd made online. "She's a writer and lives in New York. Her girlfriend plays in a lesbian rock band."

OK, that was intriguing. But it still sounded like a whole lot of hassle just to trade messages with some friend of his.

"I think you two would hit it off," he insisted. "Her name's Lindsy Van Gelder."

"Wait," I said. "*The* Lindsy Van Gelder? Writes for *Ms.* magazine? Really funny?"

I'd read anything I saw under her byline; her articles were always smart, clever, stylish, and substantive. Lindsy had written groundbreaking investigative articles, and I remembered well her essay for *Ms.* called "Marriage as a Restricted Club," a forceful argument for marriage equality, the first of its kind in a major magazine.

I bought a modem the next day.

Robin introduced us, and Lindsy and I became fast friends over email. We talked about writing and traded excerpts of our work. She and her longtime partner, Pam, had just published a gay and lesbian travel guide to Europe with a title suggested by their friend Gloria Steinem, *Are You Two . . . Together?*

Lindsy and I commiserated about the extremely tough business of freelancing. Most writers are still lucky to be paid $1 a word, a rate unchanged since Hemingway's time. So, when a former *New York Daily News* colleague recruited Lindsy for a new Condé Nast beauty magazine, Lindsy gave it serious thought, even though the last thing she wanted to do was write about makeup for one of the glossies; she'd rather be freelancing and pursuing a degree in medieval history. But with two kids to support, the pay was too good to pass up. She took the job and tried to force herself to be interested in the latest trendy moisturizers and lip gloss.

Aghast at how little money I was making by freelancing locally, she showed some of my work to her editors at *Allure*. They were intrigued, but their next question was always, "She's good, but remind me where she lives? Somewhere in Tennessee?" Long before *remote work* or *hop on a Zoom* joined everyday vocabulary, editors were reluctant to assign stories to writers outside New York.

In fact, so few editors had email accounts that writers were still printing out their stories and faxing them or sending them by postal mail. Why take a chance on someone in the boondocks? Besides, what could anyone outside the city know about beauty and fashion anyway? The hard truth, Lindsy said, was that her editors couldn't imagine that anybody serious about writing would live in the flyover—much less in Kentucky.

"Your area code is killing you, Martha. You have to move to New York." Not only that, it would help Deb's prospects in the art world, too. It was a chicken-and-egg situation, she said. I wouldn't be able to get work that paid well unless we moved to New York, but we couldn't imagine how costly it would be to uproot ourselves and move there.

Exasperated, Lindsy finally took a different tack. "At least come up here and have lunch with my editor." I laughed out loud at that one. At the time, I was making as little as $400 per article freelancing for local publications—and for stories that could take a couple of weeks to report. The price of a plane ticket to New York? Just to have lunch? "Out of the question," I told her.

"Martha," Lindsy said. "Nobody's going to hire you because of your area code. Now listen to me: I want you to fly up here, have lunch with my editor, and SHOW THEM YOU WEAR SHOES!!!"

Again, I had to laugh. Could it really be that simple? I demurred, but Lindsy was insistent and offered to let me stay overnight at their apartment. Her partner, Pam, was a gourmet cook, and she'd make something special for us. I had to admit, it did sound like fun. At last, I gave in and blew what felt like an extravagant amount on a quick trip to the city.

Lindsy met me at the Condé Nast building and took me upstairs, where an editorial meeting was about to start. So many staffers were wearing black that I assumed they all must be leaving early that day for a funeral. No, Lindsy explained later, that was what pretty much everybody wore all the time. Much simpler that way, so you could focus on what really mattered—things like mascara, celebrity hairstylists, lip gloss, anal bleaching, and whoever was doing Madonna's bikini waxing at the time.

The conference room seemed divided between breathless young fashionistas who seemed to take all of this extremely seriously and a few others like Carol, Lindsy's former newspaper editor. Carol was clearly in on the joke, her wry comments and eye-rolling suggesting that she knew that most of the content was silly, but it was also a way for otherwise serious writers to make good money without much heavy lifting. Besides, the magazine's real focus appeared to be the photos by famous photographers and the design department's snappy layout. As the writers liked to joke, the words themselves were just "picture grout."

After the meeting, Carol handed me off to a junior editor, one of the breathless ones, impossibly skinny, dressed in all black. We went to lunch. She had this idea for an article they'd wanted to call "The Perfect Body." It would be about how actually, there *is* no perfect body, and the body that excels in one context would be a hindrance in another. They needed a writer who could interview Olympic trainers, Martina Navratilova's fitness coach, a ballet instructor, and others. The story would explain how the perfect body for gymnastics is dramatically different from the perfect body for swimming, which is different from the perfect body for running sprints. They already had an A-list photographer commissioned to take artsy photos of different types of bodies. They just needed a smart-sounding story that would end with a feel-good message about how every woman should feel good about her body, because after all, the perfect body is the one that does whatever you need it to do. Could I write that?

"Oh, yes," I said.

I walked out of that lunch with a $4,000 assignment.

Back home in Kentucky, I began researching the hell out of that story. It turned out to be truly fascinating: I learned that Olympic swimmers should be tall and broad-shouldered with big feet, like a capital Y from the front and a capital L from the side. I learned that the best speed skaters look unremarkable from the waist up, but below, as one trainer told me, "It's Arnold's legs and hips"—braided-bread calves, ginormous glutes. The ideal ballerina, on the other hand, will have a long neck and wide-set eyes. All the better if she has an overbite, because, as one dance critic told me, "legibility is everything."

The photos for that story were indeed amazing, and I had a blast writing all that picture grout. My editor called immediately with another assignment. "Can you give us two thousand words about butts?"

"Um. Butts?"

"Like, the history of the ideal butt."

"Oh."

For another $4,000? Sure, I could do that.

This one was even more fun. I knew for starters that I'd have to work in the word *callipygian*, which means "having a shapely butt," from the Greek stem *kalli-*, "beautiful," and *pygē*, "buttock." Maybe I could also throw in *dasypygal*, which describes "a hairy butt." Digging deeper into the topic of butts, I discovered that if you've used the word *buttocks* too many times in one paragraph, you can always swap it out for the obsolete synonyms *clunes* or *nates*, the latter a linguistic relative of the Spanish word for one's fundament, *nadegas*.

I chatted up celebrity trainers and the charming star of the *Buns of Steel* exercise videos, who confided her self-consciousness about her own "bubble butt." I interviewed a Hollywood plastic surgeon who told me how he slurped out fat from "banana rolls"—the butt equivalent of a double chin—so the muscles' natural shape could shine through. The process was, he explained, "like chipping away at a diamond."

I learned how over the centuries and around the world, the ideal derriere has waxed and waned like, well, the moon. I noted Jean-Paul Sartre's observations about the "involuntary waddlings" of a butt as seen from behind, and studied Yoko Ono's film *No. 4 (Bottoms)*, eighty minutes of nothing but close-ups of bare butts moving to and fro as their owners walk, those cracks and creases dividing the screen into fleshy quadrants, like great doughy hearts beating.

The editors loved it. The assignments kept coming.

When news broke of a Virginia beauty queen convicted of attempted second-degree murder, the editors figured there must be other beauty queens gone bad. Could I look into it for another $4,000? Why not?

Sure enough, rogue beauty queens around the world have indeed been charged with crimes from petty theft to treason to assault. "Beauty Queen Crowned Her Rival," read one newspaper headline.

Allure soon made me a contributing editor and bumped my pay up to more than $3 a word, and unlike most freelancers, I didn't even have to come up with ideas or pitch proposals. They just kept pitching me new wackadoodle assignments.

One of the most memorable involved Mr. Blackwell, the flashy designer-to-the-stars famous for his annual "Worst-Dressed Women List." Each year, the prospect of being included in Blackwell's count of couture catastrophes had celebrities quaking in their Manolos. "We think it'd be funny for you to go to hang out in a mall with Mr. Blackwell," my editor said. "Get him to comment on what real people are wearing. We'll take a few pictures, and you have him toss off a few quips. It'll be fun!"

Well, maybe. After all, this was the guy who dissed one pop singer as "a Martian meter maid," and another star as "a boutique toothpaste tube squeezed in the middle."

Still, I needed the work. Maybe I could make something out of it.

A few days before I flew to California, it occurred to me that maybe my Kentucky clothes weren't the best choice for interviewing the catty curmudgeon known for criticizing people's fashion choices.

Panicked, I called Lindsy.

"Wear black," she said.

I did.

As it turned out, I don't think Blackwell noticed my clothes at all. As soon as he arrived at the Santa Monica Mall, Blackwell was unnerved. The mall was a shock to his senses. He took one look at the passersby and wailed, "THIS IS AN ARMY OF

GARBAGE! I CAN'T DO THIS!" After a couple of minutes, Blackwell's longtime partner, Spencer, who'd come along for the afternoon, suggested we adjourn to a nearby deli for lunch. I put my notebook away, already fretting about how I was going to explain all those empty pages to my editors.

As soon as we slipped into a booth, Blackwell launched, unbidden, into the story of his bruising childhood in a Depression-era Brooklyn slum. He spent his teenage years as a hustler in Central Park. "How could I be ashamed of it?" He shrugged, his eyes misting over. "I was hungry, and it was a way to get a quarter."

I took my notebook back out again.

He went on like that, insisting I scrap our original plan and write instead about his new autobiography, *From Rags to Bitches*, a book at once jaw-droppingly candid and self-absorbed. It was filled with stories about Blackwell's years in Hollywood, like the time he did a sultry striptease for Mae West: "I felt Mae's eyes scan my body, sliding down my thighs."

I didn't come back with the story the editors asked for, but the one I wrote was far more interesting. It never ran—maybe the photos weren't appealing enough—so I later sold it to *Salon*, where you can still find it online.

Meanwhile, living frugally in Kentucky, financed by Condé Nast paychecks, and researching on my own, I'd soon stacked up a new set of index cards for another word book, this one about the language of food. It would address such questions as: What do they call a *danish* pastry in Denmark? (Danes call danishes *Wienerbrod*, or "Vienna bread.") Why do we call those long, thin strands of pasta *vermicelli*? (This picturesque pasta name comes from Latin for "little worms," as in *vermiculture*.) The chapter I was most excited about would show the images of food hidden inside familiar terms. *Moxie*, for example, means "courage" or "energetic initiative," but derives from the name of a tart, bracing beverage.

When that book, *Ladyfingers and Nun's Tummies: A Light-hearted Look at How Foods Got Their Names* was published, it got a bit of buzz, certainly more than *A Garden of Words*. To my surprise and delight, conservative columnist William F. Buckley Jr. wrote an enthusiastic blurb, *The New Yorker* gave it a nice review, and *People* magazine ran a big color photo of me taking a big bite of a ladyfinger. It was supposed to be an elegant photo shoot with a silver tea service and me in a colorful garden frock, but I started goofing around sticking one of the fingerlike sponge cakes between my own fingers, and the photographer snapped that instead.

PUTTING WORDS IN YOUR MOUTH

Cherry

The Normans who conquered England called this fruit a *cherise*, a forerunner of Modern French *cerise*. Speakers of Middle English misunderstood *cherise* as a plural and referred to just one as a *cheri*, later to become *cherry*. This occurred through what linguistics call a type of back-formation, where a singular word is misunderstood as a plural. A similar misunderstanding gave us the English word *pea*, which in Middle English was *pease*, as in *Pease porridge hot*. One more food name that resulted from back-formation: *caper*. The ancient Greeks word *kapparis* referred to a shrub with flower buds that could be pickled. The Romans adapted this name into *capparis*, which found its way into Middle English as *caperis* or *caperes*, which later lost that *s* sound and settled into being spelled *caper*.

Currant

In Middle English, these small, dried fruits were called *raisons of Corauntz, raysyn of Curans,* or *raysons of coraunte*—"raisins of Corinth," in other words, named for the Greek port city where they were exported to the West. The German cognate *Korinthe*, by the way, figures in a handy term for "overly pedantic person." In German, a *Korinthenkacker*, or "petty stickler," is literally a "currant pooper."

Baguette

That long, thin loaf you pick up from the boulangerie has a straight-forward name. In the sixteenth century, the French word *baguette* meant simply a "stick" or "wand," a borrowing of Italian *bacchetta*, "small rod." All these words come from Latin word for "stick," *baculum*, the diminutive of which also lives on the word for the rod-shaped bacterium called a *bacillus*.

Cappuccino

Your steaming cup of cappuccino commemorates the dull brown garb of the order of Franciscan monks known as the *Capuchins*, known for their lives of austerity and simplicity and their work with those who are impoverished. Their simple robes are topped with a long, pointed hood, or in Italian, *cappuccio*, that droops down the back. These monks also inspired the name of *capuchin monkeys*, which have a brown or black cap of hair. (Incidentally, the Italian word for "nasturtium," *cappuccina*, refers to the fact that part of this flower's blossom resembles a pointed hood.)

Cocktail

The story of the word *cocktail* most likely involves the practice of docking a horse's tail, cropping it short to make the hairs stick up like the tail of a rooster—a cock tail, in other words. Over time, the term *cocktail* was applied to the entire horse with a docked tail, an example of what linguists call *metonymy*, where one feature comes to symbolize the whole.

As etymologist Anatoly Liberman notes in *Origin Uncertain*, unpedigreed horses, not thoroughbreds, were more often the ones with docked tails. Early mixed drinks were regarded as adulterated, impure, and even questionable. After all, why dilute perfectly good alcohol with other ingredients? By the early 1800s, people were comparing those watered-down beverages to those equally less-than-purebred horses, and the name *cocktail* stuck. (By the way, did that story cock your strumples? *Strumple* is an obsolete word for "the fleshy part of a horse's tail left after docking," and *to cock the strumples* or *cock someone's strumples* means "to utterly astonish.")

Nun's Tummies

I should explain the title of my previous book, *Ladyfingers and Nun's Tummies*. In Portugal, *barriga de freira*, "nun's tummy" or "nun's belly," is a sweet, velvety pudding. It's one of many so-called *conventual sweets*, which originated in Portuguese convents in the fifteenth century as a way of dealing with egg yolks left over after the whites were used for starching habits. (How else to keep one's wimple stiff?) Religious orders later sold these treats to supplement their incomes. *Barriga de freira* is made with eggs, sugar, breadcrumbs, almonds, and butter, and dusted with cinnamon. Portugal boasts lots of similarly sweet, custardy desserts with equally playful names, including *pescoços de freira* ("nun's necks"), *orelhas de abade* ("abbot's ears"), and *papa de anjo* ("angel's double chin"). There's also *toucinho do céu*, literally "bacon from heaven," although bacon-lovers are disappointed to learn that this rich, eggy dessert contains no bacon at all, but it's so named because it used to be made with lard.

It was all going so well that Times Books decided that unlike last time with the flower book, they'd send me on a book tour. I was delighted with the idea until it hit me: On a book tour, I'd have to talk in front of microphones and cameras—and I was deathly afraid of public speaking.

A dozen years earlier, a teacher at a Louisville high school had invited me to speak to his class about being a journalist. I was glad to oblige, but a couple of minutes into my talk, I suddenly felt extremely nervous. My mouth dried out—so dry that I had to leave the room and find a water fountain before I could go on. I was baffled. I'd never had that problem before. I managed to get through that class, but now I was spooked. The problem only got worse.

Whenever I tried to give a talk now, my mouth became so parched that the insides of my cheeks would stick to my teeth, then make clicking sounds like loose dentures. If I tried to drink water, my hands shook so much that I'd fumble the bottle before it ever got to my mouth, and then water would spill down my shirt.

Over the years, I'd become far more comfortable in front of a computer screen, where I could wrestle with words in private. Now when I tried to give a talk at, say, a bookstore, I'd wrestle with those words in front of the audience, editing them in real time, restating the thought another way, then correcting myself and trying again, with lots of *ums* and *uhs* and *you knows* in between. I shudder to think what it must have been like to watch.

I'd hoped it was just a passing problem, not a full-blown phobia. One way or the other, I'd soon find out.

The publicity department scheduled some TV interviews for me in New York, starting with a live interview on a brand-new network called MSNBC. I was to appear on their morning show, a knockoff of NBC's *Today*. I was nervous, of course, but it was a fantastic opportunity to promote the book.

Early that morning, a limo dropped me off at MSNBC. The producer had suggested I bring along some props; that way, the camera operator could cut to some nice visuals during the interview. I loved the idea of props—anything to take the focus off of me. I brought along a shopping bag full of them: a coconut, a box of vermicelli, some ladyfingers, and other items.

A production assistant whisked me into makeup. Once they had me ready for my close-up, she led me to a corner of the studio behind the cameras to await my segment. While I stood there anxiously clutching my shopping bag, a producer hurried over.

"I'm so sorry," she began. "Your segment's going to be cut short."

"Oh, that's OK," I said. I didn't say aloud what I was thinking, which was *That's great! Anything to get me out of here sooner rather than later.*

She kept apologizing. "It's just that we've booked a dancing Doberman pinscher."

"A what?"

"A dancing Doberman pinscher. We didn't think that we'd be able to get her, but they brought her in today. I'm so sorry, but we're going to have to cut your segment in half."

"No problem at all," I said, trying to look at least a little disappointed. Not only was I immensely relieved, I was of course curious to see what a dancing Doberman could do.

"Thanks for understanding," the producer said. "Again, I'm so sorry." She raced off.

On camera, the host was finishing up her cheery conversation with the dog handler. Some bouncy music switched on, and the woman and her Dobie began their routine.

Or tried to, anyway.

They were supposed to be doing all these lively moves to the music, the dog weaving through the woman's legs, spinning, prancing, jumping over her outstretched arm, with a little waltzing and cha-cha-cha thrown in for good measure. The woman was doing fine in her rubber-soled shoes, but the poor dog was not. The studio floor was so slick that it couldn't get any traction. The pup tried valiantly to keep up but kept slipping, pawing frantically at the glossy floor. Without a decent surface, the two of them had to settle for mostly running around the spacious studio in ever-widening circles.

The producer appeared at my side.

"Great news!" she exclaimed. "The dog isn't working out. We're going to cut to a commercial, and then you'll go on. We don't have anything else, so we're doubling your segment."

"Wait," I said. "You mean I'm going to be on for *twice* as long as you said?"

"That's right!" She beamed, then patted my arm and disappeared again. I had thought I couldn't be more jittery, but I was wrong.

During the commercial break, an assistant hustled me onto the set and introduced me to host Jodi Applegate. Another spread out all my props on a table. Jodi motioned me into a seat behind them, and before I knew it, the camera lights were on.

Jodi introduced the segment and steered me through some easy questions. I managed to explain that several pastas are named for what they resemble. *Orecchiette* is Italian for "little ears," and in Italy, bow-tie pasta is *farfalle*, or "butterflies." Long, flat *linguini* are "little tongues," an etymological relative of *linguist* and *language*.

Jodi prompted me about the word *coconut*. I pointed to the shell's three little indentations and explained that sixteenth-century Portuguese explorers first encountered these nuts, they thought they looked like a spooky little face. The Portuguese word *coco* means "goblin" or "bogeyman," hence the name of the nut.

It wasn't terrible, but Jodi surely saw how nervous I was—definitely not ready for prime time, or even a perky early-morning show. And there was still more time to fill.

She reached for another softball question and tossed it my way. "Martha, of all the food names you researched, what's your favorite?"

I was ready for this one. I'd already picked out a Dutch food and even enlisted a Dutch-speaking friend to help me practice its name, which included a distinctive guttural sound.

"Well," I began hesitantly. "My favorite food name is Dutch. Now, you have to picture this: It's a dish of string beans and navy beans. Got it? String beans and navy beans. It's called *blote billetjes in het gras*."

I'd practiced that name many times, but I was so nervous that I served up that mouthful of Dutch with a healthy helping of phlegm—so much that Jodi leapt from her chair. "Wait!" she announced, "I know the Heimlich maneuver!" She grabbed me with both hands and pretended to save me from choking.

It was a smart move. Jodi had found a way to loosen up her tongue-tied, timid guest. If I'd been worried that something mortifying would occur, well, you can't get much more mortifying than receiving the Heimlich on national TV—following a dancing Doberman pinscher, no less.

The whole thing was so funny that I finally relaxed a bit, at least enough to explain that the name of this Dutch dish—*blote billetjes in het gras*—literally means "bare butts in the grass," which makes sense if you picture rounded navy beans peeking out from a pile of green string beans.

I don't recall much more about that interview besides feeling immensely grateful to Jodi and enormously relieved to get out of there.

There were a few more stops in New York—the Food Network, some local cable shows—then on to Los Angeles for some early-morning TV and radio interviews. As the tour went on, I got a little more comfortable, but I was hugely relieved when it was over. I was happy to get back home, back to Deb, back to our growing menagerie of dogs and cats, and back to studying ancient Greek and writing silly magazine stories.

With any luck, I'd never have to be in front of a microphone again.

CHAPTER 10

ROAD TRIP! SOUTH, UPPER SOUTH, AND MIDLANDS: COME-HERES TO CHARNY

TIME TO HOP BACK INTO the Worder Wagon and continue our journey south. Again, this list is by no means comprehensive, but it's a taste of the differences in dialect you may encounter while traveling from state to state.

South

VIRGINIA

Newly arrived in Virginia? Then you're a *come-here*. If you stroll through the Blue Ridge Mountains, you can stamp on *pine shatters*. Particularly in Virginia, *pine shatters* or *pine shadows* are *pine needles* that have fallen to the ground.

NORTH CAROLINA

The chain of islands and peninsulas along part of the Virginia and North Carolina coast known as the Outer Banks has a fascinating vocabulary all its own. In the relatively isolated island community of Ocracoke, you're *mommicked* if you're bothered, frustrated, or exhausted, and if you're feeling queasy, you're *qua-mished*. Something smelly or rotting is *yethy*, your close friend is your *buck*, *slick cam* describes perfectly calm waters, and a porch is a *pizer*. The accent in those parts is distinctive as well: *High tide* sounds like *hoi toid*, *fresh* is pronounced *fraish*, *fire* is *far*, and *farm* is *farr-um*. One way to mommick someone is to *mubble-squibble* them, a local word for "giving noogies," that is, treating their scalp to a vigorous knuckle-rub.

SOUTH CAROLINA

If a South Carolina resident wants to give you a *sursee*, don't worry—it won't hurt a bit. A sursee is a small gift. Also spelled *sirsee*, *surcy*, and several other ways, this word is most likely a play on the word *surprise* and is heard throughout much of the American South.

In South Carolina, a *bloodynoun* is a bullfrog named for the sound of its call, and a *haint* is a ghost or evil spirit, and probably a variant of *haunt*. There's a long tradition of trying to ward off haints by painting parts of houses *haint blue*, the color of an American robin's egg. In folk tradition, haints can't cross water, so the patch of blue supposedly confuses them, or perhaps they mistake that blue for the sky and stay away. (Once while in South Carolina, I slipped across the state line to Tryon, North Carolina, to visit the childhood home of the great Nina Simone, and was delighted to see that the ceiling of her family's front porch was painted a lovely haint blue.)

Along the South Carolina coast, Gullah-speaking descendants of enslaved Africans echo the language of their ancestors. Many Gullah words are what linguists call *calques* or *loan translations*—that is, a literal translation of another language's term for something. For example, the English word *earworm*, meaning "a catchy tune that sticks in your head" is a literal translation of German *Ohrwurm*, and the word *rhinestone* is a calque of French *caillou du Rhin*, literally "Rhine pebble," because these sparkly fake gems were originally cut from rock crystal found in the Rhine River. In the case of Gullah, *dayclean*, meaning "dawn" or "early morning," is most likely a calque of a West African term for "daylight," and *krak teet*, or "speak," is an Africanism that literally means "crack teeth."

GEORGIA

In Georgia, many grocery shoppers will tell you they push a *buggy*, not a *shopping cart* or *grocery cart*. If it's raining but the sun's still shining on the way home, they say *The devil is beating his wife* or *The devil is beating his wife behind a red door* or *The devil is beating his wife, and the angels are crying*. We get calls from all over the South about this one, and it's unclear how such a grisly phrase would apply to such a pleasant patch of weather. Many phrases from around the world also suggest that at such times, something supernatural is occurring, but with happier results. In the Republic of Georgia, for example, if it rains while the sun shines, the devil is said to be washing his face. In South Africa, a sunshower is called a *monkey's wedding*. In Korea, it's a tiger's wedding. In several other countries, the imagined nuptials involve other creatures. In Syria and Lebanon, for example, rats are getting hitched, and in Croatia, monks are getting married.

FLORIDA

In South Florida, everyday language is changing, as English phrases are adapted to reflect Spanish syntax. In Miami, for example, you don't necessarily *get in line*; instead, you *make the line*. For many Miamians, you don't *get married to* someone, you get *married with* them, and to celebrate, you don't *throw a party*, you *make a party*. The word *super*, from Spanish *súper*, is often used instead of "very." In Florida, as the saying goes, "The farther north you go, the farther south you get," and indeed as you go back up through the state, you hear speech that sounds more stereotypically Southern.

ALABAMA

Moving on up into Alabama, a *Yankee dime* isn't currency, but a kiss—especially one offered as a reward. For example, a mom might offer to give her son a Yankee dime if he cleans his room, only to disappoint him with a measly peck on the cheek after he finishes. In Alabama, as in much of the South, if you order a *coke*, your server will likely want to know what kind you want—a *Grape coke? Orange coke? A Dr. Pepper?* There, a coke is simply any flavored, carbonated beverage, unlike in the northern and north central states, where it's more often *pop*, and toward the California coast and also the Northeast, where it's more likely to be called *soda*.

MISSISSIPPI

In Mississippi, you don't want your *bobbasheely* to be *low sick*. The word *bobbasheely*, or "close friend," is adapted from a Choctaw term that means "my brother." As a verb, *bobbasheely* means to "saunter" or "sashay," as in *bobbasheely on back to the hotel*, a phrase that appears in William Faulkner's novel *The Reivers*. Although the use of *bobbasheely* is fading, I think this fond word is well worth reviving. If you're feeling *low sick*, it means you're very unwell indeed—in which case you might just want to nibble on some *nabs*, those square little crackers that come in packs of six and are stuffed with cheese or peanut butter. A Mississippian might describe someone who's feeling really poorly or worn out as looking *like death eatin' on a nab*, a variant of the more common expression, *like death eatin' a cracker*. If you look even worse, you might be said to look *like death eatin' a cracker walkin' backwards*, which is very bad indeed.

LOUISIANA

Dialect in Louisiana is heavily influenced by French, thanks to Louisiana Creoles, whose ancestors lived in French colonial Louisiana, and by French speakers who in the eighteenth century were driven out by the British from what was then called Acadia, now Nova Scotia. These Acadians became *Cajuns* and spoke the variety of French known as *Cajun French*.

In Louisiana, to *make dodo* (DOH-doh) means "go to sleep," ultimately from French *faire dormir*. To *make groceries* means to "buy groceries," another adaptation of a French phrase. To *get down* from a car means to "get out" of it, a relic of French *descendre*. New Orleans business owners may toss in something *for lagniappe*, that is, "a small gift given to a customer with a purchase." Ultimately it goes back to the Quechua word *yapa*, meaning "something added," and was adapted into Spanish as *la ñapa* and brought to Louisiana, where it was adapted into French, which in turn was borrowed into English. Traces of Choctaw also remain in the speech of Louisiana; a raccoon, for example, is sometimes called a *shawi* (SHAH-wee), a *bogue* is a "stream, creek, or waterway" from Choctaw *bok*, and the word *bayou* itself likely comes ultimately from a Choctaw word for "creek" or "river."

TEXAS

When tossing something out, do you *chuck it* or *chunk it*? A truck driver from the Bronx and her Texas-born husband called the show and asked us to settle that question. She said *chuck*, but her husband said *chunk*. As it turns out, they're both right. In Texas and much of the South, you *chunk something*; elsewhere, you *chuck* it. Another woman who relocated to Texas told us she was astonished at how often folks there would respond to a question with *Do what?* This phrase, which means something like "What did you say?" is commonly heard there in the Lone Star State and much of the South.

You may also hear Texans declare they're going to *tell you how the cow ate the cabbage*. The story goes that an elephant escaped from the circus, wandered into a cabbage patch, then started pulling up cabbages with its trunk and eating them. The nearsighted owner called the police: "There's a big cow in my garden pulling up my cabbages with its tail!"

"What's the cow doing with them?" the officer asked.

The owner replied, "You wouldn't believe me if I told you!" (Don't worry—it took me a minute, too.) Anyway, if a Texan says they're going to tell you how *the cow ate the cabbage*, get ready for unvarnished and often unwelcome truth.

If you're getting toward the end of negotiations, you're *down to the lick log*. Because cattle need salt and other minerals, ranchers will cut troughs in felled trees and fill them with lickable blocks of salt. To *come down to the lick log*, or *come up to the lick log*, means you're reaching the place where the herd gathers, and ideally, coming to an agreement.

Upper South or South Midlands
ARKANSAS

A woman once called our show to say that when she moved from Indiana to the Ozarks, she was surprised to hear people use the word *proud* in a surprising way. A neighbor told her that he was *so proud* that she came for a visit, and her coworkers would say *I'm proud we got that figured out* to indicate they were happy about finding a solution. Over the centuries, the term *proud* has described a variety of intense, inflated emotions in addition to pride, and that sense still survives in parts of the American South. You might also hear an Arkansan say they're *journey proud*, meaning "restless, excited, or nervous about impending travel."

In Arkansas, a *bunking party* is a slumber party or sleepover. When then-Governor Bill Clinton was asked to detail his short-comings, he said that they'd need to hold a *bunking party* to give him time to list them all. Other sayings from his childhood there include *That dog won't hunt*, meaning that idea or excuse is worthless, and *It's a bird's nest on the ground*, meaning that something's so easy and beneficial it provides maximum reward for minimal effort.

OKLAHOMA

If I hear someone use the word *larruping*, I listen for other evidence that they might be from Oklahoma. *Larruping* means "extremely good." It's heard in Texas and a few other spots in the middle of the country, but we've heard from so many Oklahomans who use this term that I tend to associate it with that state. Along with variants like *larrupin'*, *larapin*, and *larpin*, the word *larruping* is used particularly with reference to food, as in *That was larrupin' good pie!* *Larrup* means to "beat" or "thrash," and *larruping* is among the many words that correlate a remarkable quality with the idea of hitting something hard. English speakers have long used similar words such as *striking* for "notable," or *smashing* to mean "excellent," or *whopping* for "huge." More recently, *slap* functions in the same way among younger Americans, as in *This song slaps!* or *a slapping good time*.

If someone from Oklahoma mentions a *yo-yo*, they might not mean the spinning toy on a string; they may mean the kind used to cut weeds. This type of yo-yo is a long, serrated blade attached to a long handle and used in a swinging motion.

MISSOURI

How do you pronounce *Missouri*? In that state, the answer's largely a matter of age. The *Missour-uh* crowd tends to be older, while younger folks say *Missour-ee*, the exception being politicians trying to sound folksy and appeal to older voters. In Southern Missouri, you might hear someone mention hitting a *love hole* or a *kiss-me-quick*. That's a sudden dip or bump in the pavement, a reference to the fact that when a vehicle goes over such a drop, it's a chance to grab your traveling companion and maybe sneak in a kiss.

St. Louis, which lies at the confluence of the Missouri and Mississippi Rivers, is a fascinating linguistic island all its own. The city became a permanent stop for both large numbers of westbound German immigrants in the nineteenth century and in the twentieth century for African Americans heading north during the Great Migration. In St. Louis, most residents use slightly different pronunciations for the words *cot* and *caught*, while on the opposite side of the state in Kansas City, fewer than a quarter of residents still distinguish between the two. Most people in St. Louis would say they drink *soda*, while on the other side of the state in Kansas City, they drink *pop*. In St. Louis, the small road running parallel to a highway is known as a *service road* or an *outer road*, while in Kansas City, it's called a *frontage road*.

TENNESSEE

In Tennessee, you don't want *blinky* milk with your *catheads*. Catheads are biscuits the size of a tabby's head, and milk that's blinky is sour. Some people have suggested that the adjective *blinky* refers to the fact that sipping sour milk will make you blink rapidly, but it's more likely from an old Scots-Irish sense of *blink* meaning to "bewitch with the evil eye," since people once blamed witchcraft for such spoilage.

To express astonishment or call someone's attention to something, some Tennesseans will do so with an emphatic *They!* (or as one caller put it, *Thaaaaaaaaay! Myyy gooooooodness!*). It's most likely a version of *There!* as in *Look there!* without that final R sound.

A woman once called us from the mountains of East Tennessee, wondering why so many of the older white people in her area pronounce *ask* to sound like the word *ax*, a pronunciation also used by some speakers of Black English. The story of this pronunciation stretches back hundreds of years. In Old English, the verb *ascian* meant "ask" and was pronounced with the K sound before the S. In Old English and the English of Chaucer's time, a second verb, *acsian*, arose, the result of what linguists call *metathesis*, or the swapping of nearby sounds. (Similar swaps happened with *bird*, previously spelled and pronounced *brid*, and *dirt*, originally *drit*, and *third*, from Middle English *thridda*.) For a long time, both forms, *ascian* and *acsian*, existed side by side, and eventually evolved into the *ask* and *ax* pronunciations. In fact, the first complete translation of the Bible, the 1535 Coverdale Bible, uses *axe* for *ask* in the famous line from Matthew 7:7, now rendered as *Ask, and it shall be given you.*

When people from different parts of the British Isles immigrated to the United States, they brought these two differing pronunciations along with them. In the geographic isolation of the Appalachian Mountains, the *ax* pronunciation persisted among Scots and Irish immigrants. Enslaved Africans who were forced to learn English picked it up. In other words, the pronunciation of *ask* as *ax* is the result of a long linguistic history and not a measure of sophistication.

KENTUCKY

A Kentuckian once called our show to say that when a friend was complaining during a card game, she'd replied, "Just quit your *mulligrubbing* and play." She'd used it all her life, but where did it come from? Since the sixteenth century, *mulligrub* has referred to "a gloomy mood," and *to have the mulligrubs* means to have an intestinal upset. In Appalachia, *to mulligrub* means "to complain for no good reason"—to be bellyaching, in other words.

In the mountains of Eastern Kentucky, *si-goggling*, *sidegogglin'*, *sidegadling*, and *sidegartlin'* all describe something that's askew. These terms are likely from England and Scotland, where *coggle* and *goggle* mean to "cause something to wobble, sway, or totter." If you'd rather not say a crooked picture on the wall is *si-goggling*, you can always say it's *antigogglin'*, *slanchwise*, *whompy-jawed*, *whopper-jawed*, *squeejawed*, or *cattywampus*. For some reason, we get lots of calls about the last of these, *cattywampus*, so let me just say that no one knows the origin, although it may be connected to the Scots verb *wampish*, meaning "to wriggle or twist like a fish."

When it comes to the second-person plural in English, my hometown of Louisville (pronounced *LOO-ah-vull*) lies in an interesting spot. At the time of the Harvard Dialect Survey, most folks in the South—roughly from Texas through Arkansas, then up along the Ohio River to the Mason-Dixon—addressed more than one person as *y'all*. In most other places, people used *you guys*. But Louisville happens to be in a narrow swath through the Ohio Valley where people have long used a third option: *you all*. I might not have believed that, except that I have actual physical evidence.

Once when I was in first grade, I was misbehaving at dinner, and my parents sent me to my room. Full of righteous fury, I grabbed my blue-and-white-lined tablet and a fat purple crayon, and wrote in big, block letters: "You and Daddy are pigs. You are very bad pigs. *You all* are very very very very bad pigs." I slipped out of my room and left it on the living-room couch, certain my angry screed would teach those pigs a lesson. As it happened, my parents thought it was hilarious, and even had it framed. My letter to the pigs hung on the wall in my father's office for many years, and now it hangs on mine.

(I say I might not have believed it because I've long assumed I grew up saying nothing but *y'all*. In fact, I'm a big fan of that term, and increasingly, much of the rest of the country agrees. *Y'all* is becoming more widespread, partly due to its use in the music and popular culture of Black Americans, and perhaps because some people now object that the term *you guys* discriminates against people who aren't guys. Personally, I don't have a problem with *you guys*; it's used so widely, I believe that it's lost its gendered sense. As we often say on the show, you can tie yourself into knots breaking down long-established idioms into their component parts. I'm all for eradicating harmful discrimination in language, but some battles aren't worth fighting. So lighten up, guys!)

WEST VIRGINIA

A Chicago listener once called us to say he was visiting relatives in West Virginia who used a word he'd never heard: *ribey*. They'd

described singer Lyle Lovett as *ribey*, meaning "thin" or "gaunt."
Ribey comes from the Scots word *ribe*, which means "a tall, scrag-
gly plant." If you see a *ribey polecat*, stay out of the way. In West
Virginia, that's a skinny skunk. In West Virginia, you might
also hear something described as *charny* or *kyarny*. Usually said
with great disgust, *charny* means "dirty" or "filthy" and probably
comes from *carrion*, as in "carcass."

OK, time to get out and stretch our legs a bit. In the meantime, I'll tell you about my own introduction to the delights of
dialect. It began early, mostly from my father's side of the family.

CHAPTER II

APPALACHIAN ROOTS

MY FATHER, HENLEE HULIX BARNETTE, was born in a one-room log cabin in the hills of western North Carolina. He always said he had no idea how his parents came up with his name. "Probably saw it in the newspaper," he'd mutter, adding: "Don't ever give your kid a screwball name."

The Barnetts (no *e* at the end—more on that in a moment) were Scots-Irish immigrants who arrived first in Pennsylvania, then moved south to Appalachia and settled at the foot of Sugarloaf Mountain, in a small valley that came to be known as Barnett Hollow, or as they pronounced it, *holler*.

There were seven children—Dad's older sister, named Wilma Mazo, and his younger siblings, Loomis Klutz, William Baines, Evelyn Magdalene, Elroy Alexander, and Raba Colleen. Two other daughters died shortly after birth. The family had no running water or indoor plumbing. They drank from a spring and washed clothes in the creek. They were subsistence farmers who survived on corn bread, molasses, pinto beans, and fatback from a few pigs they raised. To supplement the family's income, the kids gathered sassafras bark, peach pits, and apples to sell in town. Each Christmas, my grandparents scraped together enough to buy each of the children one orange. The kids would eat the fruit, then save the peel to nibble later as if it were orange candy.

The family didn't visit doctors and got by with home remedies. My grandmother, a staunch, teetotaling Southern Baptist, nevertheless sipped an elixir called Wine of Cardui, or "Woman's Relief," which contained as much as 20 percent alcohol. During flu season, she made the children wear smelly bags on a string around their necks. The little cloth bags contained a brown, sticky resin from the asafoetida plant, which smelled strongly of garlic and, according to folk tradition, would ward off disease. They called that substance *asafidgety*, also known in Appalachia as *asafidity*, *fitiddy*, or *devil's dung*.

Just up the hill from the cabin was a small cave, which was the home of their uncle Romulus. Uncle Rom had been drafted into the army during World War I, but a few weeks later, he went AWOL. After that, my father would later say, Uncle Rom was never quite right again. He lived there in the cave, where he raised a few goats and made moonshine, also known as *white lightnin'*, *panther sweat*, or *'splo juice*, so-called because too much of it would make your head explode.

In 1914, the Barnetts left the hollow and lived in a series of small towns, where my grandfather struggled to find work to support his growing family. At last, they settled in the tiny burg of Kannapolis, named for James Cannon, the wealthy industrialist who chose it as a home for Cannon Mills, then the world's largest manufacturer of sheets and towels.

It must have been a heady time for the young family, moving to a town of several thousand, with a paved main street and puzzling words spelled out on big signs with blinking electric letters.

Dad's sister Mazo, now a teenager, bobbed her hair and started wearing makeup. Hoping to impress the locals, she also added an *e* to the end of *Barnett*, figuring it would look more Frenchified and sophisticated.

There were no child labor laws, so the older kids took jobs in the mill, marching in to work before dawn right alongside their father. The giant, deafening rooms were filled with air so thick with cotton fibers, they could reach out and grab a handful. By the end of their shift, lint coated them from head to toe. The failed farmers and illiterate mountain folk who took those jobs out of desperation were disparaged by better-off townsfolk as *lintheads*. Like so many other derogatory names, *linthead* was later reclaimed as a point of pride.

My father began working the mill at the age of thirteen. At the time, he was so malnourished, he weighed just seventy-four pounds. He was assigned to stand in one spot and cut towels by pushing down a giant blade, then tie them in bundles with twine. It was soul-crushing work. There were no legal limits on work hours, so he stood there in the thunderous cutting room repeating that motion, over and over again, ten hours a day, five-and-a-half days a week, for eighteen cents an hour. In the winter, he'd leave for the mill in the dark and go home in the dark, never seeing the sun.

Over the next few years, my father's shoes wore a hole in the solid-oak floor where he stood. Throughout his life, he had nightmares about being trapped in that mill forever, running this way and that, seeking directions, and always stopped by the guards at the gate. On the wall of my office hangs a framed photograph from those days. It's of the personnel in the cutting room where my father worked: four dozen gaunt men and boys in overalls, lined up for a company photo. My dad had scribbled on the back, "Note the children employed in the mill, and none of the workers is smiling."

On Saturday evenings and Sundays, he and his friends had little energy for anything but hanging around pool halls and playing blackjack for cigarettes, passing around jars of corn liquor, and the occasional knife fight.

By the age of nineteen, my father was weary of it all. His mother had long prayed for his salvation, and on a warm September evening, a neighbor finally managed to drag him to a church revival meeting. Sitting on a hard wooden bench and listening to a sermon about sin and forgiveness, my father felt a kind of peace come over him, a sense that he'd been forgiven of his sins, cleansed, and healed.

He resolved to change his life and was baptized in a pond. Soon he was leading informal church services himself in nearby Frog Hollow. He bought a Bible and a small dictionary and kept them by his cutting table in the mill to study during breaks. He eventually decided to become a full-time preacher, but for that, he'd need a formal education—and he had dropped out in sixth grade. So at age twenty-two, he went back and enrolled in the ninth grade, figuring that'd be as good a place as any to start.

At night, studying by the light of a kerosene lamp, he puzzled through grammar lessons, memorized Bible verses and long passages of poetry, taught himself algebra, and managed at last to graduate high school. The day he quit his job, he left his well-worn dictionary and Bible on his table in the cutting room for the next worker who took his place.

In 1936, he headed to Wake Forest University. He reveled in history and religion courses, along with biology, English, Latin, and Classical Greek. From there, he went on to the Southern Baptist seminary in Louisville, where he earned a doctorate in theology. There he met and married his first wife, Charlotte, a church organist. Their son John was born a year later, and three years after that, his brother, Wayne.

My dad took a teaching job at what is now Samford University in Birmingham, Alabama, preaching part-time at local churches. His impoverished childhood and years of being treated as nothing more than a "hand," literally, in the textile mill, had left him with a keen sense of social justice. He was appalled by the overt racism and legal segregation he witnessed on a daily basis. In 1947, he and a white colleague joined Black preachers to form Birmingham's first interracial organization of Baptist ministers. The group met regularly at the Sixteenth Street Baptist Church; many years later, that same church was bombed by the KKK.

Increasingly, my father's participation in anti-racist activism drew so much attention in the local community that the college's president refused to speak to him. Administrators warned my dad that he was "teaching a dangerous subject," and after my dad's first year there, they refused to renew his contract.

Eventually he and the family returned to Louisville, where my father took a job teaching ethics. Soon, Charlotte was pregnant with their third child. Just days from her delivery date, she told her doctor she was having severe pains in her abdomen and breaking out in a cold sweat. The doctor assured her it was nothing. Hours later, she suffered a cerebral hemorrhage caused by eclampsia. My dad rushed her to the hospital, but it was too late. She died that evening, along with the baby.

My father had expected to bring home his wife and a new child, but instead returned home alone. Once the offers of help and casseroles left on the doorstep faded away, he and the boys were left to fend for themselves. Though widely admired as an educator, my dad was also something of an absent-minded professor. There were many breakfasts of nothing but doughnuts and orange juice, and in the evenings, many kitchen disasters.

My father's older sister, Mazo, left her job at a drugstore in Kannapolis and moved to Louisville to help look after her brother and the boys. She took a job managing the seminary's cafeteria, which meant she could live in the seminary's apartment building next door to my father's house.

The following year, a bright young student named Helen enrolled in my father's class. She was a preacher's daughter from the tiny town of Buchanan, Virginia, studying for a master's in religious education. One day early in the semester, she stopped by his office to get some information about an upcoming event. The two of them began talking, and time slipped away. As my father would later tell it, he had the information she needed in his desk drawer, but it took him two hours to retrieve it. They just kept talking—so long that she missed her next class.

In hindsight, it's easy to see what drew them together. They were both thoughtful, well-read, service-minded, open to a wide range of ideas, and each had a wry sense of humor. A romance quickly blossomed, one they kept secret at first.

She was twenty, he was forty. And yes, I know how that sounds. But it wasn't like that, and here's how I know: Shortly before my father died at the age of ninety-three, he handed me a stack of papers, worn and well-thumbed, about two inches thick.

"These are the love letters between Helen and me," he said. "You'll want these someday."

A dozen years earlier, my mother had died of colon cancer. She'd always taken excellent care of her health, so her diagnosis two years earlier had been a devastating shock to the whole family. She had been half my father's age when they met, after all, and the two of them had methodically planned for her widowhood. With my father's encouragement, she earned a doctorate in education so she could teach at the college level after he was gone. Instead, he was widowed for a second time.

Now as my father handed me the stack of letters, I knew that they were mine to do with as I pleased. The unspoken implication was that sometime I might want to write about them. It was many years later, though, before I could bring myself to read them. And when I did, I was flabbergasted.

For one thing, Dad had carefully included photocopies from his office diary from the autumn when they met—page after page as my father the professor realizes, to his wonder and worry, that he is falling deeply in love with a student half his age.

Even more astonishing were the letters from my mother to him. As a twenty-year-old, she knew exactly what she wanted and was determined to get it. She was vivacious and popular, but bored out of her mind with the young men in her class at the seminary. She was drawn to his maturity seasoned by grief, his intellect, his gentle manner, and his devotion to social justice. To my great surprise, the letters show clearly that she was the one aggressively pursuing the relationship. It was my dad who was constantly hesitating, telling her they needed to slow down, reminding her again and again of her own plans to become a missionary or a teacher, warning her about the practicalities of living on a seminary professor's modest salary and what people would think, not to mention the challenge of helping raise two little boys still traumatized by the sudden death of their mother.

But she wasn't having it.

I keep trying to imagine what that must have been like, a secret love affair in the 1950s between a professor and student at a Southern Baptist institution. When my mother informed her parents, a Baptist minister and his church-organist wife, that their now twenty-one-year-old daughter was going to marry her Christian ethics professor, they were scandalized.

"He's just a wicked widower wantin' a woman!" her mother fumed. My mother told her and anyone else who'd listen, "I'd rather be his widow than any other man's wife."

Because her family was vehemently opposed to the relationship, my mother and father agreed to spend a year apart to prove to them—and perhaps also themselves, or at least to my father—that their romance was more than mere infatuation. My mother finished her master's degree, then moved back to Virginia to work as assistant dean of women at her alma mater, Radford University. But, she declared, at the end of that year, they were going to get married.

They did just that at her parents' home in Virginia, with my grandfather officiating. By now, my father's gentle manner, dry wit, and kindness had won over both her parents. It didn't hurt that by now he was becoming a well-known theologian in Southern Baptist circles. When my grandfather invited him to fill the pulpit in their little country church one Sunday, the parishioners were impressed.

A year and half later, I was born. Aunt Mazo was still living next door. In fact, I spent most afternoons with Aunt Mazo until I was in elementary school. When I was very young, I'd don my cowboy boots and cowboy hat, buckle a leather holster around my waist, and with my toy Colt .45 by my side, I'd clomp up the stairs to her third-floor apartment. Together we'd watch westerns, Aunt Mazo forever yelling at the TV, warning the hero when a guy was sneaking up from behind a boulder or commenting on his love interests. I yelled right along with her, absorbing the cadences, words, and phrasing of my aunt's mountain roots.

For starters, I learned to pronounce the word *Aunt* the way she said it, so that it sounded like the word *ain't*, and pronounced the word *can't* as *cain't*. Aunt Mazo put the accent on the first syllable in *guitar* and *cigar* so they sounded like *GHEE-tar* and *SEE-gar*; a *piano* was a *pye-ANN-ah*. In her mouth, *where* sounded more like *hwur* and *there* sounded like *thar*.

She'd refer to things at a distance as being *over yonder* or *right yonder*. When she needed to retrieve something from over yonder, she said she was *a-goin' to fetch it*. If she'd brought it back already, she'd say, *I fotched it*. If she was looking all over for something, she'd ask in frustration, *What went with it?*

If Aunt Mazo thought I was hungry, she'd say, *You want you some liver mush?* or *You want you some pork and beans?*, that extra *you* being part of a grammatical construction that I'd later learn linguists call the *dative of interest*. Or she'd say *I might could find us somethin' to eat*, the *might could* being an example of *multiple modals*, which include such phrases as *shouldn't oughta*, *may could*, and *may might can*.

Typical of Southern Appalachian speech, she'd say *clumb* instead of *climbed* and *drug* instead of *dragged*. If she was embarrassed about something, she *liked-ta died* over it.

Aunt Mazo didn't press a button to turn on the TV, she *mashed* it. When she was helping me to get dressed to go someplace, she'd tell me, *Gitcher britches on!*, pronouncing the *on* like "own." If we were riding in a car and she wanted me to close the window, she'd say, *Run yer glass up!*

If somebody did something stupid, she'd tsk-tsk with, *Lawd, you ain't got brain one!* or *He ain't got brain one in his head!* If she had little regard for someplace else or the people in it, she'd hiss, *I ain't lost nothin' over there!* She naturally used multiple negatives, as in *He weren't no count* to describe someone unimpressive. Being a good Southern Baptist, she'd express disgust or frustration with *Foot!*—nothing else, just *Foot!*

To Aunt Mazo, a large number of anything was *forty-eleven of 'em*, or *a whole mess of 'em*, or a *passel of 'em*, the word *passel* being a variant of *parcel*. She had a whole passel of folksy sayings like that. Describing a fastidious neighbor, she told me he liked his shirts ironed *slick as snot*. She said that another man who kept relocating from town to town chasing work *moved around like a worm in hot ashes*.

While many of these locutions reflect the speech of Scots-Irish immigrants who settled in Southern Appalachia in the eighteenth century, the culture in that part of the country is not monolithic. Although my dad's paternal lineage goes back to Northern Ireland, his mother's family came from the many Germans who settled in those mountains. In addition, some 10 percent of people living in Appalachia are African American, also now known as Affrilachians. And of course, the region is still home to the original Appalachians, the Cherokee. (It's a myth, by the way, that people in Appalachia speak Elizabethan English. There may be the occasional vestige of such speech here or there, but nobody in the hills talks like Romeo or his girl-friend. If there were such a place, wouldn't thou thinkest that by now there would be a theme park staffed by underpaid folks in period costumes who speaketh thus?)

Knowing what I know now about Appalachian dialect, I ache to go back in time and luxuriate in these sounds and speech patterns I heard each day growing up. As it was, this language was simply the music of my childhood, the sounds and speech patterns I absorbed at a tender age. Any time I hear that accent or those turns of phrase now, I just melt—which brings me to one more story.

Early in his career, my father came to admire the civil-rights activism of a young minister in Atlanta, Dr. Martin Luther King Jr., and invited him to come lecture to his classes. King had led the successful Montgomery bus boycott just four years earlier.

My father knew King's visit would be controversial. It was 1961: Louisville was still deeply segregated, and tensions were running high. Just days before King's arrival, protesters held sit-ins at ten different lunch counters around the city. Two years later, a Gallup poll would show that only about four in ten Americans viewed the civil-rights activist favorably; by 1968, his disapproval rating rose to nearly 75 percent, a finding reflected in the fact King was sometimes referred to as "the most hated man in America."

King arrived at the seminary that day accompanied by a police escort, and went to my father's office to meet with my father and his fellow professors. Dad presented Dr. King with a copy of the first of his fourteen books, called *Introducing Christian Ethics*. At the time, this textbook was widely used in seminaries, and King said he was grateful for the inscribed copy, but indicated he'd already read it. Before his lecture, he and my father posed for photographs. One of those black-and-white photos shows the two of them standing together, as King holds the book my father wrote. That picture now sits right above my desk.

More than a thousand people showed up for King's lecture in the seminary chapel. As my father would remember it, the young preacher from Atlanta seemed a bit nervous at first—not quite the assured orator we now picture. But he soon warmed to his topic, arguing forcefully for an end to racial segregation, a firm commitment to nonviolence, and the importance of staying "maladjusted to the evils of this age." At the end of his lecture,

King received a standing ovation, the first ever for a speaker in that chapel.

Afterward, King and my father and several others walked over to take a break in the seminary cafeteria. Aunt Mazo helped serve them coffee as students, activists, and professors crowded around. A newspaper photographer snapped a picture of King and my father deep in discussion about civil-rights strategy in the South. A framed copy of that photo now hangs on my wall as well.

King was scheduled to speak afterward to a few dozen students in my father's combined ethics classes, followed by a Q&A, but again, far more people than expected showed up. By the time the crowd reached some five hundred people, they hastily moved that session to the chapel as well.

King's visit was so controversial at the time that my father nearly lost his job. The seminary's board of trustees, along with the seminary president, issued a public statement of regret for "any offense caused by the visit of the Rev. Martin Luther King Jr. to the campus." The seminary president told my father that King's appearance there had cost the seminary as much as $500,000 as churches in the Deep South began canceling their donations to the school. My dad's response was to smile, shrug, and say in his usual plainspoken way, "Well, that was money well spent!"

These stories became the stuff of family lore. Just last year, though, I was stunned to learn of something I never knew existed. A friend emailed me a link to an audio recording of Dr. King's visit with my father's class and the Q&A afterward. Dad had shared with me the recording of King's first lecture to the audience of more than a thousand, but I had no idea there was a recording of this second talk to the smaller group.[*]

---

[*]   It's inspiring. You can listen to it here: hdl.handle.net/10392/2761.

It was stirring, of course, to listen to Dr. King warmly thank my father, then offer some informal remarks before deftly fielding questions from students. He spoke at length about nonviolent resistance to oppression, the history of civil disobedience, and the ethics of boycotts, reminding them of what Gandhi called the "amazing potentialities for goodness within human nature."

What I wasn't prepared for, though, was hearing my father's voice as he introduced the great man. Those familiar soft syllables, his dry wit, and that gentle, Carolina drawl—it all took me back instantly to a sunny afternoon when I was ten years old. That day, Dad took my younger brother Jim and me for the first time to the weathered, one-room cabin up in Barnett Hollow where our father was born. I recalled how Jim and I drank cold, clear spring water from a metal ladle that still hung from a hook. I was reminded how we poked around the cabin, its roof now falling in, and gathered a few empty bottles lying around inside, then trudged up the hill to Uncle Rom's cave to peek inside at his dilapidated still.

Hearing the sound of my father's voice again, his unassuming manner and his soft Southern accent, whisked me right back to that afternoon, the way the slightest whiff of something can whisk you back decades in an instant.

And, as the mountain folk say, *Don't that knock yer hat in the creek?*

MORE FAVORITE APPALACHIAN EXPRESSIONS

Handful of minutes

Something small, as in *She ain't no bigger than a handful of minutes.*

Knee baby

A knee baby is the next-to-youngest child in a family, tall enough to lean against a parent's knee and older than an arm baby, one still held in the arms. A set-along child, also known as a sit-alone baby, is a toddler who's able to sit up but still can't walk.

Come nigh as a pea

To barely miss doing something or come very close to, as in *He come nigh as a pea gittin' thar*, meaning "He almost got there."

Footercooter

To *footercooter* means to "waste time," or "behave lazily," as in *Quit your footercooting and get to work!*

Study bee

A small fly or bee that tends to hover over flowers, as if studying it. This behavior also earned it the name *steady bee*.

Hot as brinjer

If the weather's particularly warm, you might say it's *hot as brinjer*, an expression that may go back to a Scots word that means "to rush forward recklessly" or "to beat." In Appalachian dialect, *brinjer* is part of phrases suggesting something extreme or striking, such as *hot as brinjer* or *it's brinjin' cold today*.

Sunpain

A morning headache that gets better as the day goes on.

Upscuddle

A noisy quarrel.

The hind wheels of destruction

If you look like the hind wheels of destruction, you look just terrible. A variant form is *like the hind wheels of bad luck*. Either way, you're disheveled and not in good shape, like you were run over by something awful. In other words, you look like death eatin' a cracker.

Take one's foot in hand

If someone *took his foot in hand*, he set out to walk someplace.

CHAPTER 12

ROAD TRIP! INLAND NORTH AND THE HEARTLAND: DOPPICK TO PUPPY CHOW

GRAB THE COOLER AND THE snacks—I'm revving up the Worder Wagon again! We're off for a trek through the midsection of the United States.

Inland North

PENNSYLVANIA

The language of much of this state is heavily influenced by Pennsylvania German, also known as Pennsylvania Dutch, the word *Dutch* here originally referring to speakers of various German dialects.

A veterinarian once called our show to say that when she moved to Central Pennsylvania, she'd been puzzled when clients told her their dog was *doppick* or their kitten was *nixie*. Along with variants such as *doppling* and *dopsy*, the word *doppick* comes from the Pennsylvania German *doppich*, meaning "awkward." A misbehaving kitten is *nixie*, probably from German *nichts*, which means "nothing" and the source of English *nix*. The kitten might also be *grexing*—that's a word used in Pennsylvania Dutch to mean "complaining," and if you try to pick her up, she might *rutch* around. To *rutch* or *rutsch* in that part of the country means to "slip," "slide," or "squirm," another German-inspired word. Finally, if a Pennsylvania kitten could talk, she might grex by exclaiming *The kibble's all!*, in which case you better fill that empty food bowl. *The kibble's all* (or worse yet, *The coffee's all*) is a calque of German *alle*, meaning "finished" or "all gone."

In Pittsburgh, you'll often hear the second-person plural rendered as *yinz* or *yunz*, a contraction of *you ones* or *you 'uns*—often enough that Pittsburghers are sometimes called *Yinzers*. Then there's *n'at*, a shortening of *and that*, tacked on to the end of a sentence to mean "and such things," as in *We were watching the Steelers and drinking beer, n'at*, sometimes celebrated on T-shirts as *N'@*. In Pittsburgh, someone who's nosy is *nebby*, something slippery is *slippy*, a *gumband* is a rubber band, bologna is *jumbo*, a vacuum cleaner is a *sweeper*, a *jagger* is a thorn, and *jaggin' around* is poking fun, playing tricks, or otherwise goofing around. And of course, you toss towels into the laundry when they *need washed*. (And hey, stop it, spell-check! *They need washed* is a perfectly fine.)

OHIO

I remember how puzzled I was as a kid one year when a new girl came to our school. Her family had moved to Louisville from Cincinnati, and whenever she heard something she didn't understand, Jackie wouldn't say *What?* or *Excuse me?* She'd say *Please?* It was years before I learned that this response is a distinctive feature of that Ohio city, where large numbers of Germans settled in the nineteenth century. That polite *Please?* is a vestige of German *Bitte?*

A different Ohio city figures in one of the greatest stories in the annals of forensic linguistics. Illinois police were struggling to narrow down a list of subjects in a kidnapping case and asked linguist Roger Shuy to analyze the ransom note. The kidnapper demanded that $10,000 cash be left in a trash can "on the devil strip at the corner of 18th and Carlson." Shuy asked if they had any suspects from Akron, Ohio. Stunned, the police replied that one of the suspects was indeed from Akron. The linguist explained that although around the country, the grass strip between the sidewalk and curb goes by lots of different names, including *berm*, *tree lawn*, *parkway*, *curb lawn*, *boulevard*, *grass strip*, *hell strip*, and *verge*. As it happens, the term *devil strip* is used almost exclusively in Akron. The cops confronted the suspect, and he confessed.

INDIANA

A listener named Rosemary moved from the East Coast to her husband's hometown of Evansville, Indiana, and called us to share a puzzling experience. Her mother-in-law asked her to go out to the garden and pick some tomatoes and mangoes to make chili sauce. "I was confused," Rosemary said. "You don't grow mangoes in Southern Indiana." Her mother-in-law insisted that indeed you do, and they were right out there in the garden. In fact, many people in that area refer to green peppers as mangoes— the result of some fascinating history: British colonizers in India encountered many unfamiliar fruits. But to send them back to England, they had to pickle them first. One such fruit was the mango. These new delicacies became so closely associated with this process that the noun *mango* became a verb that meant "to pickle," as in *to mango a melon*. The word *mango* was later reapplied to imported vegetables that were also pickled, particularly green peppers. No one knows why the name happened to stick in that part of the country, but the bottom line is that in Indiana, having pizza with sliced mushrooms and mangoes isn't nearly as weird as it sounds.

ILLINOIS

In Illinois, as in much of the middle of the country, you'll hear what linguists call the *positive anymore*, which means "nowadays." Yet another vestige of Scots-Irish migration, it indicates continuing action, as in *Anymore, winters are warmer*.

If a Chicagoan's on *LSD*, they may just be on Lake Shore Drive, the expressway running along Lake Michigan. A traffic jam there will be made worse by *gaper's delay* or *gaper's block*—rubbernecking, in other words. Once home, they'll probably take off their boots before going into their *frunchroom*, the front room overlooking the street, usually reserved for company.

In Chicago, or *Chi-town* (say *SHY-town* to sound like a local), a youngster might put on her *gym shoes*, not sneakers, and head outside, then walk through the *gangway* to meet friends in the *prairie*. A *gangway* is a sidewalk running through a narrow space between houses, and a *prairie* is a vacant lot. Then again, *the Hawk* might prevent that. Originating in the city's African American community, *the Hawk* is a nickname for a particularly cold wind off Lake Michigan that moves in as swiftly as a hawk, bringing a bitter cold as sharp as talons.

MICHIGAN

In Michigan, you can walk right through a *doorwall*. In parts of that state, a doorwall is simply a sliding glass door. If you step out into the snow, you can use the back of a shovel to *pank* it down, *pank* being a word of uncertain origin.

In the majority-Black city of Detroit, the casual *Whatupdoe?*, a multipurpose slang expression particular to that city's culture and vernacular that means "What's up?" or "How are you?" *Yoopers*, who live in the Upper Peninsula or *U.P.*, are particularly proud of their lingo, which includes *Holy wah!*, used to express surprise, delight, or awe. Since the Upper and Lower Peninsulas are separated by the Mackinac Bridge, or *Mighty Mac*, *Yoopers* call those living south of the bridge *trolls*, an allusion to the fairy tale about a troll who takes up residence under a bridge.

Michiganders sometimes refer to tourists as *fudgies* since they tend to head home with armfuls of the local fudge, or *conelickers* because they're forever sampling the ice cream. Some *fudgies* and *conelickers* head out to Michigan's Beaver Island for a few days of *boodling*. There, *boodle* means to wander about the island in a carefree manner, often with a fermented beverage.

Inland North (North North Central)
WISCONSIN

If you tell me you've been *drinking from bubblers from little on up*, I'm going to guess you're from Wisconsin. In parts of the Badger State, a drinking fountain is called a *bubbler*. (In fact, the Wisconsin Historical Society sells T-shirts with a picture of such a fountain. It reads: "It's a bubbler—Fountains are where you throw coins." No one's sure why, but this usage of *bubbler* is also heard in parts of Massachusetts and Rhode Island.) *From little on up* means "from a young age" and reflects Wisconsin's German heritage, as does *Let's go buy some bakery* for "Let's get some baked goods." On your way to *get bakery*, you watch for *stop-and-go lights*, not traffic lights. Of course, you shouldn't drive at all after a *whoopensocker*, or "large, strong drink," a term that Wisconsinites use to denote "anything extraordinary of its kind."

MINNESOTA

If I suspect someone's from Minnesota, I ask if they ever played *Duck, Duck, Goose*. No one's sure why, but most Minnesotans played *Duck, Duck, Gray Duck*. Minnesota is also one of those states where you're likely to hear *Uff-da!* used to express several things—surprise, annoyance, or exasperation, or what you might exclaim when lifting heavy furniture. This handy expression is borrowed from Norwegian *uff da*, which means the same thing, and is now heard mostly in areas of Norwegian settlement.

Minnesotans grow up eating *hot dish*, a casserole of various ingredients such as cream of mushroom soup, green beans, and tater tots. A Minneapolis woman once called us with a funny story about how she welcomed her new pastor from Alabama by telling a joke ending with *hot dish*. The clergyman looked terribly confused until his parishioner realized she needed to explain that in Minnesota a *hot dish* isn't a vixen but a beloved culinary tradition. Uff-da!

NORTH DAKOTA

In North Dakota, you have to hope your *slushburger* isn't *ishy*. A *slushburger* is a kind of meat sandwich, much like a sloppy joe, and *ishy* means "revolting." *Ishy* and *Ish!*, an interjection of disgust, most likely relics of Swedish and Norwegian. You also don't want your *knoephla* to be ishy. *Knoephla* is related to German *Knöpfle*, or "button," and *knoephla* is a hearty dumpling soup for those long winter nights in the Flickertail State, *flickertail* being a type of ground squirrel abundant there.

Inland North (Heartland)
SOUTH DAKOTA

In South Dakota, if you gun a car's engine to make the car spin in a circle, you're said to be *spinning cookies*, *making cookies*, or *cutting cookies*. Elsewhere, this type of fun is called *cutting dough-nuts* or *doing doughnuts*. Speaking of cookies, when South Dako-tans tire of making them, they might switch to *scotcheroos*, a local favorite made with Rice Krispies, peanut butter, chocolate, and butterscotch.

IOWA

In Iowa, you might go out for a *tavern sandwich*, a sort of sloppy joe without the tomato sauce. It's also called a *loose meat sandwich*, or a *Maid-Rite*, after the restaurant chain that popularized it. If you can't park on the street, you might leave your car in a *parking ramp*. The earliest parking facilities back east were buildings where cars were driven by a valet into an elevator to be parked on different floors. Hence, the term *parking garage* lodged in the language of the East Coast early on; the term *parking ramp* followed later out west.

Once you arrive at the sandwich shop, here's hoping no one tries to *budge* in line before you. On the way home, make sure you don't run over any *squinnies* or *grinnies*, which is what many Iowans call chipmunks. Need a pit stop? Keep your eyes peeled for a *kybo*, or "portable toilet," a term that probably doesn't derive, as some suggest, from the acronym *Keep Your Bowels Open*.

NEBRASKA

When is a pickle not a pickle? When it's in Nebraska. There, *pick-les* are pull-tab lottery cards. This name recalls the use of pickle jars in bars to collect illegal gambling tickets; if the cops busted in, the bartender could quickly whisk the jar out of sight. In addi-tion to pickles, Nebraskans like their *runzas*, yeast dough bread pockets filled with seasoned meat, grilled onions, and sauerkraut or cabbage. For dessert, they might watch for *the ding-ding man*, a local term for the driver of an ice cream truck.

KANSAS

Like many Midwesterners, Kansans take special pride in the exclamation *Ope!* It works in all kinds of situations, as when you accidentally bump into someone (*Ope! My bad!*) or you need to get by (*Ope! Let me just sneak past you here.*) or someone hands you something you dropped (*Ope! Thanks.*) However much Kansans would like to claim this expression, it's not at all unique to this area and its use extends far beyond the Midwest. It's probably just a *P* sound tacked onto an *Oh!*, as in *yep*, *nope*, and *welp*. Kansans, at least, can console themselves with some tasty *burnt ends*, *puppy chow*, and *concrete*—savory bits of barbecue; a sweetened peanut-butter snack mix; and frozen custard blended with fruit, candy, cookies, and nuts.

CHAPTER 13

THE ALLURE OF RADIO

OK, BACK TO HOW I ended up in front of that microphone—and stayed there for twenty years.

With the book tour over, I settled back into life in Kentucky and supporting my etymological habit with more freelance writing. Fashion Week in New York was coming up, and *Allure* flew me there to cover it. "We want a new perspective," my editor said, "and we know you don't care about fashion." They had that right.

Editors at other magazines were pitching me work as well. One sent me to do the first magazine interview with Jessica Lynch, the U.S. Army private captured during the 2003 invasion of Iraq and retrieved from a hospital by special forces in a dramatic rescue. As we spoke quietly in her childhood bedroom filled with stuffed animals, at her home in a West Virginia hollow, she seemed surprisingly tiny and girlish, but at some points slipped into what appeared to be the so-called "thousand-yard stare"—the fixed, unfocused gaze of a soldier who's endured unspeakable trauma.

For another, I spent a day with author Barbara Kingsolver on her farm in the rolling hills of Southwestern Virginia. Since she was graciously letting me invade her writing time and had lots of laundry to do, we drove into town. There in a stuffy laundromat, as she folded clothes and shooed away flies, we talked about her most recent acclaimed novel, *The Poisonwood Bible*. It would be another twenty-three years before her *Demon Copperhead* would win a Pulitzer, but her outrage over anti-Appalachian and anti-gay prejudice were already abundantly clear.

I also spent months writing a fascinating story for a now-defunct Condé Nast magazine, *Women's Sports and Fitness*. A woman in Louisville named Tori Murden was determined to become the first woman and first American to row a boat across the Atlantic Ocean entirely alone—no motor, no sail, no support vessel traveling alongside her. More people had walked on the moon than had accomplished what she wanted to do. Only five, all men, had successfully rowed the Atlantic west-to-east; four others had died trying.

During her first attempt, Murden set out from North Carolina for France in a twenty-three-foot boat designed to right itself if capsized. But a rare North Atlantic hurricane formed and began making its way toward her, whipping up fifty-foot-waves, capsizing the boat repeatedly and nearly killing her. She gave up that attempt, but tried again a year later, this time going east-to-west, from the Canary Islands to the Caribbean. After more than eighty days at sea, she glided up to a dock in Guadeloupe, where a small group of us were waiting for her, astounded at how healthy she looked. It was an epic story, and I was captivated—enough that I took up sculling myself and fell in love with the sport.

Not long after, I heard about a little radio show that sounded too good to be true. Produced by the San Diego public radio affiliate KPBS, it featured a lively hour of chats with callers about word origins and grammar, plus wordplay and puzzles, riddles, bloopers, and more. *A Way with Words* aired locally in San Diego and, for some reason, it was also heard throughout the state of Wisconsin.

The show's hosts were Richard Lederer and Charles Harrington Elster. Richard was the author of the bestselling *Crazy English*, a playful, rambunctious look at the quirks of English that asked questions like: Why do we drive on a parkway and park in a driveway? Why do our noses run and our feet smell? In what other language do people play at a recital and recite at a play? Why is it that when we transport something by car, it's called a shipment, but when we transport something by ship, it's called cargo? Good questions, come to think of it.

Richard's counterpart on the show was the buttoned-down Charles Harrington Elster, the author of *The Big Book of Beastly Mispronunciations* and *There Is No Zoo in Zoology*, among others. Charlie's deep, resonant voice gave his strong opinions about the proper use of language an even more authoritative air. KPBS launched the show in 1998, and this linguistic odd couple quickly built up a local following. One had a vaudevillian's sensibility, the other was a Yale-educated stickler, and both had firm opinions about how people should speak and write. They regaled listeners with stories of word origins and dispensed unequivocal advice on pronunciation, punctuation, and grammatical pet peeves—all peppered with plenty of puns.

Richard and I had met briefly a few years before when he was in Louisville to give a speech, and he was kind enough to write blurbs for my first two books. I was thrilled to learn that now he had a radio show about words, and moreover, there was even an audience for such a thing. When my third etymology book came out in 2003—this one focused on animals—*A Way with Words* was at the top of my wish list for places to try to publicize it despite my, shall we say, distaste for public speaking. I had streamed enough episodes to know that when they did interviews with authors, it was usually by phone. I figured I could handle that much. After all, I could do the interview from the comfort of my office in Kentucky with my notes in front of me, and if necessary, even write out my responses in advance and read them. With a phone interview, no one would be the wiser. Besides, the show already had a ready-made audience of word nerds, so I wouldn't have to try to win them over.

The interview indeed went well. I told Richard and Charlie that when I'd been researching my first two books about flowers and food, I was struck by the fact that, etymologically speaking, animals lurk everywhere in language, if only you know where to look. Those examples piled up, and the result was *Dog Days and Dandelions: A Lively Guide to the Animal Meanings Behind Everyday Words*. The word *muscle*, I explained, comes from Latin *musculus*, or "little mouse," because if you make a fist to show off your bicep, that muscle twitches like one under your skin. The word *merlot* means "young blackbird" in French; the wine's dark color probably inspired its name. *Melissa* is the Greek word for "honeybee," and the Hebrew word for "bee" buzzes inside the name *Deborah*.

I knew all these stories well, and Richard and Charlie put me at ease. Since it was a three-way conversation with two highly verbal hosts, I didn't have to talk that much anyway. Afterward, I kept thinking what a blast it must be to have a job that involved communing with fellow linguaphiles.

A few months later, I heard that Charlie had decided to leave the show amid a contract dispute with KPBS, and the station was doing a nationwide search for a replacement. Should I apply? Well, I was deathly afraid of public speaking. But then again, I couldn't imagine anything more fun than getting to share my passion week after week with people who actually wanted to hear about it. After all, I'd briefly derailed so many dinner conversations when I was struck by an etymological connection. "Did you know . . . ?" I'd ask, then proceed to explain that, for example, *lignin* is a chemical compound in plants used for making paper, and it has a chemical structure similar to vanilla's, which is why some old books smell so wonderful. Or I'd pipe up with the helpful observation that if you need a fancy word for "nail-biter," it's *onychophagist*, from the Greek word for "fingernail," *onyx*, the source also of the English word *onyx* because the variety of this stone used for carving cameos resembles the pink and white of human fingernails.

Just imagine if I could drop etymology bombs like these into conversations each week and instead of being perplexed (as so many of those dinner party guests probably were), listeners would be as excited about them as I was! There was no way I could pass up this opportunity. There had to be a way to make it work.

I reached out to the producer, Stefanie Levine, who asked me to send some sample audio. Some friends of mine who worked at the local public radio station in Louisville helped me record a few paragraphs from my book *A Garden of Words*. At that point, people still recorded things on CDs, so I put one in an envelope and sent it off to KPBS. A couple of weeks later, Stefanie emailed to set up a phone chat.

What I remember about that interview is that we talked for hours—two, maybe even three. Stefanie was nothing if not thorough. We also laughed a lot. She was a fantastic interviewer, with long experience producing a daily arts show before she took over at *A Way with Words*. Before that, she had worked at a bank evaluating loan applications, so she knew how to vet a potential hire and get them to spill all, drilling down on their strengths as well as their weaknesses.

At one point, Stefanie got me talking about how I spent my time outside of work. I hadn't expected to share this with her, but I mentioned in passing that I also played keyboards in a lesbian rock band. Our band was called Yer Girlfriend (and our fans wore T-shirts that read "I'm with Yer Girlfriend," causing some entertaining double takes). Our repertoire consisted mainly of original songs, most of them with a political edge at a time when it was still legal to fire gay people from their jobs and deny same-sex couples access to the public institution of civil marriage. We also played covers of artists like Melissa Etheridge and had a spirited homage to Nancy Sinatra that segued nicely into the Rolling Stones' "Satisfaction."

It was a time gay people were still starved for representation, and many celebrities were still closeted—it was nearly a decade before Ellen DeGeneres came out, and even longer before *Will & Grace* hit the airwaves. For that matter, I wasn't entirely out myself at first, and initially played under a stage name, Patty O. Veranda (a nod to my mother's maiden name, which was Poarch—get it?). At one large march for gay rights, I even performed in sunglasses and a Tina Turner wig, partly out of fear someone from work might recognize me.

In any case, it wasn't at all unusual for a couple hundred people to show up at our gigs. Many of our fans were still closeted or from rural areas where it was hard if not impossible to connect with like-minded folks. At our shows, they had a safe space where they could be themselves and enjoy some lively and affirming entertainment.

We also had regular gigs at a former funeral home that had been converted into a gay bar. We performed at lots of rallies and benefits for the Fairness Campaign, a local group fighting discrimination based on sexual orientation, gender identity, and race. From time to time, we'd hit the road and perform for thousands of women at music festivals throughout the South, and from Key West to Chicago.

I'd originally joined the band as a flute player, mainly because I enjoyed spending time with the other women. I'd had piano lessons as a kid and flute lessons in high school, so they invited me to sit in on a couple of slower songs. But we quickly realized that unless we were going to cover a bunch of Jethro Tull, a flutist wasn't much use. We had two talented singer-songwriters on guitar, an excellent drummer who'd played professionally for years, and a bass player who also played a mean banjo.

What the band really needed was a keyboardist. For that matter, we also needed a keyboard. At the time, I was the only one in our group with a credit card, and I wanted to keep playing, so I splurged on a Roland D-50 keyboard. Soon I was picking out notes on the synthesizer, like the simple trumpet part on "These Boots Are Made for Walkin'."

I went on to take lessons from a jazz pianist but never really got very good—not that that mattered much. Our fans would tell me, "I love to watch you play"—the operative word, I realized, being *watch*, not *hear*. And the fact was, we were fun to watch. Laura, Carol, Phyllis, Kathy, and I were all having a blast up there. Toward the end of each show, our bass player switched to banjo, and I'd take over the bass on "Foggy Mountain Breakdown" and a couple of two-stepping country tunes. I'd switch back to flute for our final, signature song, an original sing-along with a soaring melody and lyrics that painted a picture of a more just, equitable world.

Goofing around in the band, I learned to make up in showmanship what I lacked in musicianship, which was quite a bit.

And to my surprise, performing with my bandmates was fun, not nerve-racking. On the contrary, after long days of solitary writing and research, playing music out in public was a welcome contrast.

I was surprised to catch myself talking about my years in the band during a job interview for a show about grammar and etymology, but in the end, that may have been what tipped the scale. There just weren't that many candidates who were knowledgeable about language, were willing to do a little radio show for very little financial reward, and who had at least some kind of performance chops. I didn't mention my speaking phobia—not in so many words, anyway—although there was ample evidence out there in the form of previous radio and TV interviews that a diligent researcher like Stefanie could easily find. But she would later tell me that my years in a band gave her an inkling that despite being a halting, unsure speaker, I still might be worth a gamble. "I'd rather have to turn down the flame than have to turn it up," she said. "It seemed like there was something that I might be able to work with."

A few days after that chat, she phoned again to ask if I'd like to come to San Diego for a weeklong tryout.

Would I? I couldn't say yes fast enough. What's the worst that could happen, anyway? I'd take a flying leap and maybe, just maybe, that net would appear.

When Stefanie breezed into the spacious KPBS lobby to greet me, she was almost exactly as I'd pictured her: a tiny dynamo, warm and efficient with a hearty, ready laugh. Soon after, I learned a Yiddish word that described her perfectly: *berrieh*. Also spelled *berya*, *beria*, or *berye*, it denotes "a woman of remarkable energy and talent" and "a woman of extraordinary competence."

You'd think a word this useful would be as well-known as other Yiddishisms like *schlep* and *maven* and *chutzpah*. I've never come across *berrieh* in an English dictionary, but if this word ever does become so common that lexicographers decide to include it, they could do worse than illustrate it with a picture of Stefanie.

When Stefanie took me into the studio to see Richard, he threw open his arms and welcomed me as warmly as she had, delighted to be continuing the show with a female counterpart.

Tall, deep-voiced, effervescent, Richard lived up to his reputation as a self-declared verbivore. "Carnivores eat meat, herbivores eat plants and vegetables, and verbivores devour words," he liked to say. He earned a Ph.D. in linguistics at the University of New Hampshire, then spent a year at Harvard Law School before taking a job teaching at St. Paul's, an elite prep school in New Hampshire. In 1998, he published a playful collection of bloopers and other commentary about language. *Anguished English* became a national bestseller. After twenty-seven years at St. Paul's, he left for San Diego and embarked on a career of speaking and writing. He would go on to author scores of other books about language, showcasing them in public appearances with a borscht-belt comedian's timing and wit. At the 1989 O. Henry Pun-Off World Championship, he was crowned "Punster of the Year" and playfully referred to himself as "Conan the Grammarian" and "Attila the Pun." He promoted his appearances as "learning and language dressed up to have fun." His publicity photo featured him wearing a tuxedo with a giant jester's hat.

Richard accepted every speaking invitation he could, especially if it meant he could sell his growing inventory of lighthearted books about language. His calendar was crammed with appearances at libraries, schools, Rotary Clubs, conferences and conventions, cruises, Mensa gatherings, dinner parties, you name it. The joke going around was that given a chance, Richard would speak at the opening of an envelope, as long as he could sell his books there.

When he wasn't punning for audiences or explaining a point of grammar, he might be sharing some favorite palindromes:

SIT ON A PAN, OTIS!

TOO BAD I HID A BOOT

GO HANG A SALAMI, I'M A LASAGNA HOG

He had a store of words and phrases at the ready for every occasion, regularly hauling them out and reassembling them while riffing on the oddities of English. He regaled anyone who'd listen with a steady stream of rapid-fire quips. "The word *politics* derives from *poly*, 'many,' and *tics*, which are blood-sucking parasites. What does that tell you?"

He was constantly puzzling aloud about this or that linguistic quirk—"Why doesn't *Buick* rhyme with *quick*? Why is it that after a number of injections, your jaw gets number? Why are boxing rings square?" On the air, he'd remind listeners, "We get our audio radiance from our radio audience," then launch into more wordplay, anagrams, jokes, grammatical curiosities, and trivia.

When Richard wasn't riffing on language, you might catch him expounding upon two of his other passions: tennis and poker. An avid tennis player, Richard delighted in San Diego's year-round warm weather. He also indulged that competitive streak at the poker table. Two of his grown children, Annie Duke and Howard Lederer, were world-champion poker players who had won millions at the table. Richard proudly basked in his kids' success and jokingly boasted that he was history's most successful breeder of world-class poker players.

Naturally, he and I connected over our love of language and our shared nerdy exuberance. Still, I had a lot of ground to cover in that first intensive week, starting with a crash course in radio production and cohosting. For one thing, I was dealing with a whole new vocabulary.

First, I was surprised to learn that *A Way with Words* is what's known as a *call-out show*, not a *call-in show*. Unlike a call-in, where audience members phone the show hoping to talk with the hosts on the air in real time, a call-out show isn't live. Instead, it's a series of prerecorded calls that are assembled into a format that sounds as if it's live.

In fact, *Car Talk*, the long-running, wildly popular public radio show with auto experts Tom and Ray Magliozzi, was also a call-out. The original producer of *A Way with Words*, Mary Garbesi, spent a week shadowing the *Car Talk* hosts at WBUR in Boston to learn how they produced their show.

Anytime a listener phoned the show, they heard a friendly recording that invited them to leave a message. Staffers later screened those recorded messages, working like talent scouts to find messages from people who would make a good "third star" of the show, however briefly. Was the caller animated or shy? Did they speak clearly? Did it sound like they might freeze up while talking with the hosts? Was it a new topic the hosts had never addressed before? Did the caller have a good story or describe an amusing dispute that might lead to an interesting conversation? Anything else notable about the caller that might make for irresistible listening?

Once twenty or so callers were selected, a producer contacted them to ask if they could be by their phone for a fifteen-minute period on a particular day, ready with their question or story. Inevitably, several declined, whether due to work schedules, family obligations, or because on reflection, they were too simply shy to be on the air. The goal was to book ten to twelve of those callers per episode, ideally reflecting a diverse mix of backgrounds, ages, and geographic locations.

The show was then recorded live-to-tape. This means the producer already has all the callers lined up and waiting, like planes circling O'Hare. A staffer phones a caller and tells them to stand by, and almost before they know it, they're chatting with the hosts as if the show is live. The hosts take one call after another that way, with breaks in between for brief discussion while the next caller is being dialed. The whole thing takes a couple of hours. Afterward, the producer reviews the calls and assembles the show, tinkering with the order of the calls the way a band might with a set list, starting with a high-energy number and then moving through a variety of calls that complement each other in terms of content and pacing. The recorded calls are later edited and assembled into a show that sounds as if it's all happening live.

I also learned that the show's format included a billboard at the top, a scripted, thirty-second preview of the episode to entice listeners to stay tuned past the top-of-the-hour newsfeed from NPR. After national newsbreak, the show was divided into three segments, the first of which featured a scripted intro that welcomed everyone with a light, bright bit of language news or other "ear candy" that ideally kept them listening. A scripted outro at the end of each segment indicated more to come after a break. Then there was continuity, which is radiospeak for the scripted connective tissue between calls. During that tryout week, I learned that writing for the ear is quite different from writing for the eye; the sample scripts Stefanie gave me looked startlingly sparse. "Listen to someone like Robert Siegel read the news on the air," Stefanie said. "They're using short, simple sentences. Picture what those sentences look like. They look way too short on the page, but the voice expands to fill those gaps." I started listening that way and realized she was right. She also told me about bumpers and stingers, the musical interludes of varying lengths. All of that format and language remain to this day.

What doesn't remain is the type of scripting we did for the continuity. When Richard and Stefanie were showing me how the show was put together, they reminded me of a term I hadn't heard since undergraduate Greek: *stichomythia*, a series of quick, alternating one-liners spoken in rapid succession by two characters. This dramatic device is used for witty repartee in some of Shakespeare's plays, for example, or to heighten tension, whether in ancient Greek drama or Hulu's fast-talking dramedy *The Bear*.

Witty repartee was our goal, at least, although looking back on those early scripts, our own version of stichomythia was more like singsong. Here's an example of the last bit of continuity from one of our earliest episodes that focused on the topic of slang:

Martha: Well, Rich, we've been kickin' it—by that I mean we've been "hanging out together"—for nearly an hour now.

Richard: Which means it's time for us to kick up our heels and bounce—meaning "it's time for us to leave."

Martha: But we'll be back next week with another bangin', uber-verbivorous, hella-good show.

Richard: In the meantime, we invite you to share your uber-thoughtful questions and comments about language. The number to call is 1-877-929-WORD.

I know, I know. I *know*. What can I say? It was 2004, and that's how we did it.

For me, that part was far less intimidating than I feared—having a script in front of me, silly lines and all, was reassuring, and reading them into a mic in a small studio, snug in my headphones, with Richard sitting across from me and Stefanie on the other side of the glass along with engineer Jill Fritz felt surprisingly comfortable. It didn't really feel like talking to the tens of thousands of listeners we had at the time.

It was the conversations with callers, the unscripted parts, that were far more difficult for me. For one thing, I'd spent a lot of time researching answers to their questions and then trying to come up with a clever, engaging way of presenting them, all the while fearing that the caller might toss in an extra question I couldn't answer or take the call in a direction I wasn't prepared for. For another, Richard and I had vastly different speaking styles—he was a longtime professional speaker with bubbly zeal and a seemingly endless supply of words, while I was a hesitant, uncertain writer who was used to wrangling words in private, searching through trial and error for *le mot juste*, writing and rewriting for hours to find out what I was thinking. Oh, and did I mention I was deathly afraid of public speaking?

I lost count of the times I heard Stefanie in my headphones saying, "Martha! Jump in! Jump IN!" The flow of words from Richard was often so steady that there really wasn't even a place to jump in—one of his favorite palindromes comes to mind: NIAGARA, O ROAR AGAIN. Other times I just sat there gaping with amazement that he could go from discussing the pluperfect in past-contrary-to-fact conditions, then drop in a quote from Shakespeare or Shelley, then toss in a joke from one of his books, such as *Sleeping Dogs Don't Lay* or *Get Thee to a Punnery*. He could be loads of fun to listen to, but then again, sitting there listening in bewildered silence is not what a cohost is supposed to do.

On the other hand, I slipped easily into the role of fellow stickler. The answers Richard and I gave listeners during that tryout week were similarly traditional and straightforward: a word or phrase was either right or wrong. After all, we had it on good authority from a couple of dozen grammar books that sat on a rolling cart right there in the studio: A couple of hefty dictionaries, a usage manual or two, and some word-origin books for popular audiences. What more would you need? Callers wanted yes-or-no, black-or-white answers, and we had them. Listeners who joined us came away either satisfied that their way of speaking or writing was correct or chastened if we declared they were wrong.

By the end of my tryout, I desperately hoped that the team at KPBS had seen at least enough of a spark, if not a flame, to convince them I could grow into the job. A few days later, Stefanie and program director John Decker called to offer me the gig, I couldn't help thinking that every year thereafter, I'd celebrate August 4 as a second birthday; it felt that right. Sure, there were logistics to work out. KPBS was willing to fly me out from Kentucky every month for two-and-a-half-weeks or so, and we'd try to record as many shows as possible during that time. They'd put me up in an extended-stay motel and help me rent a car, and would a payment of $400 an episode be OK? "Of course," I said. I knew I could still live frugally in Kentucky with Deb and maybe take on an extra magazine assignment each month. It didn't really matter, though. I'd figure the rest out later.

Thus began my monthly commute between Kentucky and San Diego. Everything about the new job was exciting. Stefanie was an excellent teacher, and working together was a joy. I was learning so much every single day and luxuriated in getting to share what I loved about language with word nerds who felt the same way.

If you're like me, you can barely stand to hear a recording of your own voice. But if I was ever going to get better, that was going to be part of the job. During our postrecording listening sessions, Stefanie patiently but firmly pointed out the spots where I should have jumped into the conversation or avoided a pointless etymological tributary, or where I should have guided the call to a conclusion. As cringey as those early sessions were, Stefanie made them fun. Best of all, I began to hear what she heard, and how a call should sound, even if I couldn't quite achieve it yet. She assured me that most radio professionals confess they, too, wince to hear their own early recordings. (In fact, a couple of years later, KPBS brought NPR host Terry Gross to San Diego for a live appearance with me as emcee. As part of her speech, Terry played sound clips of her early days in radio that were so bad—high-pitched, tentative, and so very different from her later on-air presence—that they were hilarious, but also inspiring. She was incredibly gracious about doing so, and incredibly kind to me before we took the stage, as I'm sure it was obvious how nervous I was to introduce one of my radio heroes to an audience of eight hundred.)

Richard was also a generous teacher. Shortly after I arrived in San Diego, he invited me to join him one evening for his presentation to a group of retirees in an upscale part of town. His first bit of advice: Authors make a living selling books, not just writing them. So, he told me, arrive early with all the books in your inventory and set them up at a table near the entrance. This allows people to look them over, and ideally buy a copy or two and get you to sign them, right then and there. "That way people buy the books, and other people see them carrying them around. They're already advertising for you before you ever step up to the mic," he said. Afterward, some of those same purchasers would end up buying another book or two on their way out.

So, before the first attendees ever arrived, I helped him set up a couple of long tables by the entrance, each covered with stacks of his books. Richard was all too happy to chat up buyers and sign books for them, all the while reminding each of them that this or that holiday was coming up, and if they had another word lover in their life, they might want to buy this other book as well. He had several titles to choose from, although his most recent book caught my eye: *The Cunning Linguist: Ribald Riddles, Lascivious Limericks, Carnal Corn, and Other Good, Clean Dirty Fun.*

Seriously? I thought.

Richard caught me eyeing the cover. "You watch," he said, nodding to the fans slowly shuffling in. "That's the book that's going to sell out."

Wait, *The Cunning Linguist?* This crowd of retirees? I didn't believe it.

Just then, a white-haired woman picked up a copy. She flipped through it, giggled, then bought it, carried it off with her, and took a seat. I watched as she passed it down the row to show each of her friends.

For the next hour, Conan the Grammarian entertained with his exuberant patter—puns, wordplay, and bloopers from student papers, funny newspaper corrections, literary trivia, riffs on Mark Twain and Will Rogers, and his usual assort-ment of jokes and riddles. He gleefully reeled off words like *floccinaucinihilipilification*, defined in the *Oxford English Dictionary* as "the action or habit of estimating as worthless," and *pneumonoultramicroscopicsilicovolcanoconiosis*, often bandied about as the name of an occupational lung disease, although it's actually just a word that was invented mainly for inclusion on lists of long words like *floccinaucinihilipilification*.

Richard was irrepressible, enjoying every second of it, and his audience clearly was as well. He told them he was having a great time. "After all," he said, "as one frog said to another, 'Time's fun when you're having flies!'" Still more laughter.

He regaled them with the story of Reverend William Archibald Spooner, the Oxford don who supposedly had a habit of accidentally switching consonants and syllables. The story goes that Reverend Spooner once raised his glass to toast Queen Victoria with "Three cheers for our queer old dean!" He also supposedly officiated at a wedding where he told the happy couple, "It's kisstomary to cuss the bride." He was also said to have reprimanded a rebellious student with "You have hissed all my mystery lectures. You've tasted a whole worm!" That's the story, anyway, although most of these tales, amusing as they may be, are probably as fanciful as *pneumonoultramicroscopicsilicovolcanoconiosis*.

For his big finish, Richard launched into his high-energy version of a Spoonerized fairy tale about Prinderella and the cince. (To get the full flavor of his performance, I strongly suggest you read these next two paragraphs aloud as quickly as you can. Go ahead—I'm not listening.)

"Prinderella lived with her sticked wepmother and her sugly isters. They made her pine all the shots and shans and do all the wirty dirk around the house. Isn't that a shirty dame?"

He went on, faster and faster. He told how Prinderella's gary fodmother came along and turned "a cumpkin into a poach, four hice into morses, and turned Prinderella's irty drag into a drancy fess." She rode off to the drancy fess ball, where "Prinderella pranced with the dince all night long, but at the moke of stridnight she ran down the stalace peps and slopped her dripper."

The audience was in stitches. Sure enough, by the end of the evening, those long tables by the entrance were nearly empty, and there were no copies at all of *The Cunning Linguist*.

CHAPTER 14

A HOUSE ON FIRE

THOSE FIRST FEW MONTHS OF working on *A Way with Words* were thrilling. I had so much to explore about radio and real-time performance, about prepping for a show and editing it, and of course, so much more to explore about language. And I was forever pinching myself at my good luck. I told friends I was studying at the Levine School of Broadcasting, and I imagined this was what it's like for a newborn, laying down so many new neural networks every hour of the day.

Another thing I learned was that cohosting and coproducing a show was close to a full-time job, a job that included screening calls, researching topics, preparing to present them, listening to recordings and studying my mistakes, writing scripts, and learning, learning, learning. KPBS hired a well-known local actor to give me voice lessons. Around that time, I was also delighted to learn the term *infopig*, a bit of slang for anyone who's insatiably curious and obsessed with information-gathering. For an infopig like me, I was happily wallowing in every second.

One thing still terrified me, though. As one of the show's hosts, I knew it was only a matter of time before I'd have to get out and do speaking engagements before live audiences. About six months in, Richard eagerly booked our first joint appearance. It would be at a five hundred–seat theater at San Diego State University, just steps away from KPBS.

Gulp.

He and Stefanie assured me it would all go fine. He and I would step out onstage together, each with our own microphone. We'd read from a stichomythic script he'd written, which welcomed the audience to "an outrageous, courageous, contagious, glorious, notorious, uproarious, tremendous, stupendous, end-over-endous evening." After that, we'd take turns making our individual twenty-minute presentations. They encouraged me to tell my story of falling in love with Greek for my first part, and later share some favorite words from my recent dictionary-diving. We'd leave time for Q&A—Richard was all too happy to do most of that—and then we'd close by reading the rest of his script:

Martha: Well, fellow logolepts and verbivores, it's been an alphabet soup from aardvark to zebra, from the eggs to the apples and the alfalfa to the omega . . .

Richard: Martha and I like to alliterate, and we often expatiate, and occasionally we pontificate, but we try not to expectorate . . .

"It'll be easy!" Richard merrily assured.

I didn't begin to share his confidence, so over the next several weeks I read everything I could about public speaking, trying to answer all my questions. Should I practice hand gestures in front of a mirror? Should I take anti-anxiety medication, or would that dull my responses? Should I try to imagine the audience in their underwear, as some sources suggested, to calm my nerves? For that matter, what was *I* going to wear? What if they asked a question in the Q&A and I didn't know the answer? Should I bring along a dictionary to keep behind the lectern? Was there any way to get out of this?

Deb had been planning for some time to visit me in San Diego, and I was so consumed with dread about our performance that she arranged for her visit to overlap with it. That day, instead of our planned trip to the beach, she spent part of the hours leading up to the event trying to coax me out of the fetal position on the floor of the extended-stay motel room.

I remember little about that evening except the tremendous relief when it was over. Richard, of course, relished the spotlight and all the laughter, and no doubt he sold lots of books. As for me, I remained baffled why anyone would ever want to speak in front of hundreds of people, much less revel in it. But I'd gotten through it, and that was what mattered.

For the next several months, our recordings went well. The show aired twice weekly in San Diego to some sixty thousand listeners in total. Increasingly, as Richard and I worked out our chemistry on-air, there was talk of the show going national. At one point, KPBS station manager Tom Karlo and I even flew to Washington to pitch the show to the Corporation for Public Broadcasting. Nothing ever came of that, though. And soon there was another troubling development.

Richard, whose calendar was perpetually crammed with speaking engagements of all types, began having trouble with his voice. A vocal-cord condition made it increasingly raspy. His voice was fine for his public performances, but often it wasn't broadcast quality. Not only that, its condition was variable. Sometimes we'd have to cancel a recording at the last minute, which meant Stefanie would have to notify all the callers and then try to convince them to commit to a future date, which they couldn't always do. Plus, there was no guarantee that Richard's voice would be radio-ready that day either.

It was heartbreaking. This ebullient educator, a guy who lived by his speaking ability, who advertised himself with the tagline "Have Tongue, Will Travel," was struggling with the instrument that had entertained so many for so long. His voice became less and less reliable. At one point, he took off time for surgery to try to fix the problem, so we tried recording three episodes with me hosting the show by myself. But without Richard there to balance me out, those shows were nearly unlistenable. It was clear I couldn't carry the show alone.

Something had to change. Although Richard would go on to write many more books as well a regular newspaper column and continued to keep up a busy schedule of speaking engagements all around the country, he retired from the radio show he'd helped start, and KPBS began searching for a replacement.

They soon found one who couldn't be more different: a thirty-six-year-old in New York City named Grant Barrett.

Grant had been mentioned in a *New York Times* article the year before about the new wave of "young, hip lexicographers" in the relatively small, tradition-bound world of dictionary editors. The story described him as "looking like he'd just as soon fix a car as edit a dictionary," which, I would come to learn, was very much the case.

Like so many professionals in the world of language and lexicography, Grant had followed a circuitous path, driven by a passion for reading and writing. He grew up in rural Missouri, the son of a cop and a homemaker. Besotted with books at an early age, he read everything he could get his hands on—his younger sister's *Sesame Street* books, his older sister's school textbooks and trashy romance novels, the family's *World Book Encyclopedia*. At the local library, he liked to start at one end of a bookshelf and work his way down the row, devouring whatever books he encountered along the way, then switch to the next shelf and read in the other direction.

As a kid, he listened endlessly to old-time radio dramas and comedians like Burns and Allen, Nichols and May. At thirteen, he took apart an AM radio and figured out how to wire it to convert it into shortwave, which meant that after dark, he could listen to sounds that cracked open his world—the Voice of America, the Received Pronunciation of announcers on the BBC, the rhythmic cadences of Radio Havana Cuba, and the mystifying programming of Radio Moscow.

He went on to study at the University of Missouri, working at the college radio station and writing music reviews of new bands. Later, Grant went to Columbia University, earning a degree in French, and spent a year in Paris studying at the Université Paris Diderot. Afterward, he traveled in South America, lived for a time in the U.S. Virgin Islands, and worked at a variety of jobs. He also indulged a fascination with computers and the internet, developing an extraordinary facility with both. Eventually, he took a job as a computer technician at a three hundred–person ad agency in New York City. He was, if not a digital native, one of the earliest new immigrants online. He'd often say that he was already blogging when most bloggers could sit around a table in New York—and did.

Grant was also a fast, prolific writer, always casting about for ways to make his writing even better. Hoping to improve at his craft, he joined the American Dialect Society, an organization of academics and language professionals founded in 1889. Studying the discussions on their email LISTSERV and devouring their quarterly publication, he ended up giving himself a thorough education in linguistics and sociolinguistics.

He began to participate on their LISTSERV and engage in antedating, a friendly sport among linguists that involves producing hard evidence that a word or phrase was in use even earlier than currently documented in dictionaries or by colleagues. Eventually, Grant became the society's Vice President for Communications and Technology.

He read voraciously and extensively—hip-hop journals, scholarly articles, general-interest newspapers and magazines, special-interest forums in obscure corners of the web, and books of all kinds. He developed vast expertise regarding slang, neologisms, jargon, and eventually lexicography itself when he was recruited to work as project editor of the *Historical Dictionary of American Slang* for Oxford University Press. His first book, *The Oxford Dictionary of American Political Slang*, defined hundreds of terms involving politics, such as *neverendum*, "a series of referendums initiated until the desired outcome is achieved"; and *blue goose*," the bulletproof lectern with a gooseneck microphone used by the president and vice president. His second book, *The Official Dictionary of Unofficial English*, defined hundreds of terms from the fringes of English, like *gleek*, a verb that means "to squirt liquid through the teeth or from under the tongue."

During one of the periods when Richard was still out from vocal surgery, Stefanie recruited Grant to fill in for a couple of episodes, patched in from a studio in New York. He was a quick study, sharp, and often unpredictable. His vast, eclectic reading meant that one minute he might be talking about some lesser-known work by Mary Shelley, and the next he'd be referencing a passage from *Little House on the Prairie*. He was perfectly comfortable talking about *semantic satiation*, the linguist's term for the psychological process in which saying a word over and over makes it seem to lose all meaning and sound like nonsense. But he was just as happy to describe it with his own term, the *Gnarly Foot Phenomenon*. "Take off your shoe and look at your foot for a really long time," he told a listener. "After a minute, you're going to go "WHY IS THIS UGLY THING CONNECTED TO MY BODY? THIS IS HIDEOUS!" It was a great way to make his point: Stare at a word or anything else too long, and it just looks weird.

If I was an infopig, Grant was a prize infohog. I'd never seen anything like it. I'd mosey into the studio, certain that I'd done a thorough job researching a caller's question, only to find that Grant had done a deep dive into some primary sources and ante-dated all current dictionaries' entries by dozens of years. Or he'd uncover solid evidence that completely debunked a word-origin story that had persisted for years in the popular books we used for looking up etymologies.

Grant brought a rigor to the research and a modern linguist's sensibility to the show. His approach was far more descriptiv-ist than prescriptivist. Linguistic prescriptivists emphasize the importance of traditional rules of grammar and argue that such conventions help ensure clarity and mutual understanding, partic-ularly in such contexts as publishing and professional communi-cations. While acknowledging that a fundamental understanding of grammar is important, descriptivists argue that language is inherently dynamic and always evolving. A linguist's job, they believe, is to describe such changes—to be descriptive—without judgment. A dictionary, they say, is less like a set of command-ments and more like a weather report—a snapshot of what's going on with language right now. Dictionary editors don't tell people how to speak and write as much as report how they do. As linguist Anne Curzan puts it in *Says Who?: A Kinder, Funner Usage Guide for Everyone Who Cares About Words*, they're just trying to keep up with all of us.

Like most linguists, Grant couldn't abide pet peeves about how other people spoke and wrote. He was also quick to point out that some of the rules that Richard and I championed on the show were, in fact, not rules at all. If you look at the evidence, for example, you can see that not only do people have different ways of saying the word *water*, there are at least fifteen different pronunciations in the United States alone, to say nothing of those in other English-speaking countries. There's Philadelphia's *wooder*, for starters, as well as Boston's *wah-tuh*, and *wah-der* in California. The more I heard from Grant, the more I noticed those differences myself and began to celebrate their variety rather than bristle at them.

Also, the more I heard from Grant and the more widely I read, the more I began to understand that some of the grammatical finger-waving I'd been doing was the result of arbitrary, unnecessary rules laid down by self-styled grammarians in the seventeenth and eighteenth centuries. There really was no good reason, for example, to avoid a preposition at the end of a sentence. That rule was an attempt to fit the swollen foot of English into the too-tight shoe of Latin grammar, which didn't need prepositions in that spot because that information was contained within the form of the noun itself. Ditto for splitting an infinitive. In Latin—and for that matter, in Old English back in the time of *Beowulf*—the infinitive form is a single word, so there's no way it could be "split." In Modern English, however, the infinitive is made of two words, and it's fine to stick an adverb between them if you like, as Captain Kirk did when he mentioned that the mission of the *Enterprise* was to boldly go where no one had gone before.

At times my growing awareness that grammatical rules weren't quite so hard and fast could feel a bit vertiginous. Ultimately, though, it was far more interesting. The answers to listeners' questions weren't quite so black and white, and the diversity of English was something to be valued, not complained about.* I came to agree that grammatical pet peeves were the least interesting thing about language. Over time, voicemails and emails to the show that began "Don't you just hate when people say . . . ?" all but disappeared, and we didn't miss them.

Once Grant joined the show full-time, he continued to record his part of the program from a studio in New York. It was a relief to have a cohost again, but having one who was invisible made those sessions extra-challenging for us both. Not only that, our conversational styles were vastly different. I'd been raised to be what linguists call a *high-considerateness speaker*, someone used to polite turn-taking and reflective pauses. In contrast, Grant's style, like that of so many longtime New Yorkers, was fast and energetic. He was what linguists call a *high-involvement speaker*, whose interruptions and bursts of words might be read as rude, but actually signal enthusiasm and full engagement. Sociolinguists will tell you that neither of these styles is inherently superior, and in fact, being attuned to that difference and adjusting one's own speaking style and expectations can go a long way toward more effective communication.

Part of Grant's challenge was to distill the vast amounts of research he did into just a few minutes, while also allowing room for greetings, goodbyes, and playful conversation. Just as when

---

* Did you have a problem with that final preposition there? I didn't think so.

I cohosted shows with Richard, part of my challenge was to find enough places to "jump in!" Often, I'd again find myself open-mouthed, fascinated by whatever information Grant was relaying, or taken aback by one of his clever, completely unexpected analogies, or laughing at something he'd made me think of that I wasn't fast enough to articulate in real time. But again, just mouthing, "Wow!" without adding to the conversation myself was fine if I wanted to be a listener, but not if I wanted to be a cohost. I had to learn to be more spontaneous with my responses, without first writing and rewriting it in my head, and that didn't come easily at all. It was like the difference between a fire hose and a trickling faucet.

Speaking of fire hoses, the good part was that, as Grant liked to tell people, the two of us "got along like a house on fire." His sense of humor was quirky, unexpected, off-the-wall, sometimes downright dazzling. We were infoswine luxuriating each week in piles of information, digging out lots and lots of fascinating bits of research we couldn't wait to share.

Meanwhile, I'd kept doing a half month in San Diego and a half month in Louisville, and perhaps not surprisingly, my relationship with Deb had begun fraying at both ends. She had the job of her dreams, on track to become a full professor of painting at Indiana University Southeast. Not too shabby for a visual artist; a position like that was almost impossible to come by. And I had my own dream job with the radio show. True, it paid almost nothing, but I knew it was where I needed to be. I'd never forgive myself if I didn't try.

With our lives moving further and further apart, Deb and I agreed to go our separate ways, and in 2006, I moved to San Diego permanently.

I continued to do freelance writing on the side and tried to make ends meet by trying a bit of voice-over work. In January 2007, the berrieh who produced our show managed to get me hired full-time at KPBS as a cohost and assistant producer. It was a dream come true. Grant continued to plug away at his demanding IT job in New York while recording with us every other week.

Over the next several months, our listenership kept expanding. We were now fielding a couple hundred emails and calls each week with the most heartwarming feedback from listeners. They seemed as happy as we were to have a little niche on the airwaves for talking about words and how we use them. We all were beyond pleased to be nurturing this little community of language lovers, providing a little on-air oasis of thoughtful and lively conversation about language in all its diversity. Podcasting was brand-new then, and we began picking up more listeners that way, from all over the world.

In addition to San Diego and Wisconsin Public Radio, a few other broadcasters began airing us. Indianapolis picked up the show, then my hometown of Louisville, and a couple of smaller stations. Soon there was talk of adding many more as word of the show got around. So when program director John Decker called me in the summer of 2007 and asked me to come to the station that day to meet with him and the KPBS general manager, I was excited. It was finally happening. The show was about to be picked up for national distribution! As it happened, I was busy that afternoon, but I told him I could drop by tomorrow for a meeting. No, he said, we needed to talk right away, so we agreed he'd call me shortly. I was glad they were as excited as I was.

The conversation was brief. "I've decided to cancel *A Way with Words*," the general manager said crisply.

I was incredulous. "What?? Wait—the show's doing so well! Didn't you look at the numbers? Our audience is expanding, not shrinking! People tell us they love it! *WHAT?*" He was joking, right?

He wasn't. The next few minutes were a blur. I remember sputtering that our ratings had never been higher, that more stations had expressed interest in the show, that he should see the calls and emails we get from listeners . . .

None of that mattered. The bottom line was that a recession was underway, and KPBS had a massive budget shortfall. The beans had been counted. They were canceling not only our show but a popular public-affairs program as well, and laying off a dozen staffers.

I hung up in shock. Minutes later, Stefanie called. She'd been on vacation in Wyoming when they reached her with the news. Soon, we had Grant on the line from New York. For once, even Grant was almost speechless.

I don't recall much of that conversation either, except that the three of us assured each other there was too much good here, way too much potential, to just walk away from it. There was the joy we all took in producing the show, not to mention our growing relationship with our marvelous listeners, and our mission to show how language can connect people rather than divide them, and so much more. Call us delusional, or naïve, or stubborn, or all of the above, but we never questioned that we'd find a way for the show to go on. It had to.

But how?

CHAPTER 15

ROAD TRIP! MOUNTAIN WEST AND FAR WEST: FOURTEENERS TO DA KINE

PUT ON YOUR SUNGLASSES AND buckle up! This time the Worder Wagon's going to wend our way west . . .

Mountain West
COLORADO

Colorado's majestic landscape has inspired several local terms. A *fourteener* is one of Colorado's fifty-eight peaks at least fourteen thousand feet high. *Flatlanders*, not surprisingly, are from lower elevations. There, a mountain valley is a *park*, as in *South Park*, a valley basin that's surrounded by fourteeners—and, of course, the cartoon created by a couple of guys who met at the University of Colorado. A *hole* is smaller than a park, as in nearby *Jackson Hole*. Of course, as in other ski-loving states, the snowy slopes of Colorado have inspired a whole lexicon of their own. A *gaper* is a newbie who wanders around looking clueless while gaping at the spectacular scenery.

WYOMING

When is a *biscuit* not a biscuit? When it's in Wyoming, where a *biscuit* is the horn on a saddle. If you're a cowboy, you don't want to be seen *squeezing the biscuit*, lest someone question your horsemanship. They may also assume you're a *greenie*—not necessarily a *greenhorn*, but a Coloradan, so called because of that state's distinctive green license plates. Also in Wyoming, to extinguish a fire, you *dout* it or *dout it out*. The word *dout* is a shortening of *do out*. (In the same way, the verb *don* and *doff*, which is what firefighters are said to do with their equipment, come from *do on* and *do off*.)

MONTANA

If a Montanan compliments your new *outfit*, they might not mean your fashion sense; they may just be admiring your car or pickup truck. This usage reflects hundreds of years of history, when an *outfitter* in the American West would supply a group about to embark on a trip with gear and transport, and *outfit* came to mean the vehicle itself. And just as an *outfit* is not necessarily clothing, *ditch* doesn't always refer to a hole in the ground. In Montana, *ditch* is also water added to a drink, as in *Give me a bourbon and ditch*.

We once had a fascinating call from a woman from rural Montana asking about an expression she and her classmates used whenever a teacher reprimanded one of them. The other kids would say *Ah VERRR*, drawing out the syllables and rising in pitch, as if to say, "You're in trouble!" Many listeners in the Mountain West have reported similarly ominous versions, including *umber*, *uhver*, or *ombers*. Its origin remains a puzzle, although it could be from Spanish *a ver*, or "Let's see," as in "Let's see what happens next!"

IDAHO

In Idaho, there's a load of history tucked inside every *jockey box*. That's the part of a car or truck that other people call the *glove box*, *glove compartment*, or *cubby hole*. The term *jockey box* is a linguistic relic of the days when westward-bound covered wagons had a box under the driver's wooden seat for storing tools and supplies.

Idaho is known for its potatoes, and knowing about two particular preparations will mark someone as being from that area. *Funeral potatoes* are a cheesy mix of potatoes, onions, creamy soup, and sour cream, topped with corn flakes or crushed potato chips—so called because they're often brought to dinner following a funeral. *Ice cream potatoes*, on the other hand, aren't really potatoes at all. They're sundaes disguised as a potato, with a vanilla ice cream shaped to resemble a spud, dusted with cocoa powder to resemble its brown skin, then loaded with whipped cream and garnished with chocolate shavings or green sprinkles.

UTAH

Eavesdrop on Utahans and you may hear *Oh my heck*, a euphemistic result of that state's strong Mormon influence. You might hear older folks refer to safe drinking water not as *potable water*, but as *culinary water*. You might ask if they ever had a *flipper crotch*, a local term that's well on its way to obsolescence, considering that almost no one seems to use slingshots anymore. More than any other western state, Utah features some distinct pronunciations, which makes *sale* sound more like *sell*, *jail* like *jell*, and *born in a barn* sound like *barn in a born*.

NEW MEXICO

One of the oldest dialects of Spanish has persisted for more
than four hundred years in what is now New Mexico and Colorado, and the Spanish language continues to flavor some of the
English spoken there as well. In parts of New Mexico, when
you fill a car's tank with fuel, you're said to *put gas*. You may
also hear debates over the name of the lunch-size paper bags
with candles that traditionally light up the nights during the
Christmas holidays. In northern New Mexico, they're *faroli-
tos*. In the south, they're *luminarias*. Speaking of Christmas,
if you're asked *Red, green, or Christmas?* in a restaurant, you're
being asked to specify whether you want red or green chili
sauce, or a mix of the two.

ARIZONA

Many of Arizona's distinctive terms are inspired by the weather,
including *chubasco*, *haboob*, and *swamp box*. The word *chubasco* is a
borrowing from Spanish and refers to a sudden, violent squall or
thunderstorm during the rainy season. An intense dust storm is
called a *haboob*, a name originally applied to similar winds in the
Sahara Desert, from Arabic *habūb*, which means "blowing furi-
ously." Arizonans try to beat that dry heat with a *swamp box* or
swamp cooler, a device that uses a fan to push hot air over wet pads,
cooling it several degrees through evaporation.

   If you're ever in Tucson, you might spot a *ganga* on a *stravenue*. The Spanish word *ganga*, or "bargain," has been borrowed
whole into English, and a *stravenue* is a street running diagonally
between an east-west street and a north-south avenue. It's a combination of *street* and *avenue*. This term is apparently unique to
Tucson, where it's used enough that the U.S. Postal Service has
designated an official abbreviation for it: *STRA*.

Far West
NEVADA

In Nevada (rhyme that second syllable with *add* if you want to sound like a local), a *pogonip* (rhyme that first syllable with *dog*) is a dense, icy fog in deep mountain valleys. A pogonip at sunrise makes everything glitter like diamonds. Warm up later in the day with a *picon* (rhyme that first syllable with *pea*), the state's unofficial drink, a cocktail created by Basque immigrants who settled in the northern part of the state.

CALIFORNIA

Here in my adopted state, Southern Californians are known for a peculiar use of the word *the*. When giving directions that involve traveling on the freeway, we'll say *Take the 405* or *Head west on the 8*. Adding *the* before the names of freeways reflects their history. At first, these thoroughfares weren't numbered—they just had names like *the Ocean Beach Freeway* or *the Pasadena Freeway*. Even after freeways were assigned numbers, Californians hung on to the *the*. We dread hearing about *Sig alerts*, or warnings about major traffic delays. Those are named for "Sig" Sigmon, an engineer who developed a system that let police send such alerts directly to radio stations to get them on the air quickly.

In California, you'll occasionally hear *hella* used to mean "extremely" or "a lot of." *Hella* seems to have originated in Northern California, specifically in the Black community of Oakland, but is now found throughout the state, as in *During rush hour, there are hella Sig alerts*.

OREGON

While Californians *go to the beach*, Oregonians *go to the coast*. On the way, they may snack on *jojos*, thick potato wedges covered with seasoning or lightly breaded, then cooked. Jojos are a tasty substitute for more expensive fare, which an Oregonian is likely to describe as *spendy*.

WASHINGTON STATE

In Washington State, people don't *go to the beach* or *to the coast*—they *go to the ocean*. On their way, they might stop at a *jumble sale*, which is what some Washingtonians call a *garage sale* or *yard sale*. If something's good, strong, or powerful, they might say it's *skookum*, from Chinook jargon, as in a *skookum drink*.

ALASKA

What other Americans call *the lower 48*, Alaskans simply call *outside*. If you're traveling along the Alaskan coast, watch out for *williwaws*, those sudden, violent gusts of wind coming down from the mountains. The crescent-shaped knife that Alaskans call an *ulu* is useful for all kinds of activities involving cutting or scraping, not to mention being a handy word for cruciverbalists. The name of this traditional blade was borrowed whole from the language of the Indigenous Inupiat.

And although the term *breakup season* sounds ominous, in Alaska, it's a happy time—that point in early spring when snow and ice begin melting. After breakup comes *greenup*, a sudden, spectacular burst of green as new shoots break through soil almost overnight. *Greenup* means no more riding *snow machines*, which is what most Alaskans call *snowmobiles*. That also means it will be months before they'll see *termination dust*, the light, high-altitude snowfall that signals summer's end.

HAWAII

With its rich mixture of people of Filipino, Japanese, Chinese, and Native Hawaiian descent, Hawaii boasts an incredibly diverse linguistic landscape. In fact, it's the state with the highest proportion of residents who speak a non-European language at home—primarily Tagalog, Japanese, Hawaiian, and Ilocano, a language of the Philippines. That mix is made even livelier by Hawaii Pidgin English, a combination of Hawaiian, Chinese, Japanese, and English.

In Hawaii, *da kine* is an oft-used multipurpose word, most likely adapted from *the kind*. It serves as a placeholder similar to *whatsit* but also describes something good, as in *The waves were da kine!* Similarly, *small kine* means "just a little bit," as in *I was small kine unhappy*. Food, especially local food, is *grinds* or *grindz*. And of course, in Hawaii, *aloha* is both a greeting and farewell.

This is a mere sampling, of course, of the words and phrases you might encounter while traveling around the U.S. Some of them are now fading away and may be gone in another generation, which is a shame.

I'm reminded of an email we received from a listener in Upstate New York. She wrote to say that listening to our show had helped inspire her ninety-six-year-old mother to compile a list of words and phrases that their family used when their kids were growing up. Many were terms that family members made up—a kid's adorable misunderstanding that was added to the family lexicon or some funny bit of family shorthand. But there were also charming words and phrases used by the family's older members and now rarely heard. That list grew to thirty-three pages, a sort of verbal family photo album that all of them now cherish.

Why not do the same? These words and phrases are a great way to start an older person reminiscing. Ask your elders about some of these dialectal words and phrases or the funny sayings they always used. Do they know where they might have picked it up? What stories do they remember about them? Were they ever surprised when they traveled someplace and used an expression that no one else there understood? Did a newcomer to their area use a word or phrase they'd never heard before?

Get them talking and record those conversations. You never know what kind of memories you might jog loose if you ask.

CHAPTER 16

TOO SMALL TO FAIL

FOR A FEW WEEKS AFTER the cancellation of *A Way with Words*, KPBS aired archive editions of the show while Stefanie, Grant, and I scrambled to figure out what to do next. We knew that for one thing, we'd have to secure ownership of the show. We also knew that we'd have to begin churning out new episodes immediately; otherwise, we'd also lose the few stations that did broadcast us. But prepping, recording, and editing the show had been a full-time job in itself—and now we had to do all of that without any of the infrastructure we'd enjoyed at KPBS. In other words, we were building the plane as we were flying. No, it was more than that. We had the two copilots and the air traffic controller, but otherwise we were starting from scratch, building out the plane, the runway, the air terminal, and who knew what else. I was hardly any way to launch a national radio show.

For starters, we had no place to record. Studio space at KPBS was already at a premium, so we couldn't do it there. Stefanie called all over San Diego, scrambling to find another studio that could accommodate our weird setup with two hosts and a dozen callers. After some early leads fizzled, Stefanie found a recording facility called Studio West, about twenty-five miles away, which specialized in recording facilities for musicians, voice-over artists, and video-game producers. But Stefanie is nothing if not resourceful and persuasive. The owner of Studio West agreed to give us a hefty discount and adapted a space that we could use twice a month to record episodes. Because the show was a call-out, coordinating phone lines with callers in addition to the mics of the two hosts, the arrangements would be more complicated than a simple podcast. But the staff at Studio West was moved by our predicament and intrigued by the idea of recording a radio program, so they generously shared advice, equipment, and technical expertise.

Stefanie also managed to recruit a talented sound engineer and editor, Tim Felten, a laid-back local musician who played keyboards in several soul and funk bands. (Check out his group, Sure Fire Soul Ensemble, at sfsemusic.com.) Tim would join us for studio sessions, then edit the show and put it back together, and add his own musical sensibilities to both the spoken content and the musical interludes in each episode. In addition, Stefanie found two New York–based members of the National Puzzlers' League to serve as Quiz Guys for the show's weekly puzzle segment. One was Greg Pliska, a talented composer and arranger who went on to work in theater, film, and television, and John Chaneski, a former writer for *Who Wants to Be a Millionaire?* who remains with our show to this day. Patching them in from a studio in Manhattan added yet another layer of production to be coordinated.

We were beginning to assemble a homemade, rickety production line, but we had to start producing episodes right away. There are few things that public radio program directors dread more than inconsistency; their listeners are notoriously resistant to changes in schedules and hosts. Even changing a show's theme music can invite vociferous complaints, at least initially. No station manager wants to promise that listeners hear a program in its regular time slot, only to get a nasty surprise when that show suddenly disappears. So, if we were going to keep those stations happy, we'd have to make sure our listeners experienced no interruption in service. Could we pull that off?

Grant put all of his tech chops to work, setting up a toll-free phone line and email system to accommodate hundreds of communications a week, building an online presence with the new website and expanding it with social media feeds, and diving into the then-new world of podcasting—all of this in addition to his full-time IT job in New York. Meanwhile, Stefanie and I raced to plan new episodes and edit them, all the while seeking paid sponsorships through cold calls and attempts at networking. It was as if our little group of three were part of a start-up—with zero venture capital or investors—a start-up that was also frantically trying to do the full-time work of continuing to pump out new episodes. Our severance pay quickly ran out, and I started draining my savings. Stefanie's husband, Michael, an attorney, helped us negotiate with KPBS to assume ownership of the show. We agreed that in return, we'd provide the show to KPBS to air just as before, totally free of charge. We've continued that practice to this day, making the show available free of charge to any NPR affiliate or community radio station that wanted to air it. Some of the shows with a big following, like *A Prairie Home Companion*, could command a fee from stations; not so for smaller programs like ours that could be easily replaced by another. We figured our best bet was to supply the show for free and rely primarily on listener support to keep producing it.

Call us passionate, naïve, or plain old pigheaded—yes, we were all those things. The cancellation of *A Way with Words* felt manifestly unjust, and we believed we were all working hard to right a wrong. Besides, we received so many heartfelt calls and emails of support from listeners that convinced us to keep going no matter what.

Now that we were on our own, without a fundraising or marketing department, we'd also have do all that on our own as well.

In hopes that the show would be commercially viable, we formed an independent production company operating as an LLC. None of us had ever done sales—much less wanted to—but that didn't stop us from trying to learn. Some months before, my predecessor on the show, Charlie Elster, had kindly recommended me to be the female voice for a local company that sold vocabulary-building CDs. I'd done a few recordings for them on a freelance basis and somehow managed to sell the company owner a $20,000 sponsorship. That helped sustain the show for a while. However, the annual budget for the show at KPBS— for salaries, studio time, and staff support—had been closer to $250,000. We weren't sure how we would ever make up that gap. All we knew was that we had a show to produce, and we couldn't *not* keep going.

In those early months, it seemed we were working nonstop from dawn until late at night, determined to produce an hour of polished content that was still entertaining as it was educational. What we weren't so sure of was how in the world our little three-person operation would ever be able to sustain it or how any of us would avoid burning out ourselves.

I brought in a few more small sponsorships with cold calls here and there. One year stretched into two, but we still hadn't found a way to make the show financially viable. We decided we might do better as a nonprofit, which would allow us to accept donations and apply for grants. Again, with Michael's help, we formed a 501(c)(3) we called Wayword, Inc., assembled a kitchen-table board of trustees, and began seeking financial support from listeners and granting agencies.

Those first three years, none of us took any income from the show at all. None. After basic production costs, there was simply no money left. We joked grimly that our little operation was "too small to fail" and consoled ourselves that things had to get better soon, reminding each other that, after all, "you can't fall off the floor."

Fortunately, each of us had additional skills that complemented those of the others. With her banking background and years of experience producing radio, Stefanie handled the finances and the business of the nonprofit, as well as all the complicated tasks of making sure the radio production line kept moving smoothly without stopping. In addition to researching and hosting the show, Grant did the heavy lifting on the tech side of things and building a presence on social media. I was the outward face of the show, cultivating relationships with donors and seeking sponsors.

During those years, it seemed all I ever thought about was hosting the show, researching the show, editing the show, or planning the next episode—all the while struggling to support it. I imagined that this must be a little like living on a submarine, a tunnel-visioned, extremely focused life. We were on a mission. Eventually, Grant moved with his wife and young son, Guthrie, to California to take a full-time job with an online dictionary in Silicon Valley in addition to his work on the show; later, he took a marketing job in San Diego, making it easier for the three of us to work together.

Meanwhile, we faced another daunting challenge, one that requires a bit of explanation: Our tiny nonprofit was hamstrung by the fact that we weren't allowed to seek financial support from our very biggest pool of potential donors, those who listened to us on their local public radio affiliates. As a small, independent production company, we're not allowed to compete with the stations that include the show on their weekly schedules. That is, we're not allowed to say on the air that the nonprofit that produces *A Way with Words* receives no funding at all from KPBS, NPR, or, for that matter, any other radio station. If we were to ask for donations during our broadcast, we'd be competing directly with the stations that carry us—stations that depend heavily on the funds they raise during their own pledge drives. Because we couldn't ask for help directly from our hundreds of thousands of radio listeners, we were left seeking support from our podcast audience. Unlike the broadcast version of our show, the podcast version wasn't subject to FCC rules, which meant we were free to insert whatever kinds of ads or announcements we wanted, including our own little pledge drives and direct asks for funding to keep the show going. However, that pool of potential donors was substantially smaller than our radio audience. Three times a year, we also sent out e-blasts to solicit support directly from our followers on social media and subscribers to our monthly newsletter.

When we tried to tell people about our business model, such as it was, they were incredulous. We had to explain that public radio is a weird animal—that's just how it works. People were aghast to learn that we gave away our content for free to any station that wanted to air us. Again, we had to explain that there were plenty of other shows out there—so many that ours could easily be replaced. Only the biggest, heaviest hitters at the time could bring in decent money by charging radio stations or networks for their programs—and those programs usually had the backing of at least a home radio station or network, such as Chicago's WBEZ or Minnesota Public Radio.

Instead, we worked our way onto the schedules of radio stations one by one. Sometimes a radio-station staffer might be driving cross-country, hear our show, and recommend it to their boss. One program director read about the show in an in-flight magazine and promptly added us to his schedule. Listeners might hear about the show from a friend, then ask their local stations to carry us. Grant and I did as many media interviews as we could in hopes of drawing more attention to the show. Our team celebrated every time we added a new station, however small. Slowly, the list kept growing, as did our audience.

Meanwhile, week after week, we raced to feed the hungry production beast. Occasionally, a new acquaintance would say to me something like, "OK, I know you work one hour a week. What do you do with all the rest of your time?" If they only knew.

One great thing about working for a nonprofit is that it means you meet some of the best people in the world. One of them was Constance Carroll, the chancellor of the San Diego Community College District. When I asked a high-powered local fundraiser for advice, she told me that Constance was a smart, savvy pillar of the community and a patron of the arts and humanities. Not only was Constance delightfully witty, she said, she also had a Ph.D. in ancient Greek, so the two of us would have plenty to talk about, and I should reach out to her. I emailed Constance to introduce myself and learned that she'd listened to the show faithfully, all the way back to the Richard and Charlie days. She and I became fast friends, discussing everything from politics to pop culture, and spent many happy hours translating Aeschylus and Sophocles together. Constance understood the educational mission of our nonprofit as well as the challenges, and she proceeded to organize a group of local volunteers to help us with fundraising. The resulting Friends of *A Way with Words* group complemented our online fundraising drives by working hard to put on fundraising galas every couple of years in San Diego. The Latin phrase *sine qua non*, meaning "without which, not," comes to mind. The show simply wouldn't have survived without her wise counsel and support.

No one goes into public radio to get rich; it's truly a labor of love, and I'm sharing all this simply as a record, not a recipe. In fact, it was a dozen years before all three of us could draw a modest full-time salary for doing the show. Still, it never stopped feeling like the wolf was at the door or that the nonprofit might tank at any minute. Then again, it's felt like that for a very long time now—the nonprofit's been around for eighteen years—so I guess we did something right. At some point, even with that wolf at the door, you just learn to keep going, despite all that ominous huffing and puffing on the other side.

All this time, I'd continued to struggle with my fear of public speaking, even though it got a tiny bit easier the more I did it. I did have one memory from that first appearance with Richard that helped. During that speech, I briefly had the sense of being not a speaker trying to perform in front of people but a conduit— of being not a person but a pipeline that channeled information from somewhere else. In my case, that information was my passion for Greek and my story about the professor. I'd had a few moments like that since, when I stopped imagining what people were thinking about what I was saying or how I said it. They were like those first wobbly moments on a bicycle where you begin to find your balance and glide at last.

I also kept reminding myself of the so-called Spotlight Effect. Researchers at Cornell University once conducted an experiment in which they asked college students to go alone into a roomful of their peers and hang out. The catch was that the subjects had to walk into that room wearing a T-shirt that had a big picture of singer Barry Manilow—a sartorial choice that was, in that environment, decidedly uncool. Afterward, each student who had dared to enter the room in that mortifying shirt was asked to estimate how many of their peers had observed or commented on what they were wearing. Turns out they wildly overestimated that number. In reality, fewer than 25 percent of them had noticed the shirt with the singer on it. The lesson from that study was that people tend to notice far less about us than we think they do. Now, before stepping up to the mic, I'd picture not the audience in their underwear but me in a Barry Manilow shirt. It was a good reminder that audiences just want to get something out of your talk, something they can take home with them—a few interesting thoughts or new insights, or a feeling they won't forget. They actually want you to succeed; otherwise, they wouldn't have bothered to be there.

Still, those wobbly moments of success remained few and far between. I knew my on-air performance could use help as well. Grant and I were still working out our different radio styles. My slow-talking Southern self needed to be faster on my feet to keep up with his rapid-fire delivery and wide-ranging mind. At last, I worked up my courage and signed up for an improv class.

A quick bit of etymology is in order. The word *improv* goes all the way back to the Latin *vídeo*, meaning "I see." This Latin root gave us the English word *video* and related words, of course, but it has a few other descendants hiding in plain sight. It also provided us with *provide*, literally "to look ahead, act with foresight."

The Latin root of these words is also evident in the word *evident*, literally "plain to see." The past participle of *video* is *visus*, which means "seen," which is part of *vision*, or "something seen," and *visit*, which occurs when you go to "see someone." From this same family of words comes *provision*, "a providing beforehand," as well as *visa*, from Latin *charter visa*, or a "verified paper"—originally, a "paper that has been seen."

Now, back to the word *improvise*. The Latin stem *im-* means "not" and *pro* means "before." Combine them with *visus*, and you get *improvisus*—literally, "not seen before," and the source of *improvise*. At an improv show, the people onstage are making up everything right there on the spot; none of it is scripted. That's what can make improv so thrilling to watch. It's a show that's never been seen before and will never be seen again.

Many people have told me, "Oh, you do improv? I could never do stand-up comedy." That's when I explain that improv and stand-up are completely different. Stand-up is one person onstage, usually with a more or less scripted routine. With improv, there's at least one teammate with you onstage. Improv is a group effort, totally unscripted—and that's where the magic happens.

The truth is, we're all improvising, every minute of the day. If you go out to dinner with someone, you two don't know how it's going to go, what conversational paths you might take or not take, what might happen along the way. You say something, your companion responds, then you respond, and together you build a conversation that might take some unexpected turns. If you both knew what was going to be said, it'd be pretty boring, wouldn't it?

That's the beauty of improv. You never know where a scene is going to go. You're so focused on your teammates and reacting honestly in the moment, you can't plan what you're going to say in advance. You have to tune out the rest of the world and be completely present, stay in the moment, focus your complete attention on your fellow teammates, and listen, listen, listen.

In fact, one of the best lessons I learned as an improviser was to "bring a brick, not a cathedral." As a writer, that was a hard one for me to learn. I wanted to walk onstage with a detailed, scripted plot in my head, which is about the worst thing you can do. I had to break myself of that habit because it's a great way to choke the life out of a scene. Improv at its best means staying open to possibilities and delighting in the discoveries that your team makes together, discoveries that you'd never make by yourself. It's the method summed up as "Yes! And . . ." You start out with just a wisp of an idea, your teammate accepts that idea and adds something you might never have thought of on your own, then you add more detail or another idea. Brick by brick, you build something together that's far better than anything any one of you could have imagined, something that's indeed *improvisus*—never seen before.

Another thing people often say to me is, "Oh, I couldn't possibly do improv. I'm not funny." Again, not a problem! Improv isn't about telling jokes or coming up with smart-aleck remarks and clever lines. It's about exploring a scene with your partners and reacting honestly to what's unfolding before you—and then finding the funny together. Humans are fascinating to observe when they're put together in various situations. Give it enough time, and I guarantee the funny will show up.

A good example: Before a show, improvisers play silly warm-up games, and I'll admit that even those terrified me at first. In "Zip, Zap, Zop," one person in the circle begins by pointing to another and saying "Zip!" The receiver then randomly tosses to another player with "Zap!" and then that person randomly points to yet another with "Zop!" and then the sequence begins again. It's a simple game, but it goes faster and faster, until someone screws up and misspeaks.

It sounds ridiculous, and it is, but I can't tell you how afraid I was to be the one who messed up. In reality, though, mistakes were the best part of the whole game. That's when everyone dissolved into laughter. If you win at "Zip, Zap, Zop," then you just played the most boring game in the world. The same goes for actual improv scenes: A mispronounced word or a misunderstood statement can lead to comedy gold if improvisers pick it up and play with it. Improvisers learn not just to celebrate mistakes but to embrace and run with them.

As you can imagine, all this was hugely helpful for a self-critical, solitary writer type. Improv helps a person loosen up, squelch that inner critic, and let the creativity flow. It also helped that the artificial stakes were so low. Who cares, after all, if you didn't get an idea across the way you wanted in a three-minute scene? What are you going to do—shake your fist at the heavens and wail, "Alas, I pretended wrong!"? Improv is a great reminder that even if you fall on your face, you're still moving forward.

It's also helpful to have to be totally focused on your teammates—listening to what they're saying, delighting in what they're doing, thinking not about yourself but about how you can make them look even better. It's a great exercise in getting out of your own head and your own fears because you're focused on doing everything you can to support your scene partners. The best improv happens when everyone's doing that. The entire team is in sync with each other, like a school of fish moving this way and that.

I took all the classes and workshops I could, and then on a lark, I signed up for a musical improv class. Musical improv involves the same basic principles of doing a scene, except that within a minute or so of being in a scene, musicians off to the side start playing, and you're expected to start singing about whatever's going on—a song, of course, that's completely made up on the spot.

I'm not sure how it happened, but my classmates and I had an instant chemistry that was hard to describe. Some were half my age, and I was surprised to find it easier to keep up with them when I was singing about this or that—drawing out a verse gave me time to think and reach for oddball, witty rhymes. We formed our own team and performed around town for years afterward, and we looked forward to our Monday-night practice sessions, which were as much fun as our shows. We called ourselves "Berserkus!," a name inspired by a scene where one of us had been desperate to end a verse with a rhyme for *the circus* and at the very last second came up with *go berserkus*. (Hard to re-create that moment here, but trust me, it got a big laugh.)

Suffice it to say that as it has been for so many people, improv was a lifeline for me. I became downright evangelical about how improv can boost confidence and creativity and provide lots of life lessons about how to listen and work as a team. I went on to lead improv workshops to help writers, teachers, scientists, and corporate employees wriggle free of their inner critics, and access strengths they didn't know they had.

And between Berserkus! and Barry Manilow, I got much better at public speaking. Something else happened as well: There began to be moments where I felt I was channeling my parents. I'd be speaking in front of a group and hear my mother's laugh coming out of my own mouth, or I'd catch myself gesturing the way my father would before a congregation. I came to delight in those moments when I spoke to audiences; a secret little "hello" from the beyond.

There was a time when I never would have believed it, but to my astonishment, now public speaking is absolutely one of my favorite parts of my job.

Over the next several years, our little production team stubbornly staggered into more and more small successes. We worked with a booking agent to put on a nine-city tour, with Grant and me doing appearances before enthusiastic audiences from coast to coast. I enjoyed welcoming them to evenings I liked to call "Date Night for Word Nerds," and I loved communing with fellow worders after each show.

Still, life on the submarine was getting old. I had wonderful, cherished friends who tolerated my focus on work, but I missed the days of having a romantic partner. I spent way too much time sifting through dating apps and had a couple of false starts, but the truth is that I was lonely for quite a long time. At last, I decided that we might not be able to solicit donations for Wayword on the government-regulated airwaves, but why not use them to broadcast the fact that I was single and looking? Or at least find a tasteful way to do so? The opportunity came in early 2017, when a listener called in search of a better word than *ex* for a former romantic partner.

"This term *ex-wife* doesn't sit well with me," he said. "It feels kind of disrespectful, like they've been *X*'d out." He was looking for a term that would better reflect the idea that the former partner "is now a good friend and everybody's moving forward in a friendly way."

I jumped on that idea, telling him I agreed completely, and tossed in my own experience. My ex of seventeen years and I were on good terms, I said, then made a point of adding that recently, she'd posted something on Facebook and referred to me as her "ex." I told the caller that seeing the word *ex* felt somehow sharp and a little painful. It was the smallest of hints, but I made a point of making clear that my ex was a "she." I could only hope that maybe the right person was out there listening.

A few months later, we tried to raise a little money for the show by holding a trivia quiz at a local pub. We'd promote it as a fundraiser, and people could pay extra to be on a team with me or Grant. We'd raffle off a couple of our books and make a brief pitch about supporting the show.

By the time I walked into the pub that evening, teams were already forming and gathering around tables. And yeah, I saw her from across the room and couldn't help catching my breath. Wow. I was supposed to glad-hand my way around the room, of course, but I made a beeline for her. She looked familiar some- how, and not just because she was often likened to Jodie Foster.

"Hi, I'm Martha," I said, and stuck out a hand. "Have we met before?"

"Only on the radio," she replied. "I'm Bonnie."

I laughed. Well, yeah, most listeners probably feel like we've already met on the radio.

"No, really," she said. "You had me on the show a couple of years ago. We talked about the difference between the words *nice* and *kind*."

That rang a vague bell. Bonnie had called the show to say that she'd been talking with friends about how those two words differed. A former New Yorker, she maintained that behavior described as "kind" was internally motivated, arising from com- passion, while being "nice" was more of a performance designed to please others or meet social expectations. During that call, Bonnie had said that she wouldn't describe herself as nice, but she always aspired to be kind.

It was coming back to me now, vaguely, although the truth was that I'd found that particular call sort of boring and had been happy to move on to the next one. I realized now I'd have to reassess.

"Martha, I came here to meet you tonight," Bonnie continued. "This is my wingman, Kolin."

She had indeed picked up on my pronoun when I was talking about the word *ex* on the air. As it happened, her coworker Kolin's son was friends with Grant's son, so she'd pressed Kolin to find out from Grant if his cohost was single. Yep, said Grant—single and looking. Kolin arranged to have Grant introduce the two of us at the pub quiz, but now there was no need. The sparks were already flying.

The rest of the evening, it seemed Bonnie and I found lots of excuses to sidle past each other's chairs in that crowded space. As an attorney who ran a nonprofit herself, Bonnie could see that I was working, so she hung back except to sidle past occasionally, putting a fresh bottle of water in front of me because I was too busy greeting people to get one for myself. She was both attentive and, yes, kind. When we held the raffle for my book and I drew the winning ticket from the jar, it almost didn't surprise me that it was Bonnie's. More sparks.

At the end of that long evening, I was making the rounds of the room one last time. I thanked people for coming, talking up the nonprofit and our need for support. After saying yet another goodbye, I turned around, and there was Bonnie.

She took my hand in both of hers. "It was nice to meet you," she said. "I know you're working, so I'll let you go." I said I appreciated her understanding that I still had many conversations to go. As she turned and walked away, I realized she'd left a folded piece of paper in my hand.

That was the first and only time I ever thought to myself, *Please don't be a check for the nonprofit. Please do NOT be a check for the nonprofit!* That wolf might still be huffing and puffing at the door, but I desperately hoped that this time, it was a note and not a donation. I was so afraid that it might be the latter that I couldn't even bring myself to look. For another half hour, I kept shaking hands with our supporters, with my left hand tightly clutched the whole time.

When I walked to my car at last, my hand was still in a fist. I got in and thought one last time, *Please do NOT be a check!* It felt like a check, though. I winced and forced myself to open my hand.

It was her name and phone number. Before I started the car, I texted her. We had dinner two nights later. Two years later on the winter solstice, we were married in a friend's backyard, and believe me, it felt indescribably wonderful, legally and at long last, to step into the words *wife* and *married*.

CHAPTER 17

ORTS!

IF YOU DO LOTS OF crossword puzzles, chances are you've run into the word *ort*. An ort is a table scrap or fodder left by farm animals. A leftover, in other words. This handy three-letter corner-filler likely comes from an old Germanic source, but beyond that, its origin is obscure.

Virginia Woolf wrote of "orts, scraps, and fragments" in her novel *Between the Acts*, and in a poem, D. H. Lawrence referred to "orts and slarts," *slarts* being an English dialectal synonym for "leftovers." Speaking of leftovers, it's worth noting that since the mid-nineteenth century, English speakers have rolled the delicious word *manavelins* around on their tongues, using it to mean the same thing. Herman Melville spelled it *manavelins*, but it's also been spelled *manavilins*, *manarvelins*, and *malhavelins*. Any way you spell it, this word means "odds and ends," whether leftover food, small change, or other miscellaneous items, and it may derive from a bit of nautical slang. The verb *manarvel* is a word of uncertain origin that means "to pilfer from a ship's stores." You can just picture sneaky sailors developing a word like *manavilins* to denote the items that they've manarveled.

In this chapter, I'll share some favorite manavalins, orts, slarts, bits and bobs, and other oddments I've managed to manarvel, either from listeners or while meandering through dictionaries. (Ooo, *meandering*. Talk about fossil poetry: The Menderes River has a winding, crooked course running through what is now western Turkey. In ancient times, the Greeks called that river the *Maiandros* and used the word *maiandros* to describe anything similarly serpentine. The name of this river wound its way into Latin as *maeander*, and eventually into English as *meander*.)

Some of the following terms are rare, obsolete, or long forgotten. But I think you'll agree that they're quite worthy of being pulled out, dusted off, and stashed in your own word-hoard.

Some Useful Terms You May Never Have Heard Of
ABILENE PARADOX

It's a hot, dusty day in a small West Texas town. A young married couple and their in-laws are sitting out on the porch, sipping lemonade, trying to keep cool over the whir of a loud fan. At last, the older man pipes up.

"Let's get in the car and go to Abilene and have dinner in the cafeteria."

Mind you, this would mean a fifty-three-mile trip in a sweltering car with no air-conditioning.

"Sounds great," his daughter says, and she asks her husband what he thinks.

"Sounds good," he says. "I just hope your mother wants to go."

They turn to her mother. She answers, "Of course. I haven't been to Abilene in a long time."

So they pile in the car for the long, sweaty drive. Once they get to the cafeteria, they all agree the food is terrible.

Four hours later, they're back at the house, sitting on the porch in the stifling heat, exhausted.

The son-in-law finally breaks the silence. "It was a great trip, wasn't it?"

His mother-in-law says, "Well, I just went along because the three of you were so enthusiastic."

That's when it dawns on them that none of them had really wanted to go—including the father-in-law who suggested it in the first place. "I just thought you might be bored," he said.

The son-in-law was business professor Jerry Harvey, and that experience inspired him to coin the term *Abilene paradox* for when a group collectively decides on a course of action that contradicts the preferences of individual members, because each person mistakenly believes their own preferences are contrary to everyone else's. You might run into this term if you take a business communications class, but really, anyone who's ever been in a situation where no one wants to be the boat-rocker knows that this term has much wider applications beyond the business world.

ACNESTIS

That part of your back that you just can't reach to scratch? There's a word for it; that's your *acnestis*. Pronounced *ack-NEES-tis*, this term appears to come from ancient Greek, although its origin is a little obscure. It may come from a Greek word that means both "spine" and "cheese grater," or from another Greek word that means "to scratch." Either way, if you can't reach that itchy spot, it's at least nice to know that someone else was annoyed enough to name it.

ANACHORISM

Did you hear about the famous feast scene in *Game of Thrones* where viewers caught a fleeting glimpse of a paper coffee cup that somebody accidentally left on a table? Or the episode of *Downton Abbey* when a character plays a tune on the piano that wasn't composed until years after that episode's action supposedly took place?

Those instances where something appears out of its correct time are called *anachronisms*, from the Greek prefix *ana*, meaning "against," and *khronos*, meaning "time," the source also of *synchronicity*, or "occurring at the same time," and *chronic*, or "lasting over a long time."

But what if someone or something is out of place geographically speaking? Although the American version of the TV series *The Office* supposedly takes place in Scranton, sharp-eyed viewers have pointed out the occasional exterior scene with a stray palm tree in the background. Then there's the movie *Blood Diamond*, where the heroes are supposed to be traipsing through Africa—except that the background audio features birdsong heard only in North America.

These goofs are called *anatopisms*, from the Greek word *topos*, meaning "place." This root is also the source of *toponym*, a word derived from the name of a place (like *spa*, from the Belgian town of *Spa*, known for its healing hot springs and baths). *Anatopism* and *toponym* are also linguistic relatives of *dystopia*, a place you definitely don't want to be.

Many blunders are both anachronistic and anatopic, but not every one that's anatopic is also anachronistic. Incidentally, another word for something that's out of place is *anachorism*, from Greek *khōros*, a word that also means "place." The word *anachorism* is less specific than *anatopism*, which applies particularly to literary or artistic contexts.

In any case, if I see someone in my own life who's out of context—if somebody I know from the dog park passes me in the produce aisle at the grocery or I run into my physician at the DMV—I always think, *Yup, that's an anachorism.* Because that's how my mind works.

ANTIPELARGY

You wouldn't think a word that means "reciprocal love and kindness, especially between parents and children" would ever become rare or obsolete. But although the word *antipelargy* (*anty-PELL-urr-jee*) showed up in seventeenth- and eighteenth-century dictionaries, it soon faded away. *Antipelargy* is from the ancient Greek word *pelargos*, which means "stork." The Greeks viewed these leggy birds as models of familial devotion. Young adult storks were thought to feed and care for their parents and even carry them on their own backs after the elderly birds lost their feathers and couldn't fly. As you might guess, the *anti-* in *antipelargy* doesn't mean "against" or "versus," but rather "in return," as in *antiphonal* singing, a style in which two choirs or soloists sing alternating musical phrases.

The Greek word for "stork," by the way, also nestles inside the name of the flower called *pelargonium*, a reference to the beaklike shape of its seed pod. This blossom is also called *storksbill*. So, next Mother's Day or Father's Day, you might honor the tradition of *antipelargy* and say it with pelargoniums.

APRICITY

You know that delicious sensation when you step outside on a winter day, and it's bright and cold, and then the sun warms you up just a little bit? Did you know there's a word for that? It's *apricity*. This word that means "the warmth of the sun in winter" had a brief life in the seventeenth century, but then for some reason it melted away. Surely *apricity* deserves reviving, along with its linguistic relative *apricate* (*APP-rih-kayt*), meaning "to bask in the sun" or "expose to sunlight."

I'm reminded of another couple of warm words. One of them is *beek*, used in Scotland and Northern England to mean, according to the *Oxford English Dictionary*, "to expose oneself to, or disport in, pleasurable warmth; to bask." In other words, you might step outside to beek in the apricity of a sunny winter's day. Then later you'll want to come back inside and enjoy the feeling of warming oneself by the fire—the feeling that Norwegians call *peiskos* (*PYE-skohs*), literally "fireplace coziness."

BOUSTROPHEDONIC

If you're mowing the lawn and thinking to yourself, *There ought to be a word for a route like this that goes first one way, turns, and then heads back in the opposite direction, then turns around and heads the other way again*, well, now you have one. It's *boustrophedonic*, a word that's also handy if you ever need a rhyme for, say, *supersonic* or *mnemonic*. *Boustrophedonic* writing, for example, proceeds from right to left, then turns and goes left to right, then right to left again, like the path you use when mowing the lawn. Some ancient inscriptions in archaic Greek, Latin, and Etruscan are written in *boustrophedon* (*boo-stroh-FEE-dun*). The English word *boustrophedonic* comes from the Greek words that mean "ox turn," a combination of Greek *bous*, meaning "cow" or "ox," and *strophe*, meaning "turn," like the "downward turn" that is a *catastrophe*. In other words, a *boustrophedonic* pattern is one that resembles the path left by oxen plowing a field—or mowing a lawn.

CARDBOARD DOG

If you've struggled with a problem for a while, maybe you need a *cardboard dog*. A software developer in Indianapolis called us to discuss this term used in her industry. When struggling with a program, she told us, it helps to describe the challenge to someone else. Simply by going through the process of trying to explain the problem clearly, you may hit upon the solution—even before the listener has a chance to respond. The listener, in other words, may just as well have been a cardboard dog: "You're trying to debug something, and you call somebody over to help. Then you realize the problem yourself, and you say, 'Hey, thanks for being my cardboard dog.'"

This term stems from a story in a programming manual about a developer who kept a rubber duck on his desk for the same purpose. When a problem was particularly thorny, the developer would go through the program line by line and force himself to explain each line of code to the duck. Often simply verbalizing the problem to his bathtub toy would lead to a breakthrough. Both *cardboard dog* and *rubber duck* are now used this way in the tech world, but it's a good problem-solving technique for the rest of us, too. I don't know about you, but I find real-life furballs staring back at me work just as well, too.

ESPRIT DE L'SCALIER

You know that forehead-smacking moment when you think of the perfect witty remark or retort to something too late? The French have a term for that, and English speakers snapped it up. The term is *esprit de l'escalier*—literally "spirit of the staircase." It was apparently invented by eighteenth-century French philosopher Denis Diderot. In his essay *Paradoxe sur le comédien*, he described being left speechless by someone at a dinner party, and observed that "a sensitive man, such as myself, overwhelmed by the argument made against him, becomes confused and can't think clearly again until he's at the bottom of the stairs."

We've all been there, Denis. The French term for this shoulda-said, woulda-said sensation has also been adapted into English as *staircase wit* or *staircase thought*.

FORMICATION

Take another look; that's an *n*, not an *m*. *Formication* is the abnormal sensation that ants are crawling over one's skin. It derives from Latin *formica*, or "ant." And no, there are no ants in a Formica kitchen countertop. Formica plastic laminate was invented in 1912 as a type of insulation for electrical wiring. It quickly replaced mica, the natural substance that had been used for this purpose. The inventors of Formica called it that because this new synthetic material was literally a substitute *for mica*. In the nineteenth century, the word *formicant* was used in medicine to describe a weak pulse that's "extremely small, scarcely perceptible, unequal, and communicating a sensation like that of the motion of an ant through a thin texture."

Formica, by the way, is a linguistic cousin of the Spanish word for "ant," *hormiga*, another example of that correspondence between the consonants *h* and *f* that also produced the name *Herrera* in Spanish and *Ferrari* in Italian, *Ferrari* coming from Latin *ferrum*, "iron." Both those surnames mean "ironworker," as do their counterparts in English, German, and Arabic, which are, respectively, the familiar names *Smith*, *Schmied*, and *Haddad*.

FORSWUNK

If you're working really hard, you're said to be *swinking*. The nineteenth-century poet Percy Shelley used the present indicative form of *swink* when he wrote about:

> *A pretty bowl of wood—not full of wine*
> *But quicksilver; that dew which the gnomes drink*
> *When at their subterranean toil they swink.*

After a long day of swinking, you can say you're *forswunk*—that is, you're totally worn out from work. I can't recall where I came across this useful term, but I've certainly felt forswunk more than once and am certainly happy to have a word for it that sounds just like how it feels.

FOSSICK

Fossick means to "rummage about," whether you're in your attic or dictionary-diving. *Fossick* may be related to the English dialectal term *fussock*, which means "to bustle about" or "fidget." Most often, it refers to digging around in abandoned mining excavations in search of gemstones, particularly in Australia and New Zealand, where fossicking is a popular pastime. A synonym for *fossicking* is *bandicooting*, a reference to those foraging marsupials, bandicoots. (*Bandicoot?* It comes from the Telugu language of India, literally translating as "pig-rat." The name was first applied to a large, destructive rat, and later to the Australian marsupials that somewhat resemble it.)

GOUND

You may have your own word for the sleep crust or eye discharge that accumulates in the corners of your eyes during sleep, but if not, there's always *gound*, a word of uncertain origin, although its roots appear to be Germanic. But *gound* is just one of many options. Over the years, we've collected lots of other terms, including *sleepy dust*, *sleepy sand*, *sleepywinks*, *sleepyjacks*, *sleepybuds*, *sleepymen*, *dozy dust*, *eye boogers*, *eye jam*, *eye potatoes*, *sleep sugar*, *eye crusties*, *yampee*, and plain old *crusties*, as well as the term used by medical professionals, *hardened periocular discharge*.

HURKLE-DURKLE

We have the Scots to thank for *hurkle-durkle*, which means "to lie in bed or lounge around when one should be up and about." In Scotland, to *hurkle* means "to sit huddled in a crouched position" or "draw oneself together like a crouching animal." If you pandiculate and wipe the gound from your eyes, then opt to *hurkle-durkle* or *lie in hurkle-durkle* instead of slipping into the ruelle, you're enjoying a few extra minutes—or maybe an extra couple of hours—under the covers. Which is especially delicious if you went to bed forswunk.

OPSIMATH

From a Greek word that means "late in learning," *opsimath* refers to someone who learns or begins to study something late in life. This word once carried a whiff of disdain and served as a snooty put-down suggesting that someone finally got around to learning something they already should have known. But more recently, *opsimath* has been reclaimed by lifelong learners, and rightly so. I take pride in being an opsimath and always want to be a beginner at something. As you might guess, *opsimath* is a linguistic relative of *polymath* and *mathematics*, both of which go back to a Greek word that means "to learn."

PANDICULATION

This word has nothing to do with pandering and only a little to do with pandas. Instead, *pandiculation* is defined as "the stretching that accompanies yawning." This handy word is from Latin *pandere*, "to stretch," and thus a linguistic relative of that other stretchy word, *expand*.

PERENDINATE

One of the first words beginning Latin students ever learn is the word for "tomorrow," *cras*. So, it's a light bulb moment when they realize that *procrastinate* literally means "to put off for tomorrow." But what if you want to postpone something even longer, like until the day after tomorrow? Don't worry—the English language has you covered. The word you want is *perendinate*, from Latin for *perendie*, or "on the day after tomorrow." And if you need a word for "the day after tomorrow" there's always the obsolete term *overmorrow*, as in *Let's resume this conversation overmorrow*.

If you need a word for something pertaining to yesterday, you can describe it as *hesternal*, a relative of Latin *hesternus*, which means "yesterday's." And while we're at it, if you need a word to describe something that happened the day before yesterday, we've got you covered. You can describe that as *nudiustertian*, from Latin *nudius tertius*, literally "today the third day."

There's also *hodiernal*, which describes something "pertaining to today," from Latin *hodie*, the source also of Spanish *hoy* and the *hui* in French *aujourd'hui*. I find *hodiernal* particularly clunky, though. I suppose a boss could demand hodiernal results on a project or you could speak of all the tasks of hodiernal life or the hodiernal challenges now facing humanity.

Finally, if you want a general word for "the act of delaying" or "hesitation," there's always *cunctation*. Spell this one correctly, now. It's from Latin *cunctārī*, which means "to delay" or "hang back," and it shares a common prehistoric root with the English word *hang*. The adjectival forms that you might apply to a slow-poke include *cunctatory* and *cunctatious*. Or there's always *cunctative*, which Francis Bacon used in 1617 when he spoke for many of us, observing that "I confess I have somewhat of the cunctative." The Roman general Quintus Fabius Maximus Verrucosus was known as *Cunctator* due to his strategy of delay and guerilla tactics to weaken a much stronger opponent over time.

QUIDNUNC

Who doesn't need a word for someone who ought to mind their own business? You could call such a person a *Nosy Parker*. (And before you ask, no one knows which Parker was nosy, just as we don't know who Betsy is in *Heavens to Betsy* or who the heck the *Sam Hill* in *What in the Sam Hill?* really was.)

In any case, my term of choice for such a busybody is *quidnunc*. First recorded in the early eighteenth century, *quidnunc* comes directly from Latin, where the question *Quid nunc?* means "What now?"—which is, after all, the gist of the question that's always on the lips of gossips and other meddlesome folks.

RUELLE

Once you realize there's a word for "the space between the edge of one's bed and the wall," you'll wonder how you ever did without it. Now regarded in English as archaic, *ruelle* is from Middle French *ruele*, literally, "alley," the diminutive of *rue* or "street." In seventeenth- and eighteenth-century France, the *ruelle* was the narrow space around a fashionable French lady's large, curtained bed where she received worthy visitors, presumably while she continued to hurkle-durkle. By extension, the word *ruelle* came to denote social or literary gatherings held in the bedrooms of French aristocratic ladies who lounged. In any case, today, *ruelle* is most often used to denote a small alley or lane in French-speaking countries, but there's no reason you can't also use it to denote that part of your bedroom, as in, "Fluffy always sidles up in the ruelle before she pounces."

SKEUOMORPH

Ever wonder why blue jeans have those little rivets in the seams? Those flat metal disks may seem unnecessary, but they're left over from the days when jeans were first manufactured for miners during the California gold rush. With all that kneeling and digging, the forty-niners needed clothes that were especially durable. When the Levi Strauss company began marketing those trousers to the general public, they kept those rivets as part of the design, even though most jeans-wearers today don't subject them to nearly the same amount of wear and tear.

A design element like that that no longer serves a useful purpose but is kept to look familiar is called a *skeuomorph*. It's a combination of Greek *skeûos*, meaning "container" and *morphé*, "form."

Skeuomorphs have been with us since antiquity. The frieze that wraps around the Parthenon in Athens includes incised rectangles designed to resemble the ends of wooden beams used in older structures. Ancient clay pottery often had decorative handles that mimicked those on older wooden vessels. Other examples of skeuomorphs include: electric fireplaces with fake logs, light bulbs shaped like candle flames, plastic Adirondack chairs, a wood-grain pattern on vinyl flooring, and battery-powered wall clocks with a pointlessly swinging pendulum.

One place you'll see lots of skeuomorphs: computer software. Your "save" button is a teeny picture of a floppy disk, but who uses those anymore? To email a document, you first pull it from your desktop or from a pixelated folder that looks like the offline manila kind, then open your mail and tap a virtual paper clip to attach it to the message. The "send" button in your email program resembles a paper airplane. You toss any unwanted documents in the computer's trash can or recycling bin, and when you empty that container, your computer makes a skeuomorphic sound of paper being crumpled. When you take a photo with your phone, it makes a skeuomorphic noise; you don't really need that sound of a single-lens-reflex camera, but it's a satisfying click.

When it comes to language, the closest thing to a linguistic skeuomorph is what's called an *anachronym*. That's a word that's still used figuratively, even though its literal meaning no longer applies. You watch footage of a news event, but it's not really footage, given that *footage* originally referred to the physical length of a roll of film. You *tune in* to our show, even though you don't really use a conventional tuner to calibrate just the right spot on your radio dial. Come to think of it, I'm betting that whatever phone you most recently *dialed* didn't really have a dial either.

Gestures sometimes undergo similar changes, sticking around even though the motion no longer reflects the literal sense of what they've come to mean. For example, many adults will still mouth the words *Call me* while holding a hand to one ear with their pinky and thumb extended to mimic an old rotary handset. (On the other hand, a century ago, the sign-language gesture for *telephone* reflected the shape of an old-fashioned candlestick phone—one fist below the mouth and the other held up to the ear But American Sign Language evolves just like any other, and now to indicate *phone* in ASL, you can just hold up the curved fingers of one hand next to your ear, as if holding a cell phone.)

A North Dakota listener once called us to share a story about a skeuomorphic gesture that may be on the way out. The man had tried to signal some teenagers to lower their car window by moving his fist in a circle, but since they grew up with push-button window controls, they didn't seem to understand the motion. Will that skeuomorphic gesture survive another generation or two? What gesture might take its place? As the saying goes, stay tuned.

In any case, this old-fashioned gesture does live on in the slang of winter sports. If a skier or snowboarder is speeding downhill and hits a jump that throws them up into the air and off-balance, they'll start flailing in an attempt to right themselves, a motion that, at least for now, is referred to as *rolling down the windows*. (And if they wipe out completely, their skis flying one way and poles in another, that's called a *yard sale* because their equipment is strewn across the slope like secondhand items up for grabs.)

THROTTLEBOTTOM

The word *Throttlebottom* joined the language in the 1930s, and I'm surprised that it hasn't caught on and lost its capital *T* by now, given that it's means "an innocuously inept or incompetent public official." It comes to us from the musical comedy *Of Thee I Sing*, a political satire with music by the Gershwin brothers, which won the 1932 Pulitzer Prize for Drama. The silly plot features one Alexander Throttlebottom, who's elected vice president of the United States but is so feckless and unimpressive that people keep forgetting his name; at one point, he even has to sneak into the White House with a tour group. When *Throttlebottom* shows up at all these days, it's on lists of unusual words, but surely this one deserves wider use. I learned it from a Wisconsin listener who belongs to an online calligraphy group. Each month, they're assigned a list of words along with brief definitions, which they practice rendering in beautiful copperplate script. Any members who are proud of what they've penned can share a photo with the group. Let me just say that having observed some samples of their work myself, I can confirm that they have some exquisite *Throttlebottoms*.

TOHUBOHU

A *tohubohu* (*TOH-hoo-BOH-hoo*) is "a state of chaos, disorder, and utter confusion." This word comes from a similar-sounding expression in Hebrew that means "emptiness and desolation." It's the same phrase used early in the book of Genesis, where the Earth is described as "without form and void." The modern English adaptation of this term, useful for describing a teenager's bedroom or a Black Friday sale, is spelled in a jumble of ways itself, including *tohu-bohu*, *tohu-vavohu*, *tohu-vabohu*, and *tohu and bohu*.

UMWELT

I'm so glad that this German word has been borrowed whole into English because it illustrates an important concept. In German, the word *Umwelt* (*OOM-velt*) literally means "environment." But more broadly, it has come to mean "the world as it is perceived by a particular organism based on its own particular sensory apparatus and environment." For example, as Ed Yong points out in his fantastic book *An Immense World* about diversity of sensory perception among living creatures, a dog's nose is far more sensitive than our own, a bee can see ultraviolet light, and a catfish has taste buds all over its body. *Umwelt* is a magnificent word that reminds us that there are many, many different ways to perceive the world.

WINKLEHAWK

Chances are you've already had a pesky *winklehawk*, even if you didn't know that's what it's called. A winklehawk is "a rectangular tear in fabric," such as you might get in your jeans while trying to hop over a barbed-wire fence. (This once happened to me, so I was pleased when I found a word for it years later.) *Winklehawk* comes from *winkelhaak*, the Dutch word for a measuring tool known in English as *a carpenter's square*, which has the same right angle as that annoying rip in your pants.

CHAPTER 18

ARTHUR OR MARTHA

I LOVE THE IDEA THAT each of us carries around phrases we've adopted from other people, little shards of language that we happen upon and then hang on to because they express so perfectly something we hadn't quite articulated that way before. Many of the phrases I've now adopted for myself are ones I first learned from conversations with listeners. Here, in no particular order, are some of my favorites:

I don't know if I'm Arthur or Martha

I'M PARTIAL TO THIS ONE for obvious reasons, of course—and not just because it's such an apt way to describe being "in a state of confusion." Heard most often in New Zealand and Australia, where *I don't know if I'm Arthur or Martha* sounds more like a rhyming phrase, this expression for bewilderment has been around since the 1940s. A newspaper in Sydney used a version of it when describing a 1948 rugby match: "Players were all over the place like Brown's cows, and most didn't know whether they were Arthur or Martha."

(The *Brown's cows* here is another phrase with a strong Australian flavor. Who Mr. or Ms. Brown was, we'll probably never know, but their cows still ruminate inside various similes that mean "crowded together" or "in a chaotic mess"—*all in a heap like Brown's cows*, *all together like Brown's cows*, *like Brown's cows all in a lump*, or *all over the road like Brown's cows*. Aussies use phrases *to come in like Brown's cows* or *to go off like Brown's cows* to mean "to proceed one after another, in a file." This phrase isn't limited to Australia, however. In Ireland, you might hear *All in a row, like Brown's cows* or *All in a row, like Brown's cows, and he had only two*, whatever that means.)

It'll never be seen on a galloping horse

SPEAKING OF LARGE, FOUR-FOOTED ANIMALS . . .

A caller who grew up in Jamaica told us her mother was a fashion designer, and if a client pointed out a tiny flaw in the fabric or complained the hem was a little bit off, she would nonchalantly dismiss their concerns with *Oh, a man on a galloping horse wouldn't see it!*

I love this phrase because it reminds us that when we're too close to something, it's important to keep some perspective. In other words, don't worry about those small imperfections because from a distance, nobody's going to notice—even less so if they're going by at a fast clip.

Another version of this phrase is *It'll never be seen on a galloping horse*, which has a wonderfully galumphing rhythm to it. Our listeners have also reported other versions, including *A blind man on a galloping horse wouldn't see it*, and the even more wonderfully absurd *It'll never be seen on a galloping goose*.

Whatever version you use, though, its liberating message is the same: Relax, and don't sweat the small stuff.

Keep your tail over the dashboard

HERE'S SOME MORE ENCOURAGING EQUINE advice: *Keep your tail over the dashboard.*

The image here is a perky, energetic horse trotting along, her head held high and tail over the front panel of the wagon she's pulling.

The word *dashboard* first referred to a rectangular piece of wood or leather placed at the front in horse-drawn vehicles to keep the driver and passengers from being dashed with mud, water, or snow. Later, when cars were introduced, this word migrated to the front inside panel of a car where the gauges and controls were located. In the digital age, the word *dashboard* traveled even farther to the panel on a computer screen that helps a user monitor data and other features. (In German, by the way, a car's electronic dashboard display is sometimes called a *Mäusekino*, or literally, "mouse cinema." Can't you just imagine those little creatures sitting in a row between a steering wheel and the dashboard, all thrilling to the light show put on by the speedometer and fuel-level indicator?)

In any case, *Keep your tail over the dashboard* is a picturesque way to say "Chin up!" or "Don't let anything get you down!" But this phrase can also be used to rein a person in, as it were. Someone who's in too much of a hurry might be told, *Slow down! Don't get your tail over the dashboard.* Either way, the image here is an energetic horse in fine fettle.

Not my pig, not my farm

YET ANOTHER PHRASE ABOUT FARM animals . . .

A Texas caller told us that somewhere along the way, he'd picked up the phrase *Not my pig, not my farm* to mean "Not my problem" or "I don't want to get involved in that." This expression is probably a variation on a similarly dismissive phrase: *Not my circus, not my monkeys*. This one, in turn, appears to be a calque of a Polish saying, *nie mój cyrk, nie moje małpy*. A more elaborate English version is *Not my circus, not my monkeys, but the clowns definitely know me*. It's a more colorful way of saying, "This sorry state of affairs is none of my business, but I'm definitely familiar with it." After our conversation with the pigless Texan, a Russian professor wrote to share a phrase that's used when a disruptive event has ended but the problematic participants are still around—following a corporate takeover, for example, or an election. In such a case, a Russian might observe Цирк ушёл, клоуны остались, a handy phrase that translates as "The circus left, but the clowns remain."

Are you posing for animal crackers?

A PENNSYLVANIA WOMAN LEFT A voicemail telling us that whenever her stepmother was frustrated with what someone was doing—like when she was behind them at a traffic light and they took their time starting up after the light turned green— she'd demand, *Are you posing for animal crackers?* Those semisweet cookies shaped like lions, tigers, elephants, bears, and other wild animals have been around since the late 1800s. The expressions *Are you posing for animal crackers?* and *Are you modeling for animal crackers?* came about in the early twentieth century. Both are suggestive of behavior that's overly dramatic or exaggerated, like the whimsical, stylized poses of those little cookie critters.

Layovers to catch meddlers

A WOMAN NAMED ANNA CALLED us from Mississippi with what she called "a very odd phrase" from her childhood. Whenever she interrupted her father to ask what he was doing, "He'd say, *leyores to catch meddlers*, basically meaning 'None of your business.'" He later told her he'd learned that saying from his own mother. Anna wondered if the *leyore*—rhymes with *Eeyore*—might be her grandmother's own pronunciation of the word *lure*. Might it be her family's own phrase?

Actually, the expression goes back to the late 1600s, and is one of many phrases that parents have come up with over the centuries to deflect questions from overly inquisitive youngsters. In the case of *leyores to catch meddlers*, it's one of many variations, including *lareovers for meddlers, layovers for meddlers, layers for meddlers, larobes for meddlers, layoes for meddlers* or *medlars* or *medlos*, to name just a few. The version most often seen in print, though, is *layovers to catch meddlers*—Margaret Mitchell spelled it that way in *Gone with the Wind*—but its many variants are classic indicators of a saying that's transmitted primarily in oral form rather than written.

The roots of this phrase are a bit murky, but it likely comes from an old sense of the terms *layers* or *layovers* meaning "a light punishment," such as a soft blow to the head. Sometimes another word or phrase is substituted for the first element, swapping out that initial word for any of the following: *coppers, popovers, rows, rearovers, rareovers, a Pharaoh, a so-and-so,* and *a marrow*. Sometimes the phrase expands in the other direction, as in *lareovers for meddlers and crutches for lame ducks*.

A Florida caller reported that her own mother responded to meddlesome questions with *I'm stacking greased BBs with boxing gloves on*. Others wrote to us to say their parents had answered one too many inquiries with *I'm sewing buttons on ice cream* or *I'm making cat fur for kitten britches*.

It's hard to blame exasperated parents for resorting to a snarky or cryptic reply when a child asks, "What are you doing?"

one too many times. You can just picture a mom responding *The same thing I did last year and piling it up* or a Dad musing *Oh, I was thinking I might move the barn*.

(I suppose you could also distract a child at least briefly by telling them to quit their *rogitating*. The rare, obsolete verb *rogitate* was used in the seventeenth and eighteenth centuries to mean "to make frequent requests or entreaties." It's an etymological relative of *interrogate* and *rogatory*, or "seeking information.") Other creative answers to inquisitive kids' questions include *I'm making a silver new-nothing to put on your shoes* or *I'm making a silver new-nothing to hang on the end of your nose*. Or you might be making *a swinkle-swankle for a goose's nightcap* or a *nooden-nadden for a goose's necktie*.

And who knew that grinding smoke would be such a popular pastime for parents? Some harried adults say they're busy *making a whim-whom for grinding smoke* or making a *wigwam for a water-windmill for grinding smoke*, or *a weegee for grinding smoke*, or *a wiggly-woggler for grinding smoke*. Other quizzical craft projects include *making a hootenanny for a skywampus* or a *making fimfaddle to tie up the moon*. Still another listener reported her dad would brush her off with the phrase *I'm sandpapering a bowl of soup*.

Which brings us to the just-go-away-and-leave-me-alone answers to the nightly question "What's for dinner?" Some favorite answers include *We're having wind pudding and air sauce* or *wind pudding, air sauce, and balloon trimmings* or promising a piping hot dish of *bees' knees and fried onions*. You might also say that the evening's menu includes *Three jumps at the buttery door and a slide down* or *filet of bluebird on toast*.

Then again, maybe the best answer is just *We're having orts. Now run along*.

Who licked the red off your candy?

I'M FOREVER GRATEFUL TO A Virginia Beach listener for this one. Whenever she was sad as a child, her grandmother would tell her she looked like somebody had *licked the red off her candy*. You can just picture a pouty youngster on the verge of tears because someone ruined their precious sweet. You might say it to a small child, to get them to stop crying, or at least puzzle them long enough to change the focus of their attention. Increasingly, though, I find myself thinking of it when I'm out in public and see someone getting all huffy—an irate customer who berates an overworked barista while holding up the rest of the line, for example, or reacting all out of proportion when someone else beats them to a parking place.

When I see something like that, all I can think is *Who licked the red off YOUR candy, hon?*

Versions of this saying go back to the early 1900s, when the expressions *like somebody licked the 'lasses off his biscuit* or *like somebody licked the 'lasses off his bread* vividly alluded to how anyone would look if they'd been anticipating a tasty bite of bread, only to discover that someone had licked off all the molasses before they got to it.

The red-candy version of this phrase has been around since at least the 1920s, and was popularized in the 1960s by country music star Little Jimmy Dickens, whose song "Who Licked the Red Off of Your Candy?" goes in part:

> *You look like a little girl that I once saw*
> *Who bought a peppermint stick down at the drugstore*
> *And stopped to pet a big ol' friendly dog.*

Which of course leads into the refrain with the question in the song's title—in other words, a clever way to say, "Buck up and get over yourself!"

By the way, that song by Little Jimmy Dickens is a real toe-tapper, and I highly recommend finding it on YouTube and committing a few lines to memory. Then tuck them away for the next time you have to deal with an adult having a hissy fit over something that's way too petty to worry about. Even if you don't say it or sing it, it helps to be reminded of those wise words and jaunty melody.

To play Box and Cox

MAYBE YOU WORK IN A place where office space is at a premium, so you and a fellow employee take turns occupying the same space at different times. She uses a desk during the morning shift, but when you come in to work the night shift, that space belongs to you. If that's the case, then you two are *playing Box and Cox*. This British expression comes from an 1847 farce by John Maddison Morton called *Box and Cox*. In the play, a London landlord rents an apartment to two different men, neither of whom knows about the other. By day, the apartment is occupied by John Box, and by night it is leased to a fellow named James Cox. Hilarity ensues.

A box with five handles

BARB, A LISTENER IN MICHIGAN, told us that when she was four years old, a cousin promised that for Barb's upcoming birthday, she was going to bring her *a box with five handles*. Barb was overjoyed, and spent days turning over in her four-year-old mind just what kind of birthday present would come in a box so big that five handles were required to carry it. Unfortunately, when the big day came, Barb learned that the phrase is actually a joking euphemism for "a whomp upside the head with a hand," or in her case a "spanking." Another version of this phrase: *a box with five nails*. Either way, it's not the kind of box you look forward to.

I am sufficiently suffonsified

YOU'VE JUST TAKEN ONE LAST bite of a sumptuous meal when your host grandly asks if you'd like some more, but you couldn't possibly. So you answer "No, thank you. I am sufficiently suffonsified."

Every few weeks, it seems, a listener will ask us about this curious saying or some version of it, as in *I have dined sufficiently, and I have been well surossified*.

Such pseudosophisticated postprandial pronouncements go back at least as far as the 1840s, a time of great linguistic exuberance in the United States, when people playfully invented whimsical words that sounded like they came from Latin. Among these neologisms were *confusticate*, meaning "confuse" or "confound"; *goshbustified*, meaning "mightily pleased"; *hornswoggle*, meaning "to cheat or deceive"; and *absquatulate*, meaning "to take one's leave."

This self-consciously elegant formula of polite refusal would have fit right in. Perhaps it was a playful poke at the manners of high society, or perhaps it was a formula taught to children to ensure they'd be polite when company came over. Or maybe it was just the nineteenth-century equivalent of a Dad Joke at mealtime. In any case, because it was a phrase that was shared from dinner table to dinner table rather than codified in books, this expression underwent lots of changes and elaborations as it passed from parent to child and family to family.

Frederic G. Cassidy, former editor of the *Dictionary of American Regional English*, collected lots of variations on the verb in this phrase, including *suffancified, suffencified, suffoncified, suffuncified, suffauncified, suffonified, seffancified, serfancified, suffanciful, serfanciful, so fanciful, surancified, surencified, surrossified, surquancified, surquencified, circoncified,* and *ferancified.*

One listener reported hearing it as *I am sufficiently suffonsified. Anything more would be purely obnoxious to my taste.* Another recalled hearing *My sufficiency is fully surancified; any more would be obnoxious to my fastidious taste.* Others spin out even more elaborate pronouncements, ending with *I am full to superabundance,* or *I am full to redundancy,* or even *I am full clear up to my quiddy-quaddy.* Or as one listener reported her uncle would always say, *I have had sufficiency of all the numerous delicacies offered. Any more would be a superfluity. Gastronomical science admonishes me that I have reached a point consistent with dietetical economy. In other words, any more would be flippity flop.*

Here's hoping that you, too, have now had *an elegant sufficiency* of all this.

CHAPTER 19

IN THE CLOSET

AFTER OUR WEDDING, BONNIE AND I were eagerly anticipating a honeymoon trip to Alaska. The previous summer, we'd hiked along the Kenai Peninsula on the southcentral coast, and this time we were eager to visit the state's interior. I'd been invited to give a speech in March for KUAC, the public radio station in Fairbanks, and we couldn't be more excited to go back and experience Alaska in wintertime. We bought and borrowed lots of cold-weather gear.

But now it was early 2020, and the world began shutting down due to COVID-19. Two weeks before Bonnie and I were due to leave for Fairbanks, it became clear that KUAC was going to have to cancel my appearance, so our long-planned honeymoon turned into an even longer "homey-moon." We were both extremely fortunate to have the kind of jobs that, with a few adjustments, we could continue doing from home.

Like so many other families at that time, we also adjusted our living arrangements, refurbishing an empty nest. When I got married, I inherited two stepsons—Griffin, who was studying physics at the University of Hawaii, and Phoenix, who had just graduated from college and worked in Northern California. As schools and universities started shutting down, Griffin moved back in with us to continue his studies online, and Bonnie moved her office into the living room.

We followed the news like everyone else and did our fair share of doomscrolling. We also noted the new language springing up around this mysterious disease. There were the words and phrases that seemed to bubble up naturally and become part of everyday vocabulary, even though they'd been around for a while, words like *social distancing* and *flatten the curve* and *essential worker* and *vampire sneeze*. Some familiar words took on new meanings, like *bubble* and *pod*. Then there were the cutesy coinages, like *quarantini*, or "a mixed drink consumed alone or while socially distancing," *Zoom mullet*, or "nice clothes from the waist up, sweatpants (or less) out of view of the camera," and *coronials*, "children conceived during lockdown." I had a particular fondness for the German neologisms, like the term for "panic buying," *Hamsterkauf*, from *hamstern*, "to hoard like a hamster putting things in its cheeks," and *Corona-Fußgruß* or *Coronafussgruss*, literally, "Corona foot greeting," the toe-touch equivalent of greeting someone with an elbow bump.

Early on, when the COVID-19 vaccine was still available only to a few, I adopted the German word *Impfneid*, or literally "vaccine envy." *Impf* is the German word for "vaccine," and it has a fascinating history. *Impf* comes from a root meaning "to plant" or "graft." The same horticultural metaphor is hidden in the English word *inoculate*: The Latin word for "eye," *oculus*, was also applied by the Romans to mean "a small, round thing that resembles an eye, such as a flower bud." This sense of *oculus* produced the Middle English word *inoculate*, which meant "to graft a bud from one plant onto another." The word *inoculate* was later applied to the act of "grafting" a live vaccine into another creature. Bonnie and I both felt Impfneid while awaiting our first *Fauci ouchies.* (Remember that phrase?)

In the eerie quiet of those first few weeks of lockdown, meanwhile, it became clear that in order to keep *A Way with Words* on the air, our team would have to figure out how to keep putting out episodes without the technical equipment and support we received at Studio West. We'd have to improvise a solution—and fast.

Fortunately, options for creating audio had greatly improved in recent years. Plenty of podcasters were now recording in their own homes with very little equipment—just talking in front of a mic and recording on their own computer or laptop. As a call-out show with multiple voices, though, *A Way with Words* would require a much more complicated setup. We were extremely fortunate that once again, Grant and Tim had the technical savvy to come up with a system that, after some trial and error, resulted in a professional sound.

It worked like this: From our own homes, Grant, Stefanie, our engineer Tim, and I would all dial in to a Zoom meeting. Then, as before, Stefanie would listen in, coordinating and directing the sequence of callers. Tim would phone each caller, check their sound levels, briefly remind them of how the recording would work, then patch them in for their conversation with the hosts. Grant and I would record ourselves talking with the caller using a program on our own laptops. Afterward, we'd send that raw audio of ourselves to Tim to sync and edit our two tracks along with the callers. Tim would then do a rough edit of the show and send it to Stefanie and me for final edits and polishing.

We didn't bother turning on the video during those Zoom sessions because it would only be distracting and energy-consuming—not to mention that if we did, they'd have to see how *non*-professional my recording studio looked. In fact, it was laughable.

The "studio" was in my tiny bedroom closet, where the setup included pads of foam rubber fastened to one exposed wall to absorb sound and a heavy U-Haul blanket hanging behind me to do the same. The opposite sides of the closet had racks of clothing that, as the pandemic wore on and I rarely left the house, looked increasingly unfamiliar, as though they belonged to someone else. In the middle of the closet was a small table, and on it, a sound mixer the size of a thick slice of birthday cake next to a stack of books covered with a blanket. Atop that blanketed book pile was my laptop, connected by cords to the mixer and a microphone. Because the closet was standing-room only, I shared etymologies and dispensed advice about grammar while standing on a fuzzy, rubber-soled bath mat, surrounded by pillows strewn all around me on the floor to further reduce echo and reverb. Not pretty, but it got the job done.

To this day, that's what's my setup looks like. Once we realized we could record the show separately from our own homes, we just continued that way. It wasn't ideal; we missed seeing each other and our friends at Studio West. But after years of driving twenty-five miles in each direction to record episodes, a ten-foot morning commute to a crowded closet couldn't be beat. Plus, it helped us cut costs at a crucial time.

So once again, our listeners experienced no interruption in service, and all the while, we kept adding more stations. The broadcast version of the show now airs in forty-five states. In addition, Grant and I began making regular appearances as language experts on Christopher Kimball's *Milk Street* radio show and podcast about cooking, food, and dining, which meant that listeners to that show discovered ours, and vice versa.

As the pandemic wore on, two PPP loans and a State of California small-business grant closed some critical funding gaps. But most important, our listeners stepped up and generously responded to our online pledge drives and podcast asks for help, often with heartwarming messages about how the show offered them solace and diversion during such a challenging, uncertain time. Hundreds more emailed and called to share their questions about words and stories about language. We were always grateful for these messages, and we were deeply chagrined we couldn't respond to every single one. It was like shoveling snow in a blizzard; if we replied to all of them, we'd never be able to produce new episodes, much less do the necessary fundraising to keep the show going. Grant had set up an auto-response for email messages saying just that, and we did our best to answer as many as we could, but we felt awful that it was simply impossible to respond to them all.

I hope our listeners know how grateful we are for all their help in building and serving this community of language lovers. Their enthusiasm has moved and touched us, inspired us, and entertained and enlightened us. We're always heartened by emails like this one from a Montreal listener named Tamarah: "Thank you for waking up my brain every Saturday morning to something smart, fun, and uniting. It's been exhausting living in a world that has become so angry and ironically united in our attachment to fabricated divisions and divisiveness. You have a way of bringing together people of different backgrounds, life experiences, and manners of speaking and hearing, and creating a welcoming space in which we can better listen to and learn from each other with gentleness, respect, humor, warmth, and sincere curiosity. We need more of that."

We couldn't said it any better ourselves, Tamarah. And we're grateful to everyone who pitches in to help with that mission.

As the world began to open back up, Grant and I resumed doing public appearances around the country. Bonnie and I did make it to Alaska and had a blast with KUAC listeners. (We also hung out on a reindeer farm, chased the Northern Lights, wandered through an ice-carving festival, and visited a sled-dog rescue organization, enjoying a magical ride through a birch forest at sunset—all in near-silence except for the whisper of sled rails on snow.)

Back home in Southern California, Bonnie and I kept up the interests we developed when lockdown had rearranged everything. We live on a canyon with a large number of feral cats, and for us, one of the brightest spots during that dark time was raising litters of abandoned feral kittens and adopting them out. Two of those kittens stayed with us, increasing our brood to four. In addition, Bonnie became an adoption coach with a dog rescue group, which of course meant that soon, in addition to our Chihuahua–Jack Russell mix who'd lived with us for a while, we brought home another adorable puppy who grew into an adorable big lug.

As couples do, we continued building out our own familect, words and phrases that would make no sense to anyone else. We've mixed in my father's Appalachianisms and her mother's malapropisms. Like other worders, we also have good-natured disputes about language. Whenever Bonnie says "two pair of pants" or "two pair of scissors," I pipe up with a belated *Z* sound, supplying that final *S* for the word *pair*. (Her way is fine, but we still tease each other.) She pronounces *forward* as *FOH*-werd, declaring, "If there's an *R* in *forward*, it's optional!" If she says that the blue flower vase *lives over there in that cabinet* when it's not in use, I'll point out that the flower vase isn't alive. (OK, I did have to silently give ground on that one, after a listener pointed out that according to *Merriam-Webster*, definition 4.b. for the verb *live* is "to be located or stored" as in "the silverware lives here." The operative word in the previous sentence, though, is *silently*, so please don't tell her.)

And I expect we'll always be chewing over what prompted her to call the show in the first place—that question about the difference between being nice and being kind. Bonnie continues to insist she's not "nice"; I'm not so sure about that. What I can say with confidence after all these years, is that in addition to all her wonderful qualities, which include being patient with me, my spouse is also exceedingly kind.

CHAPTER 20

SLARTS!

WELL, WOULD YOU LOOK AT that? I still have some slarts left in my linguistic grab bag. Herewith, observations about meat, aprons, guys named Todd, bogus dictionary entries, garbled song lyrics, the weird history of flashlights, puzzling polyglot problems, along with a few other expressions that reveal something interesting about language.

meat

ONE OF THE MOST FASCINATING words in the English language is one of the most basic, with just four letters. It's the word *meat*.

The linguistic ancestor of *meat* is *mete*, and back in the tenth century, *mete* meant "food" in general, not just animal flesh. The word *meat* also came to be used as a transitive verb meaning "to feed" or "to supply with provisions." You might say, for example, that you were going to go out and *meat* the cows and horses.

By the early twelfth century, speakers of English specified the meat that came from animals with the term *flesh-meat*. Similarly, *green meat* came to specify vegetables and other edible parts of plants, and the expression *white meat* was used to specify what we'd call *dairy products*.

Over time, the word *meat* came to be used specifically as we use it today. Linguists have several terms for this process, including *semantic narrowing*, *semantic restriction*, and *semantic specialization*. Something similar happened with the word *deer*. In early Middle English, the word *deere* could refer to any of several wild animals, including ants, fish, and, yes, deer as we think of it today. *Deer* is used in this way in Shakespeare's *King Lear*, when Edgar refers to "mice and rats, and such small deer." It's thought that this sense of *deer* may be reflected in the word *wilderness*, a place uninhabited except for wild animals.

apron

HERE'S ANOTHER HUMBLE TERM THAT reveals something about how some words are formed: *apron*. This word is the result of what linguists call *misdivision* or *metanalysis*, which occurs when a term is misheard or misunderstood, resulting in a whole new word—a slip of the ear, you might say. In Middle French, the word *nape* meant "tablecloth," and its diminutive form, *naperon*, referred to a smaller cloth placed on top of an expensive tablecloth to protect it. (An even smaller version produced the English word *napkin*.) In the fourteenth century, speakers of English borrowed the French term for the protective tablecloth to mean a cloth covering that protects one's clothes and were soon spelling and pronouncing it as *napron*. Say *a napron* several times, and it's easy to see how *a napron* evolved into *an apron*.

If you complain about the officiating at a baseball game, you're probably yelling another word formed by misdivision. In the early fifteenth century, the French word *nompere* literally meant the person who is "without peer." This word was borrowed into English as *noumpere*, to mean "an arbitrator" or "the decider in a dispute." Over time, *a noumpere* became *an oumpere* and eventually, *an umpire*.

Many people refer to the early years of this millennium as *the aughts*, and that's another term formed by misdivision. The predecessor of *aught* was the word *naught*, which means "nothing." English speakers who heard *a naught* as *an aught* began saying and spelling it that way, leading to that term for the years between 2000 and 2009 with all those zeros in them. Something similar happened with Middle English *nadder*, which denoted a type of poisonous snake. Over time, *a nadder* morphed into *an adder*.

Sometimes, misdivision occurs in the opposite direction, with a word taking on an *n* from the preceding indefinite article. For example, the Middle English word *eke* means "also" or "in addition." (Back then, the verb *eke* simply meant "to increase" or "to lengthen," although today the expression *eke out* suggests the idea of attempting to do so against great odds.) In any case, *eke* as in "extra" also came to be applied to the familiar, or "extra," name for someone. Long ago, if your given name was Beatrice but people called you Bea, or your given name was Harold and people called you Hal, it was said you had *an ekename*, or "also-name." Say *an ekename* a few times, and you can see where we get *a nickname*.

The same thing happened with *notch*, from Middle French *oche*, meaning "an incision made to keep a record of something." *The phrase an oche* got mushed together in people's mouths and became *a notch*. Ditto for the word *newt*; this little animal was originally called *an ewt*, but over time, the letter *n* crawled over to the *ewt* and stayed there.

You may be reminded here of mondegreens, those entertaining misunderstandings that nevertheless make a kind of sense, especially in the case of song lyrics. Maybe you misheard

Creedence Clearwater Revival's "There's a bad moon on the rise" as "There's a bathroom on the right," or Bob Dylan's "The answer my friends" as "The ants are my friends." (If you want to read a whole book of these misunderstood song lyrics, check out Gavin Edwards's *'Scuse Me While I Kiss This Guy*, which is what lots of people heard when Jimi Hendrix sang, "'Scuse me while I kiss the sky.")

The word *mondegreen* was coined by humorist Sylvia Wright, author of the delightfully titled essay collection *Get Away from Me with Those Christmas Gifts*. In a 1954 essay in *Harper's*, she wrote about how her mother used to recite lyrics from old Scottish ballads. One went:

> *Ye Highlands and ye Lowlands,*
> *Oh, where hae ye been?*
> *They hae slain the Earl Amurray,*
> *And Lady Mondegreen.*

Young Sylvia could picture it all: the handsome, kilted earl and his lovely lady, both killed by arrows, lying together in a forest clearing, hands still clasped in death. As her mother recited those words, the girl wept for the star-crossed pair.

The thing is, there was no Lady Mondegreen. That verse actually ends with lines that refer to an actual Scottish nobleman killed in 1592:

> *They hae slain the Earl of Moray,*
> *And hae laid him on the green.*

Wright notes that historical fact in her essay, then adds, "I know about this, but I won't give in to it. Leaving him to die all alone without even anyone to hold his hand—I won't have it. The point about what I shall hereafter call mondegreens, since no one else has thought up a word for them, is that they are better than the original."

I don't know that mondegreens are always better, but that's what they're called, and Wright's wrong word *mondegreen* now resides in the *OED*, which defines it as "A misunderstood or misinterpreted word or phrase resulting from a mishearing, esp. of the lyrics to a song."

Todd

I'LL NEVER FORGET THE CALL we had from a guy named Todd, who said that for as long as he could remember, people have mistakenly called him Scott, not Todd. He recalled that even doctors would walk in holding his chart and greet him with "Hello, Scott, nice to see you again," And, he added, at parties where everyone's wearing name tags, "I am inevitably called Scott. It's happened too many times over my life for me to think it's coincidental, especially with someone looking directly at a name tag, shaking your hand and then saying, 'Nice to meet you, Scott.'

"What's up with that?" he asked. We weren't sure, so we put the question out to our listeners, and boy, did we hear from a lot of Todds and Scotts. "The hairs on the back of my neck stood up when I heard you talking about this," said one Todd, who told us the same thing happens to him. Another listener told us she went to a christening where the priest mistakenly referred to little baby Scott as Todd. Oops. Wrote another: "My name is Todd and YES this happens probably once every three months or so. I don't see the similarities except both names end in double letters. Incredibly freaky."

That last Todd may be on to something. Both are short masculine names with double letters at the end. In terms of pronouncing those final letters, they're both formed in nearly the same spot in the mouth; consider how Americans tend to pronounce *butter* as *budder*. In addition, both names have the same short vowel in the middle.

Rhythm might also play a role. We heard from several Stephanies mistaken for Jennifer or Rebecca, and Katherines who were sometimes called Margaret. We also heard about people mixing up three-letter names Pam and Amy.

So, who knows? All I can say is that nowadays, every time I meet a Todd, I ask if people ever call them Scott, and about half of them look astonished and say, "Yes! How did you know?"

flashlight

IF YOU THINK ABOUT IT, *flashlight* is a weird word. After all, a flashlight doesn't flash; it provides a steady beam of light until it's turned off. So why is it called a flashlight? The answer involves a fascinating story, one that shows how hard it can be to invent a word that has real staying power.

Portable electric lights were invented in the late 1890s. At the time, their batteries were so weak and their bulbs so inefficient that they'd emit light for just a few seconds at a time. You'd hold up the light, turn it on, and briefly see what was in front of you. Then the device would shut off for a while so the batteries could rest, after which you could turn it on again. In other words, they were literally "flash lights." That's the term that caught on in the United States, anyway. For some reason, in the United Kingdom, the preferred term was *portable electric torch*, and eventually, just *torch*.

The next several years brought improvements in these bulbs and batteries, allowing these lights to stay on for several minutes at a time. The technology soon advanced so much that the Eveready flashlight company decided it was time to come up with an entirely new name for their product. Someone there got the bright idea—very bright, as it turned out—to hold a contest to coin a new word.

In September 1916, in newspapers across the country, the Eveready company announced a contest: Come up with a new word to replace *flashlight*, and the winner would receive a prize of $3,000.

The text of the company's ad was stirring, to say the least:

> Twenty years ago, when the harnessing of electricity was still much of a novelty, when automobiles were three parts joke and one part hope deferred, a man with a vision dreamed of carrying a pocketful of electric light into the dark, ready for instant use. Out of this dream grew the first flashlight—an EVEREADY—with a battery the size of a watch and an electric bulb no larger than the end of your finger. When, for a second or so, it flashed its tiny stream of light, people cried "Wonderful! But what's it for?" Its novelty appealed. Its future world-wide usefulness was unrealized.
>
> Even after people began buying these new lights to carry around in the dark, EVEREADYS were still literally "flashers" or flashlights, and years of ceaseless effort were necessary to the development of a battery capable of giving hours of continuous

light. Also in those early days there were no min-
iature electric light bulbs on the market—and the
man with the vision had to create them. So, finally,
came the perfected EVEREADY with its long-
lived Tungsten battery and brilliant Mazda bulb—
an EVEREADY that has outgrown the old term
flashlight.

It was a brilliant marketing move. Retailers coast to coast
partnered with the company to distribute official entry blanks.
Local newspapers ran features on townspeople who participated
in the contest. That $3,000 prize—the equivalent of roughly
$85,000 today—was irresistible; more than half a million entries
from would-be neologists poured in. By January of 1917, the company was still going through the entries, a fact newspapers duti-
fully proceeded to report as the months went by. In March of
that year, they announced that an announcement was imminent.

In early April, the company took out huge ads all nationwide
to report the results of the contest to come up with a word for
what Eveready called "the product that has outgrown its name."
And there was even more news: The company had decided to pay
out $12,000, not $3,000, awarding prizes to four different contestants who came up with the same name. Meanwhile, newspapers breathlessly reported, "More surprising still is the news that
all winners are women."

And the winning entry? The word that was supposed to
replace the word *flashlight*? The momentous linguistic innova-
tion? That word was . . . *Daylo*.

That's right. *Daylo*.

I know—I don't get it either. Trumpeting its announcement,
Eveready noted that *Daylo* was "easy to remember and entirely

simple to pronounce," then went on to explain that "'DAY' suggests perfect light, and 'LO' means 'Behold!'— 'See!'"

Okey-dokey then. I still don't see how four different women in Kansas, South Dakota, New Jersey, and New York all came up a word like that, but whatever. In any case, while the company's publicity campaign surely paid off, it didn't change people's linguistic habits. Once there wasn't $3,000 involved, everyone just went back to the term they were used to. (However, as you might imagine, I now insist on calling these things *daylos* whenever I get the chance just for fun. I suggest you do, too.)

What did catch on, though, was the idea of word-coining contests. Organizations tried to raise public awareness with contests to invent names for this and that, such as "people who are careless with matches" or "hit-and-run drivers."

Seven years after the Eveready publicity bonanza, another nationwide contest was held to replace a popular word: *jazz*. That's right, the musical art form. Duke Ellington famously disliked the term *jazz* and told the *New York Times* that this word "never lost that association with those New Orleans bordellos," likening it to "the kind of man you wouldn't want your daughter to associate with." Later, Charles Mingus would say that he associated the word *jazz* with such things as "discrimination, second-class citizenship, the whole back-of-the-bus bit," and still later, Miles Davis would express his own dislike for the term, saying *jazz* was too limiting a word, preferring to call that art form *social music*.

But back to the 1920s: In 1924, bandleader Meyer Davis said he considered the word *jazz* passé and launched a nationwide radio contest offering listeners $100 to come up with a better word for such music.

More than seven hundred thousand entries to replace the word *jazz* poured in, most of them painfully contrived. They included *Fresco, Frolic, Fun Fun, Happytone, Jollio, Joystep, Mello, Mellojoy, Mellomeyer, Modage, Peptune, Polyphone, Radiola, Rhythmic, Rhythmel, Rythmore, Syncosway, Tunesway, Wafox,* and *Zando,* among many others.

The winning entry wasn't much better, though. It was . . . *syncopep.* Yes, *syncopep.* Mercifully, this neologism failed to catch on, which is a good thing, because who would want to sit through a viewing of *All That Syncopep,* or tune in some *smooth syncopep,* or hold up their palms to wiggle *syncopep hands?*

Another coining contest from the 1920s was far more successful, though, this one sponsored by Boston philanthropist and staunch anti-alcohol crusader named Delcevare King. In late 1923, King put up a reward of $200 in solid gold to the person who came up with the most efficient term for "someone who flouts the law by drinking illegal liquor." This contest drew more than thirty thousand entries to name such an anti-Prohibitionist. These entries included *klinker, bootlicker, boozshevic, patrinot, flounder, lawlesser, sliquor, wetocrat, slacklaw,* and *lawjacker.*

None of those quite worked for Mr. King, who complained to the *Boston Globe,* "Many of those who sent words . . . did not quite catch the idea. I do not seek an epithet for the drinker as such. I DO seek a word which will stab awake the public conscience to the fact that such lawless drinking is, in the words of President Harding, 'a menace to the republic itself.'"

Meanwhile, the competition also inspired linguistic creativity of the sarcastic kind. Indignant students at Harvard held a coinage contest of their own, offering $25 for the best new term for "a person who supports Prohibition." The contenders included *fear-beer* and *jug buster,* although the most common entry received to name such killjoys was *Delcevare.* The eventual winner: *spigot-bigot.*

The $200 prize even inspired a bit of petty larceny. The *Boston Globe* reported that when local police charged a man with stealing a dictionary and a scarf, he confessed that purloined the book specifically to try to come up with entries for the contest.

In any case, after digging through mounds of mail from would-be wordsmiths, King and his fellow judges decided that one word stood out above all others. Two different people had submitted it. The word was . . .

Scofflaw.

Amazingly enough, the word *scofflaw* managed to stick around. Maybe because it could be applied to so many people? Or because it could be used with either sarcasm or sincerity? Even after Prohibition was repealed, *scofflaw* remained in the language, and its meaning expanded to apply to anyone who scoffs at legal limitations, and particularly, as the *OED* defines it, "a person who avoids various kinds of not easily enforceable laws." Today, for example, someone who leaves a car parked illegally or goes a few miles over the speed limit might be considered a scofflaw.

Delcevare King's earnest efforts to better the world didn't end with inventing a word for lawless drinkers. He later tried, among other things, to rebrand his hometown of Quincy, Massachusetts, as "The City of Better Parking." This part of Greater Boston is better known as "City of Presidents," because John Adams and his son John Quincy Adams were both born and buried there. Delcevare King, anti-alcohol crusader and facilitator of a new term in English, is buried there as well. His epitaph reads simply "He tried to be helpful."

mountweazel

A LISTENER IN CONNECTICUT NAMED Mark called after a thirty-year quest to track down the origin of a word he saw once and could never find again. He'd been perusing Webster's *New*

Twentieth Century Dictionary, published in 1943 when he happened across the word *Jungftak*. It was defined this way:

> A Persian bird, the male of which had only one
> wing, on the right side, and the female only
> one wing, on the left side; instead of the missing
> wings, the male had a hook of bone, and the female
> an eyelet of bone, and it was by uniting hook and
> eye that they were enabled to fly,—each, when
> alone, had to remain on the ground.

Mark had never heard of such a thing. Intrigued, he tried to find out more about this mysterious animal. He went to his local library and looked in every dictionary he could find. He leafed through encyclopedias and tracked down books of Persian mythology. Nothing.

Could it be that this bizarre word and its definition were fake? In a word, yes.

Jungftak is an example of a *mountweazel*, a phony entry inserted into a reference work to catch plagiarists. It's a kind of verbal watermark—the lexical equivalent of marked bills in a bank. If a rival publication lifts that language and begins distributing it as their own, then it's clear that someone purloined those pages. Plagiarism among dictionary publishers was far more common in the eighteenth and nineteenth centuries, when it was easier to copy lots of pages and publish them as one's own and no one was the wiser. Modern lexicographers have also been known to sneak in the occasional mountweazel to protect against intellectual theft.

In 2001, the first edition of the *New Oxford American Dictionary* or *NOAD*, included the made-up word *esquivalience*, defined as "the willful avoidance of one's official responsibilities." The dictionary traced *esquivalience* back to the late nineteenth century and suggested it may come from French *esquiver*, "dodge, slink away"—another fabrication. That word was indeed later discovered in the pages of another online dictionary, and its editor was fired.

Such copyright traps aren't limited to dictionaries and encyclopedias. Cartographers have been known to insert nonexistent features such as so-called *trap streets* and *paper towns* in their maps to catch anyone stealing their work.

The word *mountweazel* derives from a bogus entry in the 1975 edition of the *New Columbia Encyclopedia*. The entry describes Lillian Mountweazel, supposedly a promising young photographer from Bangs, Ohio, who met a most untimely end. Clearly someone had fun writing it:

> Mountweazel, Lillian Virginia, 1942–73, American photographer, b. Bangs, Ohio. Turning from fountain design to photography in 1963, Mountweazel produced her celebrated portraits of the South Sierra Miwok in 1964. She was awarded government grants to make a series of photo-essays of unusual subject matter, including New York City buses, the cemeteries of Paris, and rural American mailboxes. The last group was exhibited extensively abroad and published as *Flags Up!* (1972). Mountweazel died at 31 in an explosion while on assignment for *Combustibles* magazine.

As much as I would enjoy paging through a photo book about American mailboxes called *Flags Up!*, or for that matter, settle in with an old copy of *Combustibles*, alas, neither one exists. Nor did poor Lillian.

Mountweazel doesn't appear in many dictionaries—yet—although lexicographers are quite familiar with it. Grant even told me he may have written a mountweazel or two himself, but he wouldn't say any more, so who knows? You'll have to ask him.

faulty language selection

WE HAD A FASCINATING EMAIL from a listener in Tennessee. She had studied French for ten years, but when she started studying German, a weird thing happened, and she wondered if she was the only one with this problem. Often if she started a sentence in German but couldn't think of the right German words to say, she'd naturally reach not for the English equivalent, but for the corresponding phrase in French. "When grasping for the German words that aren't on that top shelf in my mind, French filler feels more appropriate than English," she said. It was, she added, as if her brain knew somehow that it was supposed to be looking for a language that wasn't English, so it reached for French instead of her native tongue.

She's not alone. In fact, this phenomenon is so common among people who speak more than two languages that linguists have a name for it. It's called *faulty language selection*, and it almost always occurs when the person is speaking, not writing. No one's sure why this happens, although it may have something to do with where new information is stored in the brain.

After listeners heard our chat with about this, lots of polyglots told us they'd experienced the same thing. A Californian said that she'd long ago mastered German. Then she started learning Spanish, and when she didn't know the Spanish term for something, her brain automatically defaulted to the German word for it. Later she started learning Russian, and something else odd happened: "My German is significantly better than my Spanish, but my brain started putting in the Spanish words instead."

We also heard from a woman in Seattle who grew up in China, learned English as a second language in middle school, then majored in Japanese in college. When she talked to classmates there in English but forgot her English vocabulary, she automatically reached for a Japanese equivalent rather than her native Chinese. Eventually, she realized that a bit of role-playing could help solve the problem. "I pretended to be a stereotypical Japanese anime girl when I speak Japanese, using soft intonations and more humble body language," she told us. "When I talk in English, I would use a firmer voice and hold up my chest like a confident American young girl. I got to be back to myself when using Chinese. This helped me to separate the languages efficiently when talking and even if I got stuck, it was still in that language and wouldn't slip away to another. I guess if connections are made between body language and the language, it'll be harder to change the language you're speaking."

I think she's on to something. Many of us find our personalities adapting a bit when we switch to another language. When I speak Spanish, for example, I often sound more animated than I do in English. Maybe it's because I don't have the same range of vocabulary and tend to speak more in primary colors rather than from a more extensive palette, and I use more expressive gestures and facial expressions to help convey meaning. A lot of our listeners confirm this.

In any case, as far as linguistic problems go, I'd say faulty language selection is a good one to have, and aspiring to have even more of it in the future is a worthy goal.

CHAPTER 21

PLAIN OLD LOVELY AND UPLIFTING WORDS

WE CAN ALL USE SOME lovely and uplifting words, right? Here are a few random words that I cherish, and I think you will, too. Tuck these into your word-hoard for when you need them.

susurration

THE NOUN *SUSURRATION* DENOTES A whispering sound. The wind through the leaves of a tree, the murmur of a waiting audience, the sound of silk slippers on a hard floor, a rustle of ribbons, or the hum of bees in a glade. *Susurration* comes from the Latin *susurrus*, which means "a low, gentle noise," a "whispering," or a "muttering." In the fifteenth century, the Latin word's English progeny *susurration* carried a negative sense, suggesting "malicious whispering" or "tattling" on someone. Over time, though, *susurration* softened.

A similar shift seems to have occurred with *psithurism* (*SITH-urr-ism*). This sibilant English word means "a low, whispering sound, such as the rustle of leaves." The ancient Greek word, *psithurizein*, meant "to whisper what one dares not speak" or "to whisper slanders." Over time, however, it came to be used metaphorically to indicate things such as the rustling of boughs or the tittering of swallows.

stilliform

ONE OF THE MOST BEAUTIFUL words in the English language, *stilliform* means "drop-shaped." It's from Latin *stilla*, "drop," and a relative of the drippy words *distill* (to "drip down") and *instill* ("to put in drop by drop")—or as the *Oxford English Dictionary* puts it, "To introduce (some immaterial principle, notion, feeling, or quality) little by little into the mind, soul, heart, etc.; to cause to enter by degrees; to infuse slowly or gradually; to insinuate."

I like *stilliform* partly because of those short *i* sounds on either side of the *ll*, but also the fact that all those long, thin letters—the *t-i-l-l-i-f* in the middle—look kind of, well, drippy, don't they?

halcyon

I MIGHT HAVE INCLUDED *HALCYON* in Chapter 4, as this word references a bittersweet love story in ancient mythology. *Halcyon* is an adjective describing something "calm" or "serene," and I love it for its sweet, sibilant sound. It usually appears with *days*, the expression *halcyon days* referring to any "time of happy tranquility."

In ancient Greek myth, the name *alkyon* referred to the kingfisher, a bird with brilliant plumage and steadfast devotion to its mate. This bird was identified with the story of Alcyone (*al-SYE-oh-nee*), a Thessalian princess who married King Ceyx (*SEE-iks*) of Trachis. They were an extremely happy pair—so happy, in fact, that they took to calling themselves Zeus and Hera. As you might imagine, such hubris didn't go over well with the Greek gods. So, when Ceyx was away at sea without Alcyone, Zeus sent a storm to wreck the ship. Alcyone learned of his death in a dream. When she went down to the sea to grieve, she saw the body of her beloved wash up on shore. Despondent, she hurled herself from a cliff. Taking pity on them, the gods changed these lovers into kingfishers, birds whose devotion to each other was likewise legendary. It was said that every year during the days just before and after winter solstice, the reunited couple would charm the seas for two weeks, rendering the surface so calm that they could nest upon the waters and hatch their eggs, and their descendants would all do the same. *Halcyon days* refers specifically to that idyllic image, and more generally to a spell of pleasant weather, and more generally still to a period fondly remembered as a time of calm, happiness, and prosperity.

goethite

IN 2004, THE RED, YELLOW, or brown mineral called *goethite* (*GURR-tyte*) got NASA scientists all excited when the Mars rover *Spirit* detected its presence on the red planet. Goethite can't form without water, so the discovery raised hopes of finding water on Mars, or at least evidence that it once existed.

Wait, *goethite*? As in Johann Wolfgang von Goethe, the great German writer and polymath? Yes. In fact, goethite may be the only mineral named for a poet. In addition to his writing, the late eighteenth-century author of *Faust* and *The Sorrows of Young Werther* was intensely interested in geology—so much so that he amassed a legendary collection of more than eighteen thousand minerals, possibly the largest collection in Europe. There's something thrilling about the idea that this mineral named for a poet exists elsewhere in the solar system, and I still get a little chill every time I say its name. As Goethe himself once observed,

"Everything is simpler than one can imagine and yet complicated and intertwined beyond comprehension."

nemophilist

FROM THE GREEK WORD *NEMOS*, meaning "grove," "thicket," or "wooded pasture," comes this handy word for "someone who is fond of forests." The related English word *nemoral* means "belonging to forests" or "frequenting woodland areas."

Nemophilists—and I count myself among them—like to indulge in what the Japanese call *shinrin-yoku*, or literally, "forest bathing," the practice of spending time in a forest to breathe in its atmosphere and enjoy the health benefits of getting out into nature. There's a lovely German word for something similar, *Waldeinsamkeit*. It's a combination of *Wald*, meaning "forest," and *Einsamkeit*, which might be translated as "loneliness," except that it's a positive kind of loneliness—that feeling of solitude and connectedness with nature when you're alone in the woods.

scintillate

I'VE BEEN A FAN OF this word ever since I realized it's from the Latin *scintilla*, which means "spark," "glittering speck," or "particle of fire." A scintillating conversation, in other words, is a sparkling one. Not only that, *scintilla* was lifted whole into English as a word for something tiny, a mere glimmer, as in *not one scintilla of evidence*.

As long as we're talking about sparkly things, the Latin word *coruscare* once meant "to vibrate" or "tremble" and then later "to glitter" or "to flash." That root gave us the English intransitive verb *coruscate*, meaning to "flash" or "sparkle," and *coruscating*, traditionally used to describe something "glittering."

However, in the last few years, something fascinating has been happening with the word *coruscating*. Apparently misunderstanding its meaning and confusing it with *excoriating** and *corrosive*, some people have been using *coruscating* to mean "scathing" or "castigating." A book review in the *New York Times* labeled a brutal description of the author's father as "a coruscating portrait," and the *Guardian* once reported on a politician earnestly calling for an end to "coruscating political divisions." In fact, enough people are already adopting this new sense of *coruscating* that at least one reference work, the *Oxford Dictionary of English* (*ODE*), now includes a secondary definition of "Severely critical; scathing."

Anyone who instantly recognizes the word's Latin roots may find this new usage disconcerting. I did as well, at least at first. But the more I think about it, this new use of *coruscating* is a fascinating example of language change—and it's happening right under our feet. It's another great reminder that language is always evolving, and it's far better to be curious, not furious, about that process.

respair

THE *OED* SAYS THE WORD *respair* is obsolete and rare, but it supposedly means "fresh hope, or recovery from despair," the opposite of *despair*. I'm still surprised this word hasn't caught on because it sounds like something you'd want to have a word for and keep close at hand. The *OED*'s one citation for this word is

---

*   *Excoriate*, by the way, has a vivid and grisly etymology. In the fifteenth century, it literally meant to "pull the skin off of," or in other words, "to flay," from Latin *excoriāre*, "to strip off the hide."

from Andrew of Wyntoun, a Scottish writer who lived in the late fourteenth and early fifteenth centuries. His *Orygynale Cronykil*, or "Original Chronicle," is a history of humankind and of Scotland in particular, written completely in verse.

Besides *respair*, Andrew's work is also notable for some other things. For one, it contains one of the first mentions of Robin Hood in print. Andrew's writing is also the original source for the story of the encounter between Macbeth and the weird sisters, later immortalized by Shakespeare.

Depending on which version of the manuscript you look at, this word was spelled *respayr* or *respyre*. (That latter version may in fact have been more like an old use of English *respire*, as in *respiration*, meaning "to have relief from an unpleasant situation"—to take a breath in the middle of it, in other words—and by extension "to recover strength or courage or hope.")

In any case, a few modern writers such as Paul Anthony Jones, author of *The Cabinet of Calm: Soothing Words for Troubled Times*, have championed this obsolete term. It certainly seems like a word whose time has come again.

thin places

SOMETIMES WHEN I'M HIKING NEAR the top of a mountain, the beauty and the stillness feels almost unreal, otherworldly, as if the sky were a mere scrim that I could poke right through to the other side. Those moments create a profound feeling that's hard to describe, like being at some kind of edge or the threshold of another world.

Maybe you've had that experience gazing out into the vastness of a desert, or seeing the Grand Canyon for the first time, or wandering the west coast of Ireland, or gazing up inside a cathedral. There's a poetic term for such locales: *thin places*. The power of thin places doesn't have to be religious. Essayist Oliver Burkeman described them this way: "We're in the territory, here, of the ineffable. The stuff we can't express because it's *beyond* the power of language to do so. Explanations aren't merely useless; they threaten to get in the way. The experience of a thin place feels special *because* words fail, leaving stunned silence."

Incidentally, if you do an internet search for the term *thin place*, you're sure to see a popular story going round that it's a translation of an ancient Irish Gaelic expression. That's a very appealing notion, but I've seen no hard evidence that this term has been around more than a century or so.

Either way, I'm delighted to have a pair of words to articulate what sometimes leaves me wordless.

CHAPTER 22

A LAGNIAPPE

I'M STILL THUNDERSTRUCK THAT I HAVE HAD the good fortune of being to commune with so many fellow worders over the years.

My favorite Latin proverb, *Qui docet, discit*, means "Who teaches, learns" (*docet* being a relative of English *docent*, and *discit* being the linguistic kin of *disciple* and *discipline*). And it's true—I've learned so much from our listeners, the stories they've shared, the questions they've raised, and the topics we've explored together. I'm endlessly grateful for all those conversations, and I hope this book is just the beginning of many more.

I invite you to reach out to us any time through our website, waywordradio.org, where you'll find a contact page with dozens of ways to reach us from anywhere in the world. Who knows? You just might end up on the show yourself. On our website you'll also find hundreds of past episodes with thousands of conversations.

And you can reach me directly through my own website, www.marthabarnette.com.

But before I go, a lagniappe.

A *lagniappe*, as noted in Chapter 10, is a little something extra, a small gift tossed in for good measure. So here's a lexical lagniappe for you: *banana problem*.

If you have a banana problem, you're uncertain as to whether a project is finished, and therefore, when to stop revising. Maybe you've written and rewritten something so many times that it's wandered far afield from an earlier, better version. Or maybe you tossed in one too many pinches of salt to the broth that was already perfect. Or you keep adding so many bells and whistles to a website that the chaotic, multicolored result is the ugly mess that some web designers call *angry fruit salad*.

In the tech world, the term *banana problem* alludes to badly written code for the termination of a computer process. It was inspired by a joke about a little kid who declared, "I know how to spell *banana*—I just don't know when to stop!"

Now that I think about it, I'm wondering if maybe I have a banana problem of my own.

Then again, maybe I don't.

ACKNOWLEDGMENTS

I'm grateful, first and foremost, to the *A Way with Words* creative team—Stefanie, Grant, Tim, and John. It's a privilege to work with you to keep producing the little radio show that could.

I'm also grateful to all the listeners who invite us into their lives—who teach us, challenge us, entertain us, encourage us, and donate to support the show.

Thanks to past and current members of the board of Wayword, Inc., who share our mission to educate, inspire, and connect people through shared curiosity about language: Josh Eckels, Betty Willis, Michael Breslauer, Rick Seidenwurm, Bruce Rogow, Clare Grotting, Merrill Perlman, and Allie Akmal. Huge thanks also to the hardworking volunteers of the Friends of *A Way with Words* fundraising group founded by my dear friend Constance Carroll, who believed in and insisted upon the future of the show even when I doubted it myself.

Every writer should be lucky enough to have an editor as deft and thoughtful as Jamison Stoltz. I'm grateful for his creative guidance and to the whole team at Abrams Books. Thanks to my agent, Myrsini Stephanides, for introducing us, and for helping to turn this book idea into a reality. I'm indebted to historian Lillian Faderman, who read early versions and offered suggestions that made all the difference. Family friend Wendell Berry generously responded to my questions with helpful recollections of my parents from before I was born.

I remain thankful to my fellow Zerks—Allison Gauss, Missy Gurga, Justin Roberts, Andy Robinson, Dean Sage, and Salma Soliman—for their ongoing creative feedback. And I'm grateful to a whole word herd of friends who generously shared advice and support during the writing of this book: Christine Rufener, Jennifer Cole, Jen Parker, James Ramsay, Phyllis Irwin, Fran Ellers, Debra Clem, Lindsy Van Gelder, Eleanor Musick and Abe Ordover, Cindy Miles, Betty Peabody, Liz Anne Potamianos, Mary Norris, Hal and Pam Fuson, Al and Kathleen Steele, Jeanne Herberger, Tom Webber, Joe Dinwiddie, Janet Mueller, Esther Leeflang, and Connie Marrett.

Finally, for putting up with all she had to during the writing of this book, my gratitude to Bonnie is, well, beyond words.

INDEX